VENOMOUS REPTILES

VENOMOUS

ILLUSTRATED WITH PHOTOGRAPHS

REPTILES

Sherman A. Minton, Jr.
Madge Rutherford Minton

CHARLES SCRIBNER'S SONS · New York

Frontispiece: Frieze showing Naga divinities
flanked by snakes, Gandhara sculpture, c. 200 A.D.,
Swat, West Pakistan. (MINTON COLLECTION, ALLAN ROBERTS)

The lines from "In the Snake Park" by William Plomer
on page 54, which appeared first in The New Yorker,
are reprinted here from COLLECTED POEMS *by permission*
of Jonathan Cape, Ltd.

For

BROOKS, APRIL, HOLLY

Preface

Since the dawn of human thought, poisonous reptiles have had a powerful hold on man's imagination and have strongly influenced his beliefs and actions. In one way or another, poisonous reptiles impinge upon the lives of millions of persons. In reality they are a menace to some; as creatures of superstition and legend, they affect many more. We have tried to present the venomous reptiles both as they are and as they have seemed to be. Part of the book is a summary of scientific knowledge about poisonous snakes and lizards and their venoms; part is a glimpse of the intricate ways in which they have been woven into the fabric of human culture.

Our own relationship with reptiles has been marked by variety. We have collected them in forests and deserts from Indiana to Hong Kong. We have extracted venoms from snakes and treated victims of their bites. We have discussed with the Baluchis of southern Asia the possibility that cobras are djinns and with herpetologists the possibility that mole vipers are not really vipers. In this book we have drawn from these experiences as well as from the writings of others. When, in a few discussions, the word "I" is used, the author who is speaking is Sherman A. Minton.

Reptiles well known to zoologists, and particularly to herpetologists, are referred to in the text by their English names only.

For those who wish to know the technical nomenclature, a complete list of scientific names of the species mentioned appears as Table 3, pages 203–207.

In units of measure, the English system is used for larger measurements, such as the lengths of snakes. For smaller measurements such as fang lengths, weights of venom yields, and lethal doses, the more precise units of the metric system have been cited. The average American reader can more easily visualize a 6-foot cobra than a 180-centimeter cobra; on the other hand, it seems neater to compare weights of 50 and 100 milligrams rather than of 0.721 and 1.543 grains. For conversions of measures and weights from the metric to the English system, see Table 2, page 202.

Our thanks to the many people who have given valuable assistance, and the credits for the illustrations, are included in the Acknowledgments on pages 259–260. Photographs not otherwise credited were taken by the authors.

Sherman A. Minton, Jr.
Madge Rutherford Minton

Contents

Tables

Illustrations

VENOMOUS REPTILES

1. Evolution, Classification, Distribution

Snakes and lizards are by far the most abundant and diversified reptiles in the world today. From the standpoint of evolution, they are a success. Modern reptiles are survivors of a once dominant, extremely diversified, and numerous group of animals. The tuatara of New Zealand is the sole living representative of a group that goes back at least to the early Triassic period some 200 million years ago (see Table 1, Geologic Time Chart, pages 201–202), and the turtles are fully as ancient. The crocodiles and their allies can be traced to the late Triassic, about 170 million years ago. These three groups are holdovers from the Mesozoic Era, or Age of Reptiles, and have changed comparatively little over eons of time. The lizards and snakes arose late in the Mesozoic but have retained greater capacity for diversity and still seem to be undergoing active evolutionary change.

All reptiles have scales or horny plates, and those with well-developed limbs have toes that end in claws. All reptiles breathe by lungs throughout their life. They are "cold-blooded"—that is, they cannot maintain a body temperature much above or below that of their immediate environment. One of the reptiles' most important evolutionary advances was the development of an egg capable of maturing on land. Such an egg requires internal fertilization, which is seen in all reptiles. Many species of snakes and lizards retain the eggs within the female until development is complete. In a few species, a primitive connection between embryo and mother is seen; this foreshadows the placenta in higher mammals.

Zoologists who specialize in the study of amphibians and reptiles are called herpetologists; contrary to popular belief, they are not solely students of snakes. (We know one or two herpetologists who don't even like snakes.) Nearly all herpetologists find it necessary to specialize still further. Most of the early herpetologists were concerned with anatomy and classification; many neither knew nor cared much about amphibians and reptiles as living creatures in their natural environment. Modern herpetologists are generally much more oriented toward field work. Many are still involved with classification, or taxonomy, but their approach may employ biochemistry, immunology, or computer science. Ecology and zoogeography are popular with those herpetologists who enjoy field work and exploration, while studies in behavior are carried out both in the laboratory and in the field. Comparative physiology and biochemistry attract many younger herpetologists. Those interested in the venoms of amphibians and reptiles may affiliate themselves with the new subspecialty of toxinology, the study of toxins of plant or animal origin. Despite the wealth of myth and folklore relating to reptiles, there has been comparatively little interchange between herpetologists and anthropologists.

Although no special training or acumen is needed to enable one to tell an iguana from a rattlesnake, some kinds of snakes and lizards are so similar in both internal and external anatomy that herpetologists can find no single external feature that will invariably distinguish the two groups. Limblessness and marked elongation of the body are the most striking features that distinguish snakes from other reptiles, but nearly every major group of lizards has or has had representatives that show this body form. The evolutionary pressures that have so often forced lizards into this mold are not well known, but there are clues among living lizards.

In the dry regions of western Asia lives a group of smooth-scaled lizards, or skinks, that show a transition from small but well-formed limbs to tiny vestiges. Those with better-developed limbs live in crevices or under stones; the more nearly limbless ones glide along under the surface of fine sand with such ease and agility that they are known as sand fish. This suggests that limblessness can be of advantage in burrowing. Among the ophisaurs, a group that includes the "glass snakes" (really lizards) of North America, loss of limbs seems to be correlated with life in densely matted grass. Although not illustrated by living lizards, limblessness might also arise as an adaptation to aquatic life, especially one where swimming alternated with mud-burrowing. The true snakes undoubtedly evolved from primitive lizards. They may have evolved in response to any or all of these pressures; the answers still lie hidden in Mesozoic rocks formed about 100 million years ago.

The advantages the first primitive snakes gained by limblessness were accompanied by problems to be solved if snakes as a group were to survive and multiply. One was the capturing and subduing of food. Many modern snakes have solved this simply by remaining predators on the numerous small but highly prolific creatures that inhabit the earth. The adoption of a vegetarian diet is a hypothetical solution but one that snakes never utilized. Evidently this would require such radical changes in digestive physiology and anatomy that no plant-eating snake has ever evolved. A few snakes overcome comparatively large prey by sheer strength of their jaws. The American indigo snake does this; its tropical relatives, which may reach a length of 9 feet, have been known to eat boa constrictors up to 5 feet long. Using the long, muscular serpent body to overpower and kill prey by winding about it and squeezing evidently was adopted early in the evolutionary history of snakes and is the method used by the largest ones living today as well as by many smaller species. However, really efficient constriction requires heavy muscle masses and some sacrifice in speed and agility. Constrictors also run a risk of being severely injured by their prey before it succumbs.

Another problem facing primitive snakes was what to do with prey after it had become food. They might have evolved some method for chewing or tearing food, but it was apparently simpler and more in keeping with the habits of the ancestral lizards to swallow it whole.[1] This practice put an evolutionary premium on the development of strong and versatile digestive enzymes. Since salivary digestive enzymes introduced beneath the skin of the still-living prey could be distributed by its circulation, a further advantage was gained by the development of long teeth with grooves running from base to tip. Probably quite by accident, some of the salivary enzymes or their precursors proved to be potent toxins when injected into tissues. At this point there emerged a primitive poisonous snake with toxic saliva, venom, and large, grooved teeth, fangs, to introduce it into the tissues of the prey. Many snakes have progressed no further than this.

Further evolutionary changes are primarily a perfecting of this basic equipment. Enlargement of anterior teeth was favored over that of posterior teeth, grooves closed and became channels, bones bearing the fangs shortened, and musculature was modified so that the fangs swung forward. The snake could now embed its fangs with a stabbing motion when it struck. Meanwhile, natural selection favored production in the salivary glands of substances that quickly immobilized and killed the snakes' usual prey. The glands themselves enlarged, portions of them became reservoirs where venom was stored until needed, and their ducts became closely fitted to the fang base. Parallel modifications of the sense organs and body musculature made the strike faster and more accurate. Snakes became progressively better able to exploit for food animals previously not available to them. With such highly developed equipment, a 4-foot rattlesnake can feed regularly upon squirrels and half-grown rabbits, while a nonvenomous blacksnake of the same length, without these specialized aids, must usually be content with smaller and weaker game.

Defense against enemies is a secondary benefit derived by venomous reptiles. The bite need not be fatal to the enemy—only painful enough to discourage future aggression. Venomous and noxious animals tend to advertise: they show warning colors, make sounds such as hissing or rattling, and indulge in spectacular display and threatening behavior. In some reptiles, such as the spitting cobras and poisonous lizards, the defensive function of the venom apparatus seems to be more important than its role in food getting.

Venom is but one of many adaptations that contribute to the success of a reptile in its environment. The advantage a venomous snake gains in securing food may be offset by such factors as low reproductive capacity, less success at concealment or escape from predators, or poor ability to withstand cold or dryness. We have recorded twelve species of snakes living within 10 miles of our home on the north edge of Indianapolis, and not one of them is venomous. The only venomous snake known from this region within historic times, a small type of rattlesnake, was probably exterminated fifty years ago. Information on the composition of snake populations in undisturbed tropical regions is hard to obtain, but there is good reason to think the rear-fanged colubrids with a primitive venom apparatus are as successful in many parts of the American tropics as are the more specialized venomous species. On the other hand, several poisonous snakes are among the most wide-ranging reptile species and among the ones that have adjusted to a great variety of environmental conditions, including those brought about by man. Such a list would include the Asian and Egyptian cobras, pelagic sea snake, European viper, saw-scaled viper, puff adder, and tropical rattlesnake.

The Fossil Record

An attempt to trace the evolution of venomous snakes gets scant assistance from paleontology. Their small, delicate bones make poor fossils, and not many have been found. The earliest well-preserved snake fossil dates back to the late Cretaceous of South America, about 75 million years ago, and represents a fairly large reptile apparently akin to the nonpoisonous swamp-burrowing pipe snakes (Anilidae) found today in parts of tropical America and southeast Asia. The boas and pythons appeared next on the scene, along with some giant aquatic types that have left no living relatives. The great family Colubridae, which includes such modern snakes as the American garter, racer, and king snakes, must have arisen by the beginning of the Miocene period, about 30 million years ago, although fossil evidence is almost nonexistent. The two major groups of venomous snakes, the elapids, the best-known representatives of which are the cobras, and the viperids, typified by the adders of Europe and the rattlesnakes of America, also arose during the Miocene, but somewhat later.[2] They evidently represent two separate developments from primitive colubrid stock, the elapid branch coming off first from a center of origin in the region of Malaysia and the viperid branch evolving later in Africa and southern Asia. Evidence for this is based more upon distribution patterns of contemporary snakes than upon fossils. A typical cobra fossil is known from the middle Miocene of southern Europe. Viper fossils are known from the early Pliocene of Europe, dating from about 12 million years ago, and pit-viper fossils from about the same period have been found in the central United States.[3,4] Another small venomous group, the sea snakes, represents one or more invasions of salt water by elapid stock in the Asio-Australian region.

Although the lineage of the lizards is considerably more ancient than that of the snakes, going back some 200 million years, venom has apparently evolved in only one group. This is the Helodermatidae, a small family confined to the southwestern United States and Mexico and without close affinity to any other group of living lizards. A fossil helodermatid is known from Oligocene deposits in northeastern Colorado and is some 28 million years older than the oldest poisonous-snake fossils found in North America.[5]

Venomous Colubrids

The study of living reptiles tells more about the evolution of the venom apparatus than does an examination of fossils. Nowhere among the boas or pythons is there evidence of a venom apparatus. This is also true of the burrowing, wormlike blind snakes of the families Typhlopidae and Leptotyphlopidae and of the primitive relict groups such as the Anilidae. The Colubridae show many stages of transition in the development of venom apparatus. Enlarged grooved teeth are seen in diverse lines of colubrids throughout the world. As the family is now recognized, this modification involves the teeth at the rear of the upper jaw bone, or maxilla. Snakes that in the past successfully modified their front teeth in this manner made an evolutionary leap into other families. The composition of colubrid saliva has not been adequately investigated, but there is evidence that it shows wide variation in toxicity and chemical makeup. Toxicity for animals that make up the snakes' normal food is frequently quite specific; man and conventional laboratory animals may be little affected. An Indonesian salt-marsh snake (*Fordonia*), for example, has venom that is very toxic for crabs. The highest development of the colubrid venom apparatus is seen in the boomslang,* an African tree snake. Its fangs are large and deeply grooved and can be embedded by a brief bite rather than a prolonged period of chewing. Its venom glands are relatively large and unique among colubrid snakes in their microscopic structure.[6] The highly toxic venom resembles that of pit vipers in its effects and protein constituents.

Other snakes have a simpler pattern. The spotted night

---

* Scientific names of individual species appear in the text only when the species has no widely accepted common name, or in cases in which the same common name has been extensively applied to more than one species— fer-de-lance, for example. For the scientific names, see Table 3, pages 203–207.

snakes (*Hypsiglena*) of the western United States and Mexico have enlarged but ungrooved teeth and venom that quickly paralyzes the lizards that are their principal foods.[7] The tropical American cat-eyed snakes (*Leptodeira*) have taken another step. They resemble the night snakes in most ways, but the enlarged rear teeth have grooves.

Elapids and Sea Snakes

The elapids are a major group of venomous snakes with about 180 species. The fangs are at the anterior end of the maxillary bone and are tubular or deeply grooved; the maxillary bone is not drastically reduced in size and is capable of only slight rocking movement. The most primitive members of the family are probably snakes such as *Ultrocalamus* and *Apistocalamus* of New Guinea, small, slender burrowers without a common English name. In these species the fangs are only a little longer than the teeth just behind them (the actual length is a little less than 1 millimeter in a snake about 20 inches long), and the venom channel is a groove. These snakes are assumed to be innocuous, but precise information on this point is lacking.

Cobras are the best-known elapids; indeed the family is sometimes called the cobra family, a convenient but misleading oversimplification. The cobras include six species of the genus *Naja,* as well as the ringhals, king cobra, and water cobra. Although the largest species, the king cobra, and the best-known one, the Asian cobra, inhabit southern Asia, the majority of species are African. All are large snakes (4 to 8 feet), and the king cobra is immense—average adults run 8 to 12 feet, although the record of 18 feet 4 inches must have been based upon a most exceptional individual. The fangs of an adult Indian cobra are 4 to 5 millimeters long, but this is no longer than the fangs of a 17-inch diamondback rattlesnake. The maxillary bone may be without teeth other than the fangs, or there may be one to three tiny teeth near the posterior end. The ringhals, the spitting cobra, and some races of the Asian cobra have the discharge orifice of the fang so located that the venom stream is ejected forward and slightly upward when the snake is in its usual defensive position with the head raised.[8] The ringhals and spitting cobra are well known for ejecting a thin jet of venom at the eyes of an enemy. They are accurate at ranges of at least 6 feet, and the venom causes instant agonizing pain and temporary blindness. Flattening the neck into the characteristic hood is something all cobras do when alarmed. Indian races of the Asian cobra excel all others in this behavior, and the threat is made more dramatic by the spectacle, or monocle, mark on the dorsal aspect of the hood. However, spreading the neck as a type of threatening behavior is not restricted to cobras; it is done by many kinds of snakes, poisonous and nonpoisonous, in widely separated parts of the world.

The four species of tropical African mambas are large, whiplike snakes usually 5 to 7 feet long, although the black mamba is reported to reach 14 feet. The fangs are long and slender (6 to 7 millimeters in adult green mambas). The otherwise toothless maxillary bone is quite mobile, and the fangs lie far forward almost under the tip of the nose. Most mambas are tree snakes, but the black mamba is largely a ground dweller.

Elapids are represented in the New World by the coral snakes (*Micrurus, Micruroides, Leptomicrurus*). The fifty or so species are almost entirely tropical and subtropical in distribution;

two reach the southern United States. Their similarity to one another and to certain Oriental species suggests that coral snakes probably represent a single invasion across a land bridge from Asia. Most are medium-sized (2 to 4 feet) snakes with small heads and bright ringed patterns of black, red, and yellow. The fangs are short, about 2 millimeters in adults of the North American coral snake. Coral snakes are secretive and feed mostly upon other snakes.

Kraits are South Asian elapids with short fangs but highly toxic venom. Among English-speaking peoples they are thought of as small snakes, but actually most species are 3 to 4 feet long when adult, and two may reach 7 feet. They have vivid patterns, usually of light and dark bands.

The sixty or so species of elapids restricted to Australia, New Guinea, and nearby islands show a range of variation as great as all the rest of the family combined. Evidently they reached the island continent at a time when there was minimal competition from other kinds of snakes and proceeded to preempt most of the available habitat niches. The Australian elapids range from tiny, bright-colored burrowers to giant species, such as the 11-foot taipan. The Australian blacksnake spreads a cobra-like hood, and the death adder is a heavy-bodied, wide-headed snake that affords a striking parallel to some of the vipers. Such species as the tiger snake and Australian brown snake are best known for the high toxicity of their venoms.

The sea snakes are a group of about fifty species derived from the elapids. Some of the sea kraits (*Laticauda*) look very similar to the banded krait; the most obvious difference is the flat, oarlike tail of the former. However, most sea snakes are highly modified for marine life: the body and tail are laterally compressed to aid in swimming; the nostrils are on the top rather than on the side of the head; the large belly scutes seen in most land snakes are very small or absent; and they have salt-excreting glands. Some sea snakes have a heavy body and long, thin neck that terminates in a grotesquely small head. Sea-snake fangs are short (3 millimeters in a 38-inch beaked sea snake and 2 millimeters in a 22-inch pelagic sea snake), and there are usually several small teeth on the long, firmly fixed maxillary bone. Most sea snakes are awkward to helpless on land. None can strike when out of water, but most can turn to make an awkward snapping bite.

These reptiles are found in both Asian and Australian coastal waters, with a few species ranging well out into Oceania. The pelagic sea snake has spread across the Pacific to the western coasts of Central and South America and south to New Zealand and the Cape of Good Hope. No sea snake is known from the Atlantic Ocean, although the pelagic sea snake may eventually find its way through the Panama Canal and become established in the Caribbean.

Vipers

Vipers are the other major group of venomous snakes, having about the same number of species as the elapids. In vipers the maxillary bones are short and each bears only one tooth, the fang. The fangs are near the front of the mouth and have a wide range of rocking movement. The venom channel is a tube for at least part of its length. Most vipers have a somewhat triangular head that is distinctly wider than the neck.

This widening is often accompanied by subdivision of the large head shields seen in most snakes.

The most primitive vipers are the four species of African night adders and the almost unknown *Azemiops* of upper Burma and adjacent China and India. The fangs are short (2.5 millimeters in a 23-inch night adder, which is little longer than the fangs of a coral snake of that size), and the venom channel is a groove for about half its length. Night adders' heads are barely distinct from the neck, and the head shields are not fragmented.

Another genus of African vipers, *Bitis,* includes both large and small species, all of which have unusually wide heads and stout bodies. The Gaboon viper appears to have the longest fangs of any snake. They measure 29 millimeters in a 51-inch snake and 45 to 50 millimeters (almost 2 inches) in giant 6-foot specimens. Fangs this size are formidable weapons even without venom. The puff adder is the best-known snake of this group and is found through most of Africa and into the western part of the Arabian peninsula.

The genus *Vipera* includes the small vipers of Europe, Russell's viper of India and southeast Asia, and several Middle Eastern species. *Cerastes,* which includes the well-known horned viper of the Sahara, and *Pseudocerastes* and *Eristicophis* of western Asia are specialized desert genera. The saw-scaled vipers are small but exceedingly dangerous snakes found throughout most of the Afro-Asian desert belt.

The largest subdivision of vipers, known as pit vipers, includes about 120 species and is often placed in a separate family, the Crotalidae. The pit vipers are characterized by a deep pit on each side of the head between the eye and nostril and usually slightly below a line connecting the two. The pits may give the impression of an extra pair of nostrils, and one of these snakes is called *cuatro narices* ("four nostrils") in Mexico. The pit is actually two cavities, an outer and an inner, separated by a membrane. The pits are heat sensors able to detect temperature differences of as little as 1° C. higher or lower than that of the background. Although the range is limited to about 12 inches in adult rattlesnakes, the resolving power of the sensor is high, and objects of different temperatures can be localized within the zone of sensitivity. The pits appear to be used chiefly in directing the strike; snakes of this group that have had their other sense organs blocked out can still strike accurately.[9] The linking of heat-sensing organs with highly developed fangs and powerful venom gives pit vipers the most sophisticated weapons system known among snakes. It is especially effective against warm-blooded targets that can be tracked at night and in tunnels.

No known snakes, living or fossil, link the pit vipers to the rest of the viper family. Zoogeographic evidence indicates that the group arose in southeast Asia and rather promptly migrated via a land bridge to America, where at least three subgroups are now well established. The most primitive pit vipers are in the genus *Agkistrodon*, which includes the North American copperhead and cottonmouth as well as one Middle American and nine Asian species. The two largest genera of pit vipers, *Bothrops* in tropical and temperate South America and *Trimeresurus* in southeast Asia, are so similar that they have been united by some herpetologists. It is debatable whether the relationship is really very close or whether the two genera are showing a remarkable degree of parallel evolution. The species of both genera fall into three broad groups. One group, exemplified by the jararaca and fer-de-lance of the Americas and the habu of Asia, consists of large snakes, 4 to 7 feet long, but rather slender and of terrestrial habits. The second group is composed of species usually under 4 feet long but heavy-bodied. They are dull-colored, terrestrial in habits, and often occur in highlands. The Chinese mountain viper of Asia and the jumping viper of Central America belong to this group. In the third group are relatively small, slender, but large-headed species that are green or mottled green, brown, and yellow. They have prehensile tails and are arboreal. Examples are the eyelash viper of Central America and the white-lipped tree viper of southeast Asia. As might be expected, some species do not fit very well into any of these groups.

A fang length of 17 to 19 millimeters is average for adults of the larger species such as the fer-de-lance and habu. Some small species have proportionally very long fangs (6 millimeters in a 16-inch hognose viper). The North American *Agkistrodon* have relatively short fangs, 4 to 5.5 millimeters in adult copperheads.

Rattlesnakes are distinctively American pit vipers that probably developed on the Mexican plateau and dispersed chiefly northward. Of the twenty-seven species of *Crotalus* and three of *Sistrurus,* only one has an extensive range south of Mexico, while fifteen occur in the United States. There are both large and small species; exceptional specimens of the eastern diamond-back-rattlesnake are 7 to 8 feet long, while one of the small species of the Mexican mountains seldom attains a length of 20 inches. The rattle is an interlocking series of horny segments attached to the tail tip. When vibrated it makes a hissing or buzzing sound that serves warning that the snake is alert, annoyed, and likely to bite if the annoyance continues. Tail vibrating is a common nervous habit of snakes of many kinds. Why an elaborate organ for enhancement of this sound should develop in one line of the pit vipers is a matter for speculation. The most reasonable hypothesis assumes that it developed to discourage accidental trampling of the snakes by large grazing animals, such as bison.[10] The same hypothesis has been evoked to explain the development of venom spraying in some cobras. The rattle is not equally well developed in all species of rattle-snakes. It is so small in the pigmy rattlesnake that it would seem to have little function as a warning, while a species from Santa Catalina Island in the Gulf of California lacks a functional rattle. Fangs of larger rattlesnakes, such as the diamond-backs, measure 13 to 17 millimeters in snakes 4 to 5 feet long.

Longest of the vipers is the bushmaster of the American tropics, which is reported to reach a length of 12 feet. It is relatively slender, so exceptional specimens of the Gaboon viper and diamondback rattlesnake may exceed it in weight. It is the only American pit viper that lays eggs, and certain features of the skull, plus the presence of a curious burrlike arrangement of scales at the tip of the tail, suggest that it may have been close to the stock from which the rattlesnakes arose. However, it is certainly not a direct ancestor, and its affinities with other pit vipers are obscure.

A final, enigmatic group of poisonous snakes is the mole vipers (*Atractaspis*). Although they have long hollow fangs and reduced maxillary bones, they are markedly different from the rest of the vipers. They have large head shields and the body form of many colubrid snakes. They are subterranean in habits and have the small head, minute eyes, and polished scales common to many burrowing snakes. The fangs are not especially long for a viper (4 millimeters in a 23-inch specimen), but they appear huge in the small head. They cannot be swung far forward, but can be elevated, usually one at a time, and brought backward and downward with a stabbing movement while the mouth is closed. The small head and peculiar manner of biting make it unsafe to hold a mole viper behind the head in the usual manner of holding snakes, a fact that several herpetologists have learned to their sorrow. The mole vipers are small, rarely more than 2 feet long, and uniformly black or brown in color. The sixteen species inhabit tropical Africa and small areas of the Middle East.

Venomous Lizards

There are only two venomous lizards, the gila monster of the southwestern United States and northern Mexico and the closely related escorpion of central western and southern Mexico. They are large, corpulent, rather slow-moving reptiles that inhabit warm, semiarid country. Since their food consists mostly of nestling mammals and the eggs of birds and reptiles, their venom seems to have a defensive rather than a food-getting function. In marked contrast to that of the snakes, the venom apparatus consists of four pairs of deeply grooved and flanged teeth in the lower jaw, with ducts from the venom glands opening near their bases. In a large lizard, these teeth may be 5 to 6 millimeters long.[11]

2. Venom Glands and Venom Secretion

Structure of the Glands

Nature, or evolution, if you will, works with materials at hand. Venomous reptiles' fangs are modified teeth; glands producing the venom developed from glands that once had other functions. As they acquired the ability to synthesize new substances, they evidently still retained some of their original functions. This may explain why reptile venoms are among the most complex of biological toxins. Exceptionally well-developed oral glands are among the specializations snakes developed in order to eat comparatively large animals by swallowing them whole. The original function of these glands was evidently to secrete substances that lubricated the food for easier swallowing and speeded up digestion. After examining about 180 species in 120 representative genera of snakes, Dr. Aaron Taub of the Department of Zoology of Pennsylvania State University found ten distinct types of oral glands. No one species had all ten, but most had several.[1]

Only two types of ophidian oral glands produce venom—Duvernoy's glands in certain colubrid snakes and the venom glands of vipers, elapids, and sea snakes. These glands lie in the space between the eye and the angle of the mouth. Although sometimes considered homologous to the parotid salivary gland of mammals, they have a different nerve supply and embryonic origin. Depending upon the species of snake, the venom glands may be pear-shaped, almond-shaped, or triangular. Their surface may be smooth or lobulate. In vipers a special muscle, the compressor glandulae, helps squeeze the secretion from the glands; in elapids the superficialis muscle has this function. Ducts carry the venom to the fangs. The connection between duct and fang is of necessity somewhat loose, for the fangs are regularly shed and replaced. In vipers, a small mass of glandular tissue surrounds the duct shortly before it connects with the fang; in elapids, glandular tissue of similar type encases the duct for most of its length. This tissue comprises the accessory gland.[2] Its function is not clearly understood. However, venom taken directly from the main venom gland has been reported to be less toxic than that normally expelled through the fangs, which suggests that the accessory gland ejects into the venom stream substances that activate components produced in the main venom gland. (For a longitudinal section of a rattlesnake venom gland, see illustrations, following page 116.)

Two species of slender, brightly colored snakes found in southeastern Asia have thin, tubular venom glands that extend back into the body almost half of its length. These snakes, known as long-glanded snakes (*Maticora*), are closely related to the Oriental coral snakes. Similar, although somewhat shorter, glands are found in two of the sixteen species of mole vipers and two of the four species of night adders. Since long-glanded snakes, mole vipers, and night adders are only remotely related to one another, and since all species with elongated glands are closely related to species with conventional glands, this curious modification seems to have evolved independently in the three lineages. The elongate glands may represent a way of fitting a comparatively large mass of venom-producing tissue into the animal without widening the small, compact head that is a pronounced advantage in burrowing or pushing into crevices.

Work by Dr. Carl Gans of the Department of Biology of the State University of New York at Buffalo, Dr. Joseph F. Gennaro of the University of Louisville Medical School, and Dr. Elazar Kochva, an Israeli zoologist who has worked with Gans and also independently at Tel Aviv University, has thrown new light on the anatomical and chemical changes that take place in viper venom glands during the secretion cycle. Viewed under the microscope, the venom gland consists of clumps of tubules lined with secretory cells. These cells are mostly of the serous or protein-secreting type, but mucus-secreting cells are also found, particularly in the accessory gland. If the snake is killed 24 hours or so after it has expended a good portion of its venom and the main venom gland then examined, its cells are tall columns filled with granules that rise to the apex of the cells and are extruded into the tubule along with some nongranular material. If the snake is killed and the gland examined a week or so after the venom was expended, the tubules and central lumen of the gland are filled with venom. The secretory cells are flat and have lost most of their granules.[3,4]

Gennaro and his associates have examined the venom gland and venom of pit vipers with an electron microscope.[5] They find the venom within the gland literally packed with ultramicroscopic globules of several kinds, each surrounded by a membrane. These globules are most abundant near the cells that secrete the venom; far fewer are found in venom that has been expelled from the fangs. Some globules appear to contain ribosomes, the minute granules that synthesize protein. It seems highly probable that the globules are packages of enzymes, toxins, and other substances of the venom, neatly sealed up until needed. This would explain how mutually incompatible substances, such as protein toxins and proteolytic enzymes that would digest them, can coexist in venom stored in the gland. The mechanism that "unwraps" the packages when their contents are needed is unknown. Very likely some substance secreted by the accessory gland does this, although there is a good chance some of the globules are triggered to burst on contact with substances in the tissues of the bitten animal. Perhaps the relative immunity of snakes to their own venom may be partially explained by the failure of toxin globules to disintegrate in their tissues.

Dr. Herbert Rosenberg, a North American zoologist who worked with Gans at Buffalo and is now at the Langmuir Laboratory of Cornell University, found that the elapid venom gland has longer secretory tubules than the viper type of gland, but the cells and the general features of the secretory process seem to be similar. Sea-snake venom glands are of the elapid type.[6]

Less is known of the secretory cycle in Duvernoy's glands. A striking difference between these glands and viper venom glands is the larger amount of storage space in the latter.[7] The amount of secretory tissue in the Duvernoy's glands of a 2-foot Asian river snake (*Enhydris plumbea*) is probably greater than that in the venom glands of an American copperhead of equal size, but the copperhead has much more venom available for instant injection.

In the two poisonous lizards the venom glands also evolved

from modified salivary glands, but here the specialization involved glands just under the skin on the outer side of the lower
jaws. In the gila monster, each gland consists of three or four
lobes of secretory tissue, each having a duct that carries the
secretion to the base of one of the grooved teeth in the lower
jaw. The microscopic anatomy of the gland is similar to that
of Duvernoy's gland, and the process of venom secretion follows
the same general pattern as in snakes.[8]

Venom Secretion and Injection

Venom secretion probably begins before the birth or hatch-
ing of young snakes, for an appreciable amount of venom can be
extracted from rattlesnakes less than 24 hours old, and there
are reports of painful and serious bites inflicted by very young
snakes. Secretion continues throughout the reptile's life. The
idea that a snake will outlive its poison, which Rudyard Kipling
used in his story "The King's Ankus," seems to have no basis in
fact.

Temperature markedly affects venom secretion, as it does
practically all reptilian body functions. Poisonous snakes kept
outdoors in the temperate zone produce the greatest amount of
venom during the warmest months and little or no venom during
hibernation. Venom already in the glands may become more
concentrated. Seasonal fluctuation in venom secretion has been
observed in the serpentarium of the Haffkine Institute at Bombay, and even there the peak coincides with the oppressively
hot weather at the onset of the monsoon.[9]

Since the blood of some snakes is toxic when injected into
mammals, it has been suggested that the venom glands serve

only to filter out and concentrate substances made in some other part of the body. However, none of the toxic protein components of venom has been unequivocally demonstrated to be present in the blood, and antiserum that neutralizes venom does not neutralize the toxic effects of snake blood.[10] Although these experiments have included only a few species of snakes, the evidence indicates that the venom glands truly synthesize most of the active principles in venom. Other authorities have postulated an endocrine or internal secretion of the venom glands in addition to their external secretions. There is no very convincing evidence for this hypothesis. The idea that venom is produced in some part of the body remote from the fangs goes back at least to Pliny the Elder (*c.* 23–79 A.D.), who thought it was formed in the gall bladder. A bit of folklore occasionally heard in the southwestern United States is that the gila monster has no anus and produces its venom from food decomposing in the digestive tract.

The amount of venom a snake injects in biting is a matter of great practical importance. One of the unknown factors in every case of snakebite is the amount of toxin the victim has received. Many authorities have assumed that a snake delivers its full supply of venom when it bites. Instances of bites by deadly snakes that were followed by few or no ill effects were explained by assuming that the glands were empty or some malfunction of the venom apparatus prevented effective injection. However, in 1960 Elazar Kochva reported some simple but highly significant experiments carried out on a group of twenty captive Palestine vipers (*Vipera xanthina palaestinae*). He induced the vipers to strike dead mice that were weighed very accurately before and after each bite. Any weight increase was assumed to be due to venom injected. At the end of the experiment, the snakes were milked of any venom that remained, and it was weighed also. He found that a snake almost never expended more than half of its available venom in a single bite, and the average amount injected was 11 percent. There was great variation among his snakes. One cooperative reptile struck twenty-two times, injecting venom every time until its supply was completely exhausted. Another struck ten times, injecting no detectable venom in six of these trials. It then refused to strike and ended the experiment with 85 percent of its venom unexpended.[11] Gennaro, using cottonmouths and rattlesnakes whose venom had been labeled with radioisotopes, confirmed Kochva's observations of the great variation in amount of venom injected at a single bite. Gennaro also found that his snakes used more venom in striking a rat than in striking a mouse.[12] Some kinds of vipers, such as the arboreal pit vipers of the American and Asian tropics, grip their prey and hold it until it is dead. In contrast, Russell's viper, the copperhead, and most species of rattlesnakes usually bite and then release the prey almost instantly. Other species hold onto small prey but release larger animals. It does seem clear that vipers can control the amount of venom they inject in biting and often use very little when striking defensively. It also follows that there is a high-speed sensory feedback mechanism that allows the snake to make split-second adjustments in the force and direction of the strike and in the quantity of venom expelled from the glands. Fang erection, biting, and gland compression are all under independent nervous control.

Elapids, sea snakes, and rear-fanged colubrids all tend to bite and hold on, often chewing as they do so. This sort of bite should be accompanied by a larger injection of venom, but there is no very convincing evidence that this is true. Nor are quick defensive bites by these snakes always ineffective. A rear-fanged boomslang inflicted a fatal bite after embedding only one fang and that for not much more than a second.[13]

3. Properties and Composition of Venoms

One of the liveliest controversies of late-seventeenth-century European science revolved about the bite of the viper. Francisco Redi, an Italian biologist, ascribed its dangerous nature to a yellowish fluid that flowed from the fangs, while M. Charas, a French chemist, attributed it to the animal's "enraged spirits." Charas' view was the popular one. In the final scene of Shakespeare's *Antony and Cleopatra* the Egyptian queen says to the asp as she applies it to her breast:

With thy sharp teeth this knot intrinsicate
Of life at once untie. Poor venomous fool,
Be angry, and dispatch. . . .

Redi's position, supported by his own experiments and later by those of his countryman Felice Fontana (1730–1805), eventually prevailed.[1] However, Charas was not completely wrong; the bite of an enraged viper probably is more dangerous, because an angry snake usually injects more venom.

After three centuries of scientific and technological progress the spiritual heirs of Redi, Fontana, and Charas conduct their debates on a more sophisticated level and write a great deal more, but much remains to be learned about venoms. And no wonder. Reptile venoms often contain fifteen to twenty active substances, most of them large complex molecules impossible to synthesize or to analyze accurately in the laboratory. Their production in the reptile's body is influenced by a host of factors, most of them poorly understood. The biologically active substances in venoms deteriorate at various rates from the moment of their secretion, and this deterioration can be accelerated or retarded depending upon the way the venom is collected, processed and stored. The unique property of venom, its toxicity, can only be measured by using another living system with all its complexities and variations. Add to this all the little accidents that can happen in even a well-run biological laboratory—the misplacement of a decimal point, the colorimeter that reads too high, the subcutaneous injection that was given intramuscularly—and it is surprising there is any consistency at all in experimental results.

Venom Extraction

Since venom research presupposes the obtaining of a supply of venom, this may be a good place to say something about the extraction of venom, popularly known as snake milking. Although not without risk, it is a simple procedure. In our laboratory, one person lifts the snake from its cage with tongs or with a hook slid under its body, disturbing it as little as possible. Exceptionally active and dangerous species may be anesthetized or chilled into helplessness. The operator pins down the snake's head and grasps it just behind the jaws, while an assistant controls the body. The snake opens its mouth; if not, the mouth is pulled open with a small blunt hook, and the operator hooks the fangs over the edge of a vial or tube. At this point a liberal amount of venom is usually ejected; more is squeezed out by gentle pressure on the glands. Samples from individual snakes may be kept separate, or venom from several individuals of the same species may be pooled. We freeze the samples as soon as possible after collection. After we have about six samples, we transfer the vials without thawing them to a lyophilizing apparatus. Here water is withdrawn from the frozen material under a high vacuum, leaving a light, chalky deposit. Stored away from light and dampness in a refrigerator, lyophilized venom retains its toxicity and most of its other properties for years. In the days before we had a lyophilizing apparatus, we collected venom in shallow containers, such as watch glasses, and dried it over a chemical desiccant. Venom dried in this fashion has been reported to retain its lethal properties for 39 years, but some of its enzyme activity is lost or diminished much more rapidly. Some of our biochemist colleagues, concerned with obtaining venom enzymes with as little deterioration as possible, milk their snakes into vials chilled to about $-200°$ C. with liquid nitrogen. Many laboratories cover the open end of the collecting vessel with a membrane to prevent contamination of the venom with mouth secretions and to simulate more closely conditions of a natural bite. Some laboratories use electrical stimulation of the jaw muscles to increase the amount of venom expelled. Workers on occasion object to pressing on the venom glands because cells may be damaged and their contents expelled prematurely.

Rear-fanged snakes, very short-fanged snakes, and gila monsters present special problems. Venom samples can be obtained by inducing the reptile to bite a rubber or plastic object and washing the secretion from its surface, or by collecting droplets from the fangs with a fine capillary tube or wick of filter paper. Sometimes venom glands are dissected out, ground or minced, and extracted with saline solution. Material so obtained is obviously not the same as naturally secreted venom.

From time to time the word gets around that snake milking is a highly lucrative business. Nearly every herpetologist has in his file letters from ambitious youngsters who hope to finance a new car or a year of college by extracting and selling venom. It does look profitable. A recent price list from a well-known commercial supplier lists timber rattlesnake venom at $40 per gram, Mojave rattlesnake venom at $100, North American coral snake venom $1,000, and sea krait venom at $5,000. The project becomes a little less enticing when one learns that 200 to 500 coral-snake milkings are required to accumulate 1 gram of venom. Also, the amateur usually does not realize that the market for most venoms is extremely small; moreover, the demand in the United States is largely being filled by a few laboratories with the equipment and expertise to turn out a satisfactory product. So nearly saturated is the market that venom extracted from diamondback rattlesnakes and other common species as a part of public demonstrations at small roadside snake exhibits is usually thrown away because no purchaser can be found for it. The amateur who has access to a good supply of venomous snakes of unusual species or of species whose venom is in particular demand may occasionally do well with a small-scale snake-milking operation, but even he might be better advised to sell the snakes to larger laboratories or to individual investigators. Particularly when dealing with rare or unusual species, research workers often prefer to buy the animals and extract the venom in their own laboratories. In this way they have control over at least some of the many variables that affect the quality of a venom sample, and the animal itself can be preserved and later examined by anyone who may wish to confirm its identity.

The rate at which snakes replenish their venom after milking or biting varies tremendously, depending upon temperature and other factors affecting the animals' general condition. Kochva found that Palestine vipers required 16 days to refill their glands during the warm season;[2] a group of rattlesnakes, however, required 54 days.[3] Milking does not necessarily render a snake temporarily harmless. Three bites inflicted on snake handlers by rattlesnakes milked the previous day resulted in poisoning severe enough to require hospitalization.[4] Of course, the milkings may not have drained the snakes' glands.

We milk our snakes as soon as practicable after capture unless we know that the snake expended a great deal of venom or injured its mouth in its battle to remain free. After the first milking we allow them at least 3 weeks' rest between milkings and usually give them no food for 3 to 5 days before milking. We do not usually make more than two venom extractions from a snake that does not eat in captivity. We never extract venom from a snake that is obviously sick unless we are interested in the effect the illness may have on venom secretion.

Nearly all records from snake farms where large numbers of reptiles are kept for venom extraction show that the quantity of venom per snake declines with successive milkings. We believe that this may be ascribed to inadequate and improper diet, overcrowding with resultant rapid spread of infection, insufficient time between venom extractions, and the more or less continuous disturbance of the snakes, especially if they are on public display. Pampering snakes to keep up production is often simply not consistent with the economical operation of the serpentarium, particularly in a place where fresh snakes are easily obtained. In theory, repeated milking of a healthy snake at 15- to 20-day intervals should increase venom production, for the epithelium of the venom gland is kept in the secretory phase.

Venom Yields and Physical Properties

The maximum amount of venom that even a very large snake can produce is rarely more than 5 cubic centimeters, with a dry weight of 1 to 1.5 grams. The late C. B. Pollard, former professor of chemistry at the University of Florida, reported obtaining 6.25 cubic centimeters of venom from an eastern diamondback rattlesnake.[5] The dry weight was not recorded but would have been more than 1.5 grams if the sample contained an average amount of solids. Herschel Flowers, a U.S. Army expert on poisonous snakes and their venoms, told us of collecting 6 to 7 cubic centimeters of venom from giant specimens of the terciopelo (*Bothrops atrox*) collected in Costa Rica. These samples when evaporated yielded about 1 gram of dry venom, so the water content was high. Flowers believes that this great pit viper produces more venom than the bushmaster, although the latter is an even bigger snake. Some other exceptionally large yields from vipers are 1,530 milligrams from a jararacussu,[6] 1,094 milligrams from a cottonmouth moccasin,[7] 1,145 milligrams from a western diamondback rattlesnake,[8] and 750 milligrams from a puff adder.[9] The Gaboon viper, probably the heaviest of the world's poisonous snakes, may well produce the most venom, but no one has reported the quantity that can be obtained from really giant specimens of this awesome reptile. Three large ones milked at the serpentarium in Brazzaville, Congo, gave a combined yield of about 10 cubic centimeters with a dry weight of 2,970 milligrams.[10]

Elapid snakes generally produce less venom than vipers; however, 720 milligrams has been obtained from an Egyptian cobra[11] and almost 600 milligrams from an Australian mulga snake.[12] There is very little on record about venom production by king cobras, but our impression is that this species does not produce the quantities that might be expected from its great size. Sea snakes are poor venom producers, although no one has reported milking any really big ones. A yield of 55.4 milligrams from a beaked sea snake seems to be the largest on record.[13] Rear-fanged snakes produce still less venom. Fifteen milligrams from a boomslang is the highest yield reported. It is difficult to extract venom from rear-fanged snakes. The location of the fangs makes it hard to insert them in a collecting receptacle, and the venom often flows from the grooves rather than from the tips of the fangs and thus is lost or mixed with other mouth secretions.[14] Up to 2 cubic centimeters of liquid venom has been collected from gila monsters, but the techniques used do not prevent the venom from being contaminated with appreciable amounts of other oral secretions.[15]

Very large venom yields seem to be obtained unpredictably. In the summer of 1961, three employees of the Postgraduate Medical Centre in Karachi brought me a 62-inch cobra they had caught in a nearby rubbish dump. It was an extraordinarily handsome specimen, so I allowed it about a month to adjust to captivity before milking it early in September. At that time it gave 194 milligrams of venom, an average quantity for a big cobra. In February I milked it a second time and obtained 610 milligrams, an extremely high yield. A third milking in July, almost a year after its capture, yielded 399 milligrams, also well above average. In three milkings this reptile produced more venom than the combined single samples from twelve adult cobras, one of which was 68 inches long.

In biology, average values are of more significance than extremes. If ten healthy adult timber rattlesnakes are milked, about 4.5 cubic centimeters, or slightly over a teaspoonful, of somewhat cloudy yellow liquid should be obtained. If the liquid stands overnight in the refrigerator or is put in a centrifuge operating at moderate speed for a few minutes, a whitish deposit composed of amorphous granular material and cells from the venom glands settles to the bottom of the tube. The clear yellow fluid that remains is somewhat denser than water (specific gravity 1.08–1.09), slightly viscid, practically odorless, and very slightly acid (pH 5.9). Those who have tasted rattlesnake venom say it is weakly astringent and sweetish and causes slight tingling of the lips. Dried in a thin layer, the venom cracks and can be scraped off in yellow platelets, or needles, sometimes incorrectly called crystals. After drying, this sample will weigh about 1.35 grams, indicating a content of about 30 percent solids.

In Table 4, Reptile Venoms: Yields and Toxicity (pages 208–219), are listed average venom yields for a representative group of poisonous snakes. Yields are expressed as dry weight. The liquid volume, in addition to being difficult to measure when very small quantities are involved, tells little of the potency or activity of the sample because the water content is so variable. Rattlesnake venoms usually contain 25 to 30 percent solids, and most other viper venoms contain 20 to 27 percent. Elapids may secrete more concentrated venoms. Cape cobras on a South

African snake farm produced venom containing 37 to 43 percent solids,[16] and a range of 18 to 35 percent is reported for
coral snakes.[17] A specimen from an Australian blacksnake was
said to contain 67 percent solids and must have had the consistency of syrup.[18]

Most snake venoms are yellowish, varying from amber to
pale straw. Those of vipers are generally darker than those of
elapids. Colorless venoms that become white on drying are characteristic of sea snakes and the very young of many species.
Secretion of colorless venom may be seen in local populations of
species with a normally yellow fluid—for example, the vipers in
certain districts of France. It may also occur as an individual
aberration among cobras and other species.

While low temperature is an excellent way to preserve the
biological activity of reptile venoms, high temperature has the
opposite effect. At a temperature of about 65° C. most viper
venoms begin to lose toxicity, and exposure to 80° C. for 5 minutes renders them almost totally innocuous. Recently, however, I
have found that venom of Wagler's pit viper is unique in remaining almost fully toxic after heating in an autoclave (a sterilizer
using steam under pressure) at 125° C. for 15 minutes. With this
exception, elapid venoms are more heat-resistant than those of
vipers. Temperatures close to boiling (97° to 102° C.) maintained for 30 minutes are necessary to destroy all the toxicity of
cobra venom. The venom of the gila monster is more resistant
to heating than that of any snake, with the possible exception of
Wagler's pit viper.

Visible light has little effect on either dried or liquid venom.
However, if traces of the common biological stain methylene
blue are added to venom in solution, it is rapidly inactivated by

light.[19] Ultraviolet light and X rays also inactivate snake-venom solutions.

The Chemistry of Reptile Venoms

Early chemists were perplexed and perhaps disappointed to find that analysis of snake venoms revealed no unique or unusual substance to account for their deadly properties. In fact, they were quite indistinguishable from other "animal gums," such as egg white. As organic chemistry advanced during the nineteenth century, venoms were again examined for the presence of toxic alkaloids such as conine or hyoscine. Since these toxic alkaloids had been found in plants, it seemed logical to the chemists of the time that they might be in the venoms of animals as well. Some of the symptoms of cobra poisoning are a little like those of hyoscine poisoning. None could be found, however, and the Commission on Indian and Australian Snake Poisoning reported in 1874: "It is quite impossible to draw any deductions as to the nature of the poison. It is . . . a mixture of albuminous principles with some specific poison." [20]

The protein nature of snake venoms was established during the latter part of the nineteenth century, largely through the research of the versatile physician and novelist S. Weir Mitchell in the United States and the biochemist Norris Wolfenden in England. The latter in 1886 summed up his experiments with these comments: "The power of the venom in all these snakes appears to reside in the proteids. Why should proteids in these cases be so strongly poisonous? . . . The proteid molecule is still little understood . . . and there is no antecedent improbability in the supposition that a rearrangement of the molecule, without altering the ultimate composition of the body and without depriving it of any of the characters making it typical of the class to which it belongs, should make it a poison." [21]

John de Lacerda, a French physician living in Brazil, in 1880 was one of the first to attribute the toxicity of snake venoms to enzymes, an idea that gained increasing popularity as more and more of these biological catalysts were found in the venoms of reptiles. About twenty-five venom enzymes are now known, although no one species of reptile has all of them. Some of them clearly help the venom perform its lethal task. Hyaluronidase promotes its rapid spread from the point of injection; phospholipase A damages cell membranes; proteases liquefy tissue. Others, such as the nucleotidases, seem to be more involved with the digestive function of venom than with its toxicity. The yellow color of snake venoms is associated with the enzyme L-amino acid oxidase. Although it attacks many different substances, it has very little toxicity. Indeed, no venom enzyme has been identified with the main lethal component. For some of the more important venom enzymes see Table 5 (pages 220–222).

Isolation and Identification of Toxins

With the development of techniques such as electrophoresis and immunodiffusion that permit separation of the components of protein mixtures, it has become evident that reptile venoms are complex in comparison with other biological toxins. A substance like the toxin of the tetanus bacillus is homogeneous and specific in its action. It is a biochemical bullet that unerringly combines with its molecular target. Reptile venoms are more like hand grenades whose lethal fragments hit multiple targets.

The method I have used most frequently in studying the relative complexity and interrelationships of snake venoms is the immunodiffusion technique devised in 1948 by Örjan Ouchterlony, a Swedish bacteriologist working in the State Bacteriological Laboratory in Stockholm, to detect production of toxin by diphtheria bacilli. If a solution of a protein toxin is mixed in proper proportion with its corresponding antitoxin a precipitate forms. Now if instead of being mixed, the two are put into separate wells cut in a gel such as agar, they will diffuse outward, and the precipitate will form as a band in the area between the wells. If the toxin is a mixture of proteins, each one will form a band, providing it has a corresponding component or antibody in the antitoxin. The number of bands thus indicates the number of protein components in the toxin. This system has another interesting and useful property. If two complex toxins, such as copperhead venom and cottonmouth venom, are put in adjoining wells and an antitoxin against a mixture of the two into a third well equidistant from them both, two sets of bands will be formed. Those representing components common to both venoms will fuse as the two sets approach each other, while those representing substances present in one venom but not in the other will cross. This does not exhaust the usefulness of the gel diffusion tests. The positions of the bands reflect the diffusion rates of the components, and their curvature tells something of their molecular weight.

The method can yield a great deal of valuable information. It has been used to show existence of different components in venoms of young and adult snakes of the same species; to compare venoms before and after treatment with X rays, light, and chemicals; and to show the degree of relationship between venoms of snakes of different families, genera, or species. It has not, however, proved very successful in predicting how well an antitoxin will neutralize a particular venom. So far, my colleagues and I have had little success in associating particular bands with particular activities. We would like to be able to say: Band A represents neurotoxin, Band B, hemolysin, Band C, hyaluronidase, and so on, but this goal has not been reached.

Electrophoresis—the separation of substances by their migration through a paper strip or gel bed under the influence of an electric current—is another technique used to determine the number of components in venoms. It also permits isolation of these fractions so that their biological activities can be identified. In this respect particularly it has proved extremely useful in studying the composition of venoms.

Attempts to purify and to characterize chemically the toxins of snake venoms date back at least a century. The early preparations, such as cobric acid, ophiotoxin, and crotalotoxin, were either artifacts of preparation or substances of undefinable composition. No real success was attained until the 1930s. In 1938 Karl Slotta and Heinz Fraenkl-Conrat, German biochemists working in São Paulo, Brazil, gave the name crotoxin to an apparently pure protein extracted from the venom of Brazilian rattlesnakes.[22] This material was about twice as toxic as the crude venom. Other Latin American workers found that an even more toxic substance, which they named crotamine, could be separated from crotoxin. Crotamine has a very low molecular weight for a protein (about 10,000) and has no enzyme activity. It produces much the same shock and paralysis as the crude venom when injected into animals.[23] About the same time crotoxin was isolated in South America, Indian biochemists, notably B. H. Ghosh and S. S. De in Calcutta, isolated the neurotoxic component of cobra venom.[24] During World War II venom research was slowed or halted over most of the world, but the 1950s brought improvements in methods for separating and purifying large molecules of biological origin. Since 1954, purified toxins have been prepared from at least a dozen reptile venoms. Not all these preparations are of equal purity, and some of them may represent essentially the same substance. All are similar in being of comparatively low molecular weight and in having no known enzyme activity. For only one is the site and manner of action known. Beta bungarotoxin, from the venom of the many-banded krait, acts at the junction of nerve and muscle by competing with acetylcholine, a substance vital for nerve-impulse transmission.[25]

Most of the biochemical knowledge of reptile venoms comes from studies of a comparatively small number of elapids and vipers. Much less is known of sea-snake venoms and next to nothing of colubrid venoms. Venom of the gila monster is quite different chemically from snake venoms and is poor in enzymes, except for hyaluronidase. Its principal toxic moiety seems to be a polypeptide rather than a protein.[26]

4. Lethal Qualities of Venoms

When the average person thinks of a poison, he is likely to think first, not of its chemical formula or its site of action, but of how deadly it is. However, evaluating the killing power of biological toxins is an extremely tricky business because of the many variables involved—for an obvious example, the kind of animal used. Many early experiments used pigeons as test animals, while most recent work has been done with mice. Comparison of data makes it clear that on a weight basis the pigeon is much more susceptible than is the mouse to most venoms, especially those of vipers. Likewise, there is significant variation in susceptibility among mammals, even between closely related species such as mice and rats.

Reptile venoms are almost innocuous when taken by mouth, a fact known to the first century Roman poet Lucan who wrote:

> Mixt with the blood, the serpents' poison kills.
> The bite conveys it; death lurks in the teeth.
> Swallowed, it works no harm.[1]

Showmen sometimes demonstrate this by drinking a teaspoonful or so of freshly extracted rattlesnake venom. When rattlesnake venom is given to mice by stomach tube, the amount required to kill an animal is about 750,000 times the lethal dose by injection. However, with cobra and krait venoms, the lethal dose by mouth is only 80 to 100 times that by injection. Thus a generous sip of cobra venom could cause fatal poisoning.[2]

For most toxicity assays, the routes of injection used are intravenous, intraperitoneal, or subcutaneous. Intravenous injection is technically the most difficult, for the needle must be inserted directly into a vein, a neat trick in an animal as small as a mouse, but when properly performed it gives the most uniform results. Intraperitoneal injection, in which the needle is inserted into the abdominal cavity, is easy to do, and results are fairly consistent. Injection just under the skin, subcutaneous injection, is also simple, but the effects are less predictable. Since this is the usual mode of injection when a snake bites a man, it is often used in experiments testing serums or other methods of snakebite therapy. For nearly all venoms, the intravenous lethal dose is smallest, the subcutaneous largest, and the intraperitoneal intermediate. The ratio among the three is by no means constant, however. With cobra venoms there is little difference in the lethal doses established by the three routes of injection. However, the intraperitoneal lethal dose may be as little as 1/25 that of the subcutaneous one in the case of the massasauga rattlesnake and practically equal to the subcutaneous dose in some samples taken from the timber and Mojave rattlesnakes. The intravenous lethal dose of boomslang venom is 1/125 the subcutaneous lethal dose, and the difference is almost as great with some viper venoms.

Among snakes, is the female of the species more deadly than the male? This is one of the questions I tried to answer in an experiment testing individual venom samples from seven adult timber rattlesnakes and eight copperheads. About all the experiment really showed was that there is wide and unpredictable variation in toxicity among timber rattlesnakes. The most powerful sample was about five times as toxic as the least powerful one; both came from gravid female snakes collected the same day on the same hilltop. Copperhead samples showed less variation, but there was no obvious correlation with sex, nutritional state, or gestation.[3]

A chance to investigate whether the venom of young snakes was the same as that of adults came during the summer of 1963. While Madge and our eldest daughter were vainly hunting for diamonds in the clay of southwestern Arkansas, I bagged a large female canebrake rattlesnake, a southern subspecies of the timber rattler. That night she presented us with a litter of seventeen young. We kept several of them through their first year, during which they more than doubled their length. Periodically, we extracted their venom. Although the first sample, collected when the young were 5 days old, was less than ⅓ as toxic for mice as a sample from adult canebrake rattlesnakes, there was a steady increase in toxicity, until the sample collected at 6 months was almost 3 times as toxic as venom from adults. After that there was a slight decrease in toxicity, but the 1-year-old sample was still 1.8 times as toxic as that from adults. Venom from a cobra collected as a 13-inch baby and kept for a year in the laboratory showed an even more marked increase in toxicity, but samples from two litters of baby copperheads had about the same toxicity as those of adult snakes.[4]

An interesting sort of venom variation occurs in the tropical rattlesnake (*Crotalus durissus*) which ranges from Mexico to northern Argentina. In parts of this extensive range it has the sinister reputation of being able to break a man's neck regardless of the part of the body bitten. This is believed to be due to the neurotoxic effect of crotamine, which relaxes the neck muscles and causes the head to loll if unsupported. In examination of 530 individual snakes from Brazil, practically all snakes from the northwestern part of the state of São Paulo and an adjacent area in Paraná were found to have large amounts of crotamine in their venom, while snakes from southeastern São Paulo and Minas Gerais were a mixed population of crotamine secretors and snakes without crotamine in their venom. The snakes of Argentina were crotamine positive, but those of several localities in northern and eastern Brazil were negative, with the exception of a population in the state of Ceará that contained both secretors and nonsecretors.[5] There is little information on this topic from other parts of Latin America. The "broken-neck effect" has been reported occasionally following rattlesnake bites in Honduras and Costa Rica but apparently not in tropical Mexico. Crotamine has not been found in venoms of the numerous species of rattlesnakes found in northern Mexico and the United States, although venoms of at least two species produce paralytic symptoms in animals.

Asian cobra venom shows another sort of variation. Although samples from widely separated areas, such as Taiwan, Thailand, and the delta of the Indus have about the same lethal dose for animals, immunological studies show that their toxins are not the same. This was first noted during World War II, when cobra antivenin manufactured in India was found inadequate to treat cobra bites sustained in the Philippines.[6]

The unpredictable variation within venom of a single species has made it almost impossible to establish international standards of potency for serums used in the treatment of snakebites. After careful assay of fifteen pooled venom samples from jararacas (a Brazilian pit viper) collected in localities no more than 31 miles apart, Werner Schöttler, a German pharmacologist, concluded: "Consistent and reproducible reference preparations of snake venoms for antivenin assay can probably be obtained only from snakes that are bred and kept in captivity under constant environmental conditions." [7]

The manner in which venom has been collected, processed, and stored affects its toxicity and other properties, although the lethal factors are quite stable as biological toxins go. Dried venom of the Australian blacksnake was found to retain most of its original toxicity after 39 years of storage, and dried rattlesnake venom remained toxic after 50 years. [8]

In older works on toxicology, toxicity is often expressed as "the minimum lethal dose"—that is, the least amount of the material that will kill an experimental animal; occasionally, "the certainly lethal dose" is used—the amount that will kill all animals in an experimental group. Both of these figures are unduly affected by highly susceptible and highly resistant animals, so modern practice is to use "the 50 percent lethal dose" (LD_{50}), or the dose that in theory will kill half the animals in an experimental group. This is determined by injecting groups of animals (four is about the minimum number) with varying doses of toxins until most or all of the animals receiving the largest dose die and most receiving the smallest dose survive. Generally, a minimum of twenty animals must be used to get a reliable figure. Statistical methods are then used to calculate the LD_{50}. With the more powerful biological toxins this is usually expressed in micrograms (1 microgram is equal to 0.001 milligram) or, to facilitate comparison between species, as micrograms per kilogram of body weight.

Using the white mouse as a test animal, the LD_{50} of Asian

cobra venom is about 5 micrograms. This venom is about forty
times as toxic as sodium cyanide and considerably more toxic
than any other inorganic poison exclusive of radioactive sub
stances. It is about twice as toxic as strychnine and about seve
times as toxic as the dangerous mushroom *Aminita muscaria.*
has about the same lethal dose as the venom of the dangero
yellow scorpion of the Middle East (*Leiurus quinquestriatu*
and is about five times as toxic as that of the black widow spid
Only in comparison with some of the bacterial toxins does it m
a poor showing. While it is about thirty times as lethal as typ
endotoxin, it is only about 1/800 as toxic as diphtheria t
and 1/7,500,000 as toxic as botulinus A toxin, the most l
substance known.

Information is now available on the toxicity to m
many snake venoms. Topping the list in lethality are ven
some of the sea snakes, notably the beaked and small-
varieties. Both are about twice as toxic as Asian cobra
Close behind them are the venoms of the tiger snake, Au
brown snake, many-banded krait, and Philippine cobra;
are elapids. With a few exceptions, venoms of vipers
vipers are considerably less toxic for mice than are elapid
venoms, unless they are compared after intravenous injection.
If this method of injection is used, Russell's viper venom, for
example, is more toxic than krait or cobra venom.

Toxicity of snake venoms for man obviously is something
that cannot be determined experimentally. Nor can any very
meaningful information be gained by extrapolating from the
toxic or lethal doses for small laboratory animals. Indeed, by
this method it is possible to demonstrate that several highly dangerous species of snakes could not possibly kill a man, or con-

versely, that other species are considerably more dangerous than experience tells us they are. Lethal doses for man could probably be determined by establishing the lethal dose for monkeys and extrapolating from this. Such experiments have been done with a few venoms, but the large number of experimental monkeys needed makes this approach impractical on a very extensive scale.

Madge and I have tried to estimate the human lethal dose for various venoms by reviewing snakebite mortality statistics and correlating this information with venom yields and biting habits. For example, bites by the saw-scaled viper frequently are fatal, so an average-size snake of this species probably has several human lethal doses of venom in its glands most of the time. Furthermore, there are a few instances of death from the bite of a saw-scaled viper only 10 or 11 inches long, so a snake of this size can carry at least one lethal dose. Knowing the venom yield from a viper of this size and having reason to think that no more than half this amount is injected in a bite, we estimate the human lethal dose at about half the maximum amount of venom in the glands of a 10- or 11-inch viper, or about 3 milligrams. Of course this does not allow for the probably higher toxicity of the venom of a young snake, nor does it take into consideration the variation in susceptibility of human beings. Nevertheless it seems fair to assume that the lethal dose of this venom for man is quite small. To take another example, it is known that about 10 percent of bites by the North American coral snake are fatal. Well-documented accounts of fatal cases show that the snakes responsible were at least 20 inches long and usually either inflicted multiple bites or hung on for several seconds, thus having a chance to inject most of the venom in their glands. We can now estimate the lethal dose of this venom as close to the maximum contained in the glands of a 20- to 24-inch coral snake, or 4 to 5 milligrams.

Helio Belluomini, a Brazilian herpetologist, using venom yields and toxicity data from experiments on larger animals, has estimated the danger to man of bites by the commoner pit vipers of Brazil. He believes the tropical rattlesnake and the jararacussu capable of delivering a fatal bite in about three out of five cases. With the jararaca the chances of receiving a fatal dose are about one in five, and with the jararaca pintada about one in twenty-five.[9] Snakebite mortality statistics from Brazil tend to confirm Belluomini's estimates of the relative danger of the various species.

Effects of Snake Venoms on Animals

If a mouse is injected subcutaneously with a lethal, but not overwhelming, dose of king-cobra venom, it shows little immediate evidence of pain or discomfort. For a short time it may behave normally but soon it shows signs of weakness. Its breathing is labored, and its flanks have a peculiar, punched-in appearance; excessive saliva soaks its muzzle. Presently it can no longer get to its foot, and breathing becomes ever more difficult. As respiration ceases there is often a brief convulsion with involuntary urination; the heart continues to beat for a few minutes. An autopsy shows no reaction at the site of injection and no gross abnormalities of the internal organs. If half a lethal dose is injected, the weakness and difficulty in breathing develop and may last a few hours, but the animal recovers and is normal in appearance and behavior the next day.

If cottonmouth venom is used, the sequence of events is altogether different. The animal is obviously uncomfortable from the start; it scratches, rubs, or bites at the injection site and is generally irritable and hyperactive. Next comes a quiet period during which the animal sits huddled up but alert. The injection site is dark and oozes bloody fluid while swelling spreads outward from it. There may now be a short period of almost normal activity followed by another quiet stage that eventually terminates in collapse and death. Autopsy shows extensive hemorrhage under the swollen area. The skin around the injection site is gangrenous and may be liquefied. There may be small hemorrhages in the heart, lungs, intestines, and other organs. If the dose is sublethal, there is sloughing of the dead tissue around the injection site after a day or so. The animal is weak, eats poorly, and appears generally miserable for several days before it recovers its health.

The effects produced by these two venoms represent the ends of a spectrum of activities. King-cobra venom kills by directly affecting the vital functions of breathing and heartbeat with little effect on tissues around the site of injection or on the blood and blood vessels. Cottonmouth venom literally dissolves the tissues that it contacts. Small blood vessels are disrupted so that both fluid and cellular parts of the blood leak out. As the zone of vascular damage increases in size, the animal bleeds to death into its own tissues. The heart fails, not because of direct injury but because it can no longer pump effectively through the riddled vascular bed.

Most venoms have effects that are a blend of these extremes. In general, elapid venoms correspond to the king-cobra pattern,

although venom of the Australian blacksnake is strongly hemorrhagic with little paralytic effect. Some coral-snake venoms have a
powerful hemolytic effect—that is, they break down the red
blood cells liberating hemoglobin. Viper venoms generally are
closer to the cottonmouth pattern, but there are exceptions.
Venoms of the tropical rattlesnake and Palestine horned viper
(*Pseudocerastes*) have powerful paralytic activity but little local
effect. Venom of Wagler's pit viper causes exceptionally rapid
collapse and death without local swelling or hemorrhage. In
proportionally large doses, as when a snake strikes its normal
prey, viper venoms kill rapidly, apparently by a more direct effect
on the heart and circulatory system.

To serve the snake in securing food, the venom must be
able to incapacitate prey quickly. To a hungry diamondback
rattler about to strike a wood rat it does not matter whether the
dose of venom it is about to inject will kill ten rats or a hundred
rats in the laboratory. The task at hand is to kill one wood rat
and to do so before the bitten rodent can scurry to an inaccessible
spot or sink its teeth into the rattler's vulnerable spine. And the
rattlesnake can accomplish this. An animal of proper size for
a meal is usually struck in the chest or shoulder. It hunches up
for a second or so, gives several violent but uncoordinated leaps,
falls on its side, and kicks for a short time. It is usually helpless
within 2 minutes, dead within 5. The snake finds it by scent or by
its body heat, probes it with nose and tongue, and swallows it,
usually head first. I once did an experiment in which mice were
removed from a rattlesnake's cage soon after they had been
bitten, and animals that had just been killed by a blow on the
head were substituted. Quite by accident, one of these mice was

only stunned and revived as the snake was about to swallow it. The prey's recovery seemed to disconcert the snake completely, and it lost interest in feeding for the rest of the day.

Too little is known of how snakes use their venom in feeding or how it affects their normal prey. Some rear-fanged colubrids use constriction as the primary means of immobilizing their prey; the venom may weaken it, thus preventing the constrictor from becoming exhausted during a prolonged struggle. Sea-snake venoms are extremely toxic for mammals, which sea snakes never eat, but little is known of their effect on fish, the normal food of most sea snakes. Many elapids feed principally upon snakes and lizards, and it might be expected that their venoms would be more toxic for cold-blooded animals than for mammals. Yet experimental data indicate quite the opposite; speed of action might be more important than sheer killing power.

Snake venom is much too toxic to have a purely defensive function. It is, after all, unnecessary to kill an aggressor in order to discourage him. Indeed, for the long-term future of the defending species, it may be a disadvantage. A dead predator cannot learn from its experience, nor, if it is one of the more intelligent mammals, can it teach its young to avoid snakes that flatten their necks or buzz their tails. The whole selective advantage of warning colors and behavior is based on the premise that most of the aggressors will have an exceedingly unpleasant experience but one from which they will survive and learn something.

Anger or fright probably stimulates a different type of striking response than that seen when the snake is attacking prey, or one accompanied by a smaller injection of venom. We also think there may be a third type of strike, provoked by severe fright or injury, that results in an unusually large venom injection. Efforts to test this experimentally have not been very conclusive. I once offered a mouse to a Popes' tree viper that was feeding regularly and well adjusted to captivity. The snake was evidently not hungry and ignored the mouse until the rodent provoked it into biting. At least one fang drew blood from the mouse's nose, and it ran to a corner in obvious distress. Feeling pretty sure it would die and be eaten during the night, I left it in the cage. The next morning the mouse was alive. Although its head was badly swollen, it eventually recovered. A few days later the snake was offered another mouse that it killed and swallowed within 10 minutes. It seems clear that toward the first mouse the snake used its weapons in response to threat or annoyance; toward the second it was the aggressor and used them to kill. I have seen other incidents of this sort, including one when a large cobra struck a rat several times with its mouth closed. The rat was knocked off its feet but not otherwise harmed. Walker Van Riper, a retired banker who became Curator of Spiders at the Denver Museum of Natural History, made a remarkable series of high-speed photographs of rattlesnakes striking. He noted two types of strike when he used latex bulbs as targets. In the more common type, the fangs were used in a stabbing fashion, while the less common terminated in a definite strong bite.[10] He made no observations on the amount of venom ejected in the two kinds of strike. Van Riper felt that the way of striking was a peculiarity of individual snakes, but we think that had he used a prey animal instead of an artificial object he might have seen the biting response more frequently.

5. When Snake Bites Man

Myth and legend have made the snake man's most implacable enemy, although it is nearer the truth that man is the snakes' most implacable enemy. In the world of the late Pliocene, venomous bites may have effectively deterred curious primate hands and left some subtle trace of fear in the brains of man's prehuman ancestors. Eons later, when early hunters and gatherers experienced the unexpected, violent, and terrifying consequences of a bite by a poisonous snake, they must have seen it as a force quite beyond the ordinary order of things, inexplicable and malignant.

William Plomer's poem "In the Snake Park" expresses a contemporary view:

A man I once knew did survive the bite,
Saved by a doctor running with a knife,
Serum and all. He was never the same again.
Vomiting blackness, agonizing, passing blood,
Part paralyzed, near gone, he felt
(He told me later) he would burst apart . . .
Why should that little head have power
To inject all horror for no reason at all?[1]

Man's high susceptibility to many reptile venoms actually seems to be something of a biological accident. Almost certainly all the genera and practically all the species of poisonous snakes had evolved before man appeared. No poisonous snake today feeds upon primates, nor is there real reason to think any species has done so in the past. The Gaboon viper, which has been known to dine on small antelopes, would have no trouble swallowing a 5- or 6-pound monkey; neither would the bushmaster or some of the other very large venomous snakes of Africa and tropical America, but only very rarely would these ground-dwelling nocturnal snakes have the chance.

When a snake bites a man the effects are extremely variable and unpredictable, ranging from transient and local discomfort —scarcely more than would accompany a briar scratch—to collapse and death within a few minutes. This unpredictability has confused the thinking of biologists and medical men, to say nothing of ordinary citizens, and fostered a great deal of folklore and magic. If you are a Pakistani villager and your neighbor Ahmed is bitten by a cobra and dies after being treated at the district hospital, while your neighbor Ghulzar who is also bitten by a cobra recovers after being treated by the local snake charmer, it will be difficult to convince you that the hospital's treatment is superior to that of the snake charmer. A good many persons in the United States, including some physicians, believe that any bite by a venomous snake will end fatally unless treated. If this is the prevailing attitude, it is not hard to understand how almost any treatment, including some that are positively harmful, can gain a reputation for effectiveness.

A most interesting and significant finding of several recent studies is that many snakebites, perhaps one-third to one-half, result in little or no poisoning. These observations have been made in widely separated parts of the globe: the United States, Malaya, New Guinea, and Israel among others; and the snakes involved have been a diverse lot of vipers, pit vipers, elapids, and sea snakes, including many species that unquestionably have the potential ability to inflict a fatal bite.[2]

Archie Carr, an American herpetologist best known for his work on sea turtles, vividly describes his experiences after being bitten on the leg by a 6-foot terciopelo at a remote field station in Costa Rica. He had no ill effects other than discoloration of the skin around the puncture wounds. Although understandably apprehensive, he did not use the antivenin he had available nor did he drink the two fingers of kerosine offered by a well-meaning neighbor. Carr suggests that the terciopelo may attempt to save its fangs and venom by making abortive strikes at animals too large for food and thus using the strike to frighten rather than to kill. He adds, "And if the incidence of aborted bites is high enough, the cure would be bound to take hold as part of the folk medicine of the country. If generations keep getting 40 per cent recovery from snake brains, kerosine, and chewing tobacco, they have to be unnaturally skeptical not to stick to these as treatment."[3]

While there is no such thing as a typical snakebite, certain combinations of symptoms are seen frequently enough to be considered characteristic. Many of these are sufficiently striking to have found their way into folklore as well as into the earliest medical writings. Symptoms of cobra poisoning often begin within 15 to 30 minutes after the bite, which is usually somewhat painful but not agonizing. One of the first definite indications of serious poisoning is a drooping of the eyelids that gives the victim a sleepy or doped expression. Difficulty in swallowing and speaking, drooling of saliva, giddiness, weakness, and gasping respirations all show the effect of the venom on the nervous system, while weakness and irregularity of the pulse result from the cardiac toxin. Carl F. Kauffeld, herpetologist and director of the Staten Island Zoo, has described the sensations of serious cobra poisoning: "I was sinking into a state that could not be called unconsciousness, but one in which I was no longer aware of what was going on about me. . . . I felt no anxiety; I felt no pain; it did not even strike me as strange that the darkness was closing in on the light. . . . I am certain that I did not lose consciousness entirely at any time; I only felt a complete and utter lassitude in which nothing seemed to matter—not at all unpleasant if this is the way death comes from cobra poisoning." [4]

Recovery is complete and often dramatically rapid. In 1910 an unflappable Englishman who received one of the first doses of cobra antivenin prepared at the new institute in Kasauli, India, was playing tennis a few hours after physicians had despaired of his recovery. Despite the severe involvement of the heart and nervous system, there is no lasting damage.

Bites by other elapids, such as kraits, mambas, and coral snakes, are accompanied by many of the symptoms of cobra poisoning, but there are some significant differences. There is often a period of 1 to 6 hours after the bite during which there are no alarming symptoms or evidence of serious poisoning. This may cause unjustified optimism on the part of the patient and his physician, for the symptoms, once they begin, may progress with terrifying rapidity. A Pakistani physician told us of being consulted one night by a neighbor who had been bitten by a snake while walking in his garden a short time before. He seemed perfectly healthy and normal. The two men were discussing whether it would be better to go to the hospital for an examination or to forget the incident when the bitten man suddenly felt as if there were a great weight pressing on his chest. He was taken to the hospital at once, but died rapidly of respiratory failure. Although the snake was not identified, the circumstances and symptoms strongly suggest krait poisoning. With some krait and coral-snake bites there are shooting pains around the area of the bite and cramping abdominal pain.

Rattlesnake bite, like that of most vipers, is very painful, resembling a jab with a hot needle. Sometimes the area around the fang punctures is temporarily numb; this usually means a large injection of venom and a serious bite. Tingling around the mouth and a sensation of yellow vision are other early indications of severe poisoning. Gary Clarke, a young American herpetologist who reported his symptoms after being bitten just below the knee by a large red rattlesnake, was in excruciating pain for more than two days, the calf of his leg swollen until it was larger than his thigh and so tender that the pressure of bedclothes or the breath of the doctors examining him could scarcely be endured. For part of this time he was plagued with vomiting, and short, violent spasms shook his entire body. Although he received excellent hospital treatment, it was ten days before he could walk unsupported and about two months before he recovered completely.[5] He was, in a sense, unlucky, for many persons with snakebites of this severity lapse into shock, which spares them some of the agony.

We have already mentioned the "broken-neck effect" that follows bites by some tropical American rattlesnakes. In marked contrast to most rattlesnake bites seen in North America, these bites produce little local pain or swelling. There is intense headache and impairment of vision that may progress to blindness. The kidneys may be seriously damaged. The venom of the tropical rattlesnake is the most toxic of rattlesnake venoms although closely rivaled by that of the Mojave rattlesnake of the southwestern United States. It was a snake of this latter species that killed Dr. Fred Shannon, a well-known American surgeon and herpetologist. He was bitten while on a collecting trip and lost consciousness within 15 minutes, although he did not die until the next day. Bites by the Mojave rattler are not often reported, partly because the snake resembles the western diamondback so closely that even herpetologists have trouble telling the species apart.

Bites by vipers are often followed by the death of tissue around the bitten place. This is caused by the digestive enzymes in the venom and by damage to the local blood supply and often is made worse by improper use of tourniquets in first aid. Some of these bites result in nothing worse than an interesting scar, but sometimes the entire digit or limb becomes gangrenous and must be amputated. A Florida surgeon, Dr. Newton C. McCollough, found that 17 percent of surgical amputations performed on children in his state were done because of snakebites.[6] At herpetologists' meetings it is usually possible to tell the museum men from the zoo men by counting fingers; few of the latter have a complete set. Such vipers as the cottonmouth and eastern diamondback rattler in the United States, the urutu in Brazil and Argentina, and the puff adder in Africa are particularly notorious for their necrotizing venom. The puff adder, which must have been known to the Greeks and Romans of about 2,000 years ago, was probably the Spectaficus, a snake whose bite consumed the entire body with swelling and putrefaction. Necrosis sometimes follows bites of cobras and other elapids, although it may be overshadowed by the more alarming neurotoxic symptoms. An interesting case involved a scientist who had been immunized against cobra venom some months before he was bitten by a captive cobra. Although he had no neurotoxic or other generalized symptoms, he developed a gangrenous patch that required skin grafting. Apparently his inoculation protected him against the lethal components of the venom but not against its necrotizing power.

A dramatic and terrifying manifestation of certain snakebites is hemorrhage. It results from an impairment of the normal blood-clotting mechanism plus damage to the walls of small blood vessels. This occurs to a limited extent after most viper bites but dominates the entire picture in poisoning by such species as the saw-scaled viper, fer-de-lance, jararaca, boomslang, and Australian blacksnake. Severely poisoned victims of these snakes ooze blood from all body orifices: urine and saliva are bloodstained; red or purplish patches appear on the skin spontaneously or at the sites of slight injury, such as a hypodermic needle puncture. Death may come suddenly and unexpectedly from internal bleeding. Our esteemed friend Karl P. Schmidt, then curator of zoology at the Field Museum in Chicago, died 24 hours after being bitten by a boomslang, but only 2 hours before his fatal collapse he felt well enough to call the museum to expect him at work the next day.[7] Bites by the vicious little saw-scaled viper of the dry regions of Africa and Asia are particularly discouraging to treat. A Pakistani farmer came to the hospital a week after being bitten by one of these snakes. His loins ached, his urine was bloody, and blood seeped from his gums. Neither antivenin, blood transfusions, nor coagulant drugs such as vitamin K brought any lasting improvement. He died, apparently from a cerebral hemorrhage, 12 days after his snakebite.

The venom of sea snakes is unique in having a direct effect on muscles, causing release of the protein myoglobin, which is excreted by the kidneys. The bite itself is an innocuous-seeming pinprick; if there is any considerable pain or swelling, the injury was probably inflicted by some other venomous marine creature. Characteristically, there is a symptom-free period of 30 minutes to 8 hours. The first evidence of trouble is weakness and soreness in the muscles. The eyelids droop, and the jaws are stiff, somewhat as in tetanus. Weakness increases until the patient literally can hardly lift a finger. Myoglobin and potassium from the damaged muscles stain the urine red, injure the kidneys, and cause irregularity of the heart. Death may come within 12 hours of the bite but is usually delayed several days. Most of what we know of sea-snake poisoning in man was learned from the observations of Dr. H. Alistair Reid, an Englishman who was a physician on the staff of Penang General Hospital in Malaya for several years before he joined the faculty of the Liverpool School of Tropical Medicine.[8] Dr. Reid himself had a narrow escape when bitten while extracting venom from a beaked sea snake. An assistant milked the snake immediately afterward and obtained a near-record yield of venom. Reid could not have received much of the toxin, although one of the snake's fangs broke off in his skin. None the less, on the day after the bite he said his muscles ached as though he had played in a football match when out of condition.[9]

Gila-monster bites are quite painful because the lizards have strong jaws and often hold on with the tenacity of a snapping turtle. The venom itself contains serotonin, a powerful pain-producing substance. General symptoms reported include sweating, nausea, thirst, sore throat, ringing in the ears, weakness, rapid breathing, faintness, and collapse. The wide range of symptoms reported may be explained by great variation in the amount of venom injected and possibly by great differences in individual response to the venom. There have been several reports of fatal gila-monster bites, but only one is accompanied by adequate medical details. The victim in this case was a carnival barker with a bad heart and a history of alcoholism and drug addiction. In two other fairly well-authenticated fatal cases, highly inebriated individuals set out to test the venomous powers of the gila monster in the most simple and direct way possible—by sticking a finger within reach of its jaws. In 1953, an army officer, apparently suffering from boredom at his desert station, sought to carry on this tradition. With good hospital care, he recovered from both the lizard venom and the alcohol.[10]

6. Snakebite Around the World

As a medical problem snakebite is insignificant compared with malnutrition, overpopulation, cancer, and heart disease. Even in the field of tropical medicine, to which it is usually relegated, it is overshadowed by the dysenteries, malaria, schistosomiasis, hookworm, and many other ailments of warm lands. But snakes do kill some thousands of persons annually. A 1954 study by S. Swaroop and B. Grab of the World Health Organization's Statistical Studies Section estimated the annual mortality as 30,000 to 40,000. Assuming a mortality rate of about 15 percent, the annual number of snakebites has been estimated at 300,000.[1] There is good reason to think this figure considerably too low; the annual number of bites by poisonous snakes throughout the world may be close to a million. None of these estimates is very solidly based. Snakebite is most prevalent, and its mortality is highest, in countries where gathering of medical statistics is a haphazard business at best. In many sections of Asia, Africa, the tropical Americas, Australia, and New Guinea, births and deaths are matters only of village or tribal concern and may never find their way into an official record. In most of the villages of Pakistan, for example, deaths are reported by the police constable, a man without special training or facilities for investigation except in obvious criminal cases. In even smaller hamlets, they may be reported by the *chowkidor,* or watchman, who is usually illiterate. The best that can be expected of such officials is that they be honest and conscientious; not infrequently they fall short of this ideal.

The United States

Only within the last decade has there been an adequate, nationwide picture of the frequency, geographic distribution, age incidence, and mortality of snakebite in the United States. This information has mostly been gathered and assembled by one individual, Dr. Henry M. Parrish of the University of Missouri School of Medicine, who has applied modern epidemiological methods to a study of snakebite. His figures show that the incidence is higher than was generally believed, about 6,700 cases annually being treated by physicians, but mortality is gratifyingly low, averaging 14 or 15 deaths annually. Texas reports the greatest number of bites, about 1,000 a year, but if figures are corrected for population, the rate is highest in North Carolina.[2] Arizona, Texas, Georgia, and Florida lead in number of fatalities.[3] A distinctive feature of snakebite epidemiology in the United States is the high incidence among children and teenagers, while in most other countries incidence is highest among adult males. Carelessness and ignorance of the danger of snakes probably explain the large number of small children bitten, while bravado plays a part in many snakebites involving teen-age boys.

Between 1/4 and 1/3 of the snakebites in the United States are classified as "illegitimate"—that is, sustained while catching, killing, handling, or otherwise manipulating reptiles. It has been estimated that there are 10 snakebites in the New York metropolitan area each year.[4] Since the last wild copperhead in the Bronx died between 1945 and 1950, all these bites are inflicted by captive or accidentally introduced snakes and probably are in the illegitimate category. Herpetologists, sideshow performers, and certain religious zealots, however different their backgrounds and motives, form a natural high-risk group.

Most persons bitten by snakes in the United States are injured within a mile of their own homes; for instance, in the Midwest, children are frequently bitten by copperheads while playing around woodpiles or in old buildings. Former Vice President Alben Barkley's career was almost terminated at the age of six when a copperhead bit him as he crawled under the family cabin after a chicken. An almost identical case in southern Indiana ended fatally. In the same area a girl suffered a near-fatal bite when she jumped from a grapevine swing and landed on a good-sized rattler. Adults have been bitten while berry picking, gardening, moving rocks and lumber, and doing various household chores. Comparatively few persons are attacked by snakes during such outdoor recreation as hunting, camping, swimming, and hiking. In the southern lowlands, where cottonmouth moccasins abound, fishermen are occasionally bitten. In the past few years we have heard at least five accounts of water skiers mortally bitten by cottonmouths. Since three of these incidents were said to have happened in states where the cottonmouth does not occur, we are inclined to doubt them all, although anyone participating in water sports on southern lakes and rivers should be aware of the hazard from these belligerent snakes.

In the United States and other temperate-zone countries snakebite is a summer complaint, with the highest frequency usually during July and August. Human outdoor activity at this season may be more important than that of the snakes, for the peak hours for bites are during the day, while most poisonous snakes are active at twilight and during the early hours of darkness during hot weather.

Rattlesnakes account for most snakebites in the United States and for 85 to 90 percent of the fatalities. The eastern and western diamondbacks are the most dangerous species. Both are large snakes with extensive distribution in well-populated regions. The Mojave rattlesnake is also quite dangerous but has a limited range in the Southwest. The timber rattler and its subspecies the canebrake rattler are important in the eastern half of the country, while the Pacific, prairie and Great Basin rattlers (all subspecies of the wide-ranging *Crotalus viridis*) are dominant in the West. The pigmy rattlers in the South, the massasauga in the Midwest, and the sidewinder in the arid Southwest are small species that account for a number of bites but few fatalities. Copperheads probably cause more bites than any one species of rattlesnake, but fatalities are almost unknown. Cottonmouths are a fairly common cause of bites in parts of Louisiana, Mississippi, and Florida. The North American coral snake rarely bites but considered in relation to the percentage of fatalities it causes, it is as dangerous as most rattlesnakes. The Arizona, or Sonora, coral snake is a small and uncommon reptile that has never been known to inflict a fatal bite. Gila-monster bites are infrequent and almost always result from careless handling of captive lizards.

Europe and the Middle East

Although centuries of intensive agriculture and more recent industrialization have made most of Europe unsuitable territory for poisonous snakes, they are nevertheless plentiful in certain areas. In Finland during the summer of 1961 no less than 163 snakebites were reported, most of them among agricultural workers.[5] One physician, T. C. Morton of Cornwall, England, saw 18 adder bites between 1952 and 1959.[6] Many victims were picnickers and hikers who were apparently unaware that poisonous snakes inhabit modern Britain. France and Italy each report 17 to 22 deaths annually from venomous bites and stings, but probably no more than a quarter of these are due to snakes. Southeastern Europe presumably has a higher rate of both bites and fatalities than the rest of the continent, but there is little information available. The Middle East is a meeting place for the African and Asian reptile faunas and has a comparatively large number of venomous snakes. Snakebites were a matter of some concern in the modern state of Israel during the first decade of its existence, and this led to development of an active program of snake-venom research. Between 1951 and 1953 there were 303 cases registered, with 24 deaths; and between 1955 and 1957 there were 418 cases, with 17 deaths. Most of the snakebites in Israel occur along the Mediterranean coast and in the upper Jordan Valley.[7]

The only venomous snake of northern and western Europe is the European viper, or adder, which rarely exceeds a length of 2 feet. Four other small species occur in central and southern Europe, and two larger and more dangerous ones, the Levantine and Turkish vipers, barely enter Europe from the southeast. The Palestine viper is the most important species in Israel and surrounding territory, while the Levantine viper causes most of the serious bites in Iraq, Iran, and Russian Turkestan.

Several of the serious or fatal snakebites reported recently from western Europe and the United States have been caused by exotic species kept in zoos, other types of exhibits, laboratories, or by private individuals. These bites are likely to be bad ones, because zoos take pride in keeping large examples of dangerous reptiles and also are likely to exhibit unusual species for which suitable antivenins may not be available. Even though speedy treatment for these bites is usually possible, severity of the injury plus lack of experience may lead to an unhappy outcome.

Southern Asia

In southeast Asia, man and snake have lived together for a long time and have developed a tenuous pattern of coexistence. Here, as in no other part of the world, dense populations of humans and dangerous snakes live in close proximity to each other. This is the chief reason why southeast Asia has the world's highest incidence of snakebites and deaths from them. It does not mean that every round of golf or walk in the country features an encounter with a cobra. Extreme secretiveness is part of the snakes' scheme for survival. But here, more than in other parts of the world, man and snake confront each other suddenly and unexpectedly to the everlasting disadvantage of one or both parties.

The figure of 20,000 deaths from snakebite annually in India has become one of the more durable medical statistics and is still quoted even in technical publications. It is based on information gathered in 1869 by Sir Joseph Fayrer, one of the first Europeans to study Indian snakes and their venoms, and confirmed by further statistics for years between 1880 and 1890.[8] However, the figure was reached by making some extrapolations and with knowledge of the questionable accuracy of vital statistics in India. It was an educated guess, and Fayrer would probably be dismayed at the aura of authority it still has a century later. A more recent figure for India is 10,000 to 15,000 deaths per year with a rate of 5.4 deaths per 100,000 population. Certain districts of West Bengal located in the delta of the Ganges report rates about twice that for the country as a whole.[9] In Bombay State, between 1954 and 1958 the death toll was 1,237 to 1,788 annually; the states of Orissa and Bihar also report high mortality figures.[10]

In Burma there are about 2,000 deaths annually and a rate of 15 per 100,000. Between 1936 and 1940 some districts along the Irrawaddy and Chindwin Rivers reported rates of 31 to 37 deaths per 100,000, the highest recorded anywhere in the world. The snakebite death rate in Ceylon is a little lower than that of India, and the rate in Thailand is much lower than that in Burma.[11] No figures are available for Vietnam, Cambodia, and Laos. When this territory was under French rule there were few reported snakebite fatalities, but information from the native population was almost totally lacking. Michel Barme, former Director of the Pasteur Institute Laboratory at Saigon, wrote of sea-snake bites alone, "Each year fatal cases are numerous, but actual numbers remain unknown because of superstitions . . . and also because many villages where these accidents occur are isolated far from urban centers." [12] The

Amami Islands in the Ryukyu group may well have the world's highest snakebite rate with about 1 case per 500 population; fatalities are about 3 percent.[13] The Philippines report a fairly high snakebite mortality rate of 1.26 per 100,000 population, with most cases reported from the rice- and sugar-growing regions of Luzon.[14]

Writers have frequently noted the marked differences in the incidence of snakebites in districts of Asia that are adjoining and have similar terrain, such as the eastern and western parts of the Ganges-Brahmaputra delta. Probably human customs and attitudes toward snakes are primarily responsible for these differences. Aside from snake charming and snake rituals (see pages 131–148), such ethnological factors as methods of agriculture and fish netting or trapping, house construction, sleeping accommodations, and types of foot gear or other clothing can appreciably influence the incidence and severity of bites.

Throughout south Asia the frequency of snakebite is strongly seasonal, the peak coinciding with the rains. Writing about 320 B.C., the Cretan Nearchus, admiral of Alexander the Great, observed that in the Land of the Five Rivers, today the Punjab: "They [snakes] retreat from the plains to the villages that do not disappear under water at the time of the inundations and fill the houses . . . On this account, the people raise their beds to a great height from the ground and are sometimes compelled to abandon their homes. . . . The minute size of some and the immense size of others are sources of danger; the former because it is difficult to guard against their attacks, the latter by reason of their strength . . ." [15]

The catastrophic effect of floods which concentrate both snake and human populations on high ground is seen throughout the tropics and also in areas such as the Gulf Coast of the United States following hurricanes. In the drier parts of southern Asia, however, the monsoon brings a burgeoning of all forms of life from algae to elephants. The flooded lowlands teem with frogs and fish; lizards appear to feed upon the swarms of insects; and the snakes emerge to share in the general bounty. It is during the monsoon that krait and cobra eggs hatch, while the live-bearing Russell's and saw-scaled vipers produce most of their young at this season. Even sea snakes tend to concentrate their numbers in the mangrove swamps and around the mouths of streams. This is also a season of increased agricultural activity. In many Asian countries rice seedlings are planted at the beginning of the rains, and the crop is harvested soon after the end of the rainy season. Many persons working barefooted and bare-legged in the fields suffer snakebites.

A fair number of snakebites in the Asian tropics are inflicted on sleeping persons. Kraits are most often implicated. In one case reported by the Dutch physician F. Kopstein in 1932, a Javanese father and son were sleeping in a hut when the younger man felt a snake crawl over his hand and made a quick movement that resulted in his being bitten on the finger. He threw the snake away from him, and it fell on his father who was bitten on the leg. Both men died.[16] Of 35 krait bites reported from India by Lieutenant Colonel M. L. Ahuja and Gurkirpal Singh, 29 took place at night, and most of the victims were asleep when bitten.[17] In Sind, a province in the lower Indus Valley in West Pakistan, we were told that the Indian krait, locally called *sangchul,* does not bite, but kills sleeping persons by sucking their breath. The reason for these nocturnal attacks is unclear. Kraits may live near dwellings and are inveterate night prowlers, but they are also exceptionally inoffensive. The Englishman, Colonel Frank Wall, who had vast experience with the snakes of India and Ceylon, said the only krait he ever saw attempt to bite in anger was one that had been impaled with an iron trident.[18] We did not find the Indian krait quite so long-suffering; nevertheless it is a quiet and timid snake. Kraits feed almost wholly upon cold-blooded vertebrates, mostly other snakes, and presumably would not be stimulated to strike by the body warmth of a sleeping person. There is reason to think, however, that they do attack in response to sudden slight movements while on their nocturnal hunting forays, and the stirring of a sleeper might provide such a stimulus.

The Asian cobras probably have the dubious distinction of causing more fatalities than any other species. Basically, the Asian cobra is a timid snake that will flee if surprised in the open, bluff and bluster if escape is cut off, and bite only as a last resort. However, it does seem to have a certain degree of territorial sense, and we have been impressed with the bellicose way a well-adjusted captive cobra reacts to being disturbed in a cage where it feels at home. In addition, the Asian cobra inhabits many kinds of terrain and does not seem greatly disturbed by human activity. It is one of the more omnivorous of snakes, and the presence of large numbers of frogs around rice fields and rodents around villages may favor its increase in agricultural regions. Although wide ranging, the king cobra is an insignificant cause of snakebites. Large, with highly specialized feeding habits (it eats only snakes and large lizards), it is nowhere plentiful. Its allegedly aggressive temperament has been overemphasized. A king cobra 15 feet 7 inches long was captured on a Singapore golf course by two men who thought it

was a python. It made no effective resistance.[19] Simon Campden-
Main, a young herpetologist now at the U.S. National Museum,
had considerable field experience with king cobras while serving
with the armed forces in Vietnam. He says they are very timid
in the wild and probably only aggressive when confronted at
close quarters.

Russell's viper, also known as *daboia* and *tic polonga,* is
said to be more important than the cobra as a cause of snakebites in Burma and parts of India and Ceylon. A large and
somewhat pugnacious snake, it is often common around grain
fields, probably attracted by the numbers of rodents that are its
chief food. In the dry lands from central India westward
through much of the Middle East, the saw-scaled viper is the
most dangerous reptile and is extremely common in the semiarid
country of West Pakistan and adjoining India. Small, but exceptionally alert and irritable, it is particularly dangerous to the
inadequately shod native populations. In the Ratnagiri District
a little south of Bombay during the late 1800s government
bounties were paid on more than 225,000 of these snakes annually. When the reward was raised from 6 pice (about 2 cents) to
2 annas (about 6 cents) per head, 115,921 snakes were brought
in during an 8-day period.[20]

Pit vipers are an important cause of snakebites in the Far
East. The hyappoda, or hundred-pace snake, which derives its
name from the distance a bitten man can walk before collapsing,
causes the greatest number of such deaths on Taiwan; it also
occurs on the Chinese mainland. The Okinawa habu, largest
of the Asian vipers, chiefly accounts for the high snakebite rate
in the Ryukyu Islands; it has relatives on the Asian mainland.
The Malay pit viper is a sluggish, heavy, rather ill-tempered

snake found over a wide range in Thailand, Malaya, Vietnam, and Indonesia. In northern Malaya alone it causes about 700 bites annually, mostly among weeders and tappers on rubber plantations.[21] Several species of arboreal pit vipers, predominantly green in color, are plentiful in southeast Asia. They often bite people picking tea, cutting bamboo, or clearing underbrush, but very rarely cause serious injury.

Sea snakes are a hazard to Asian fishermen, although the degree of danger seems to vary from place to place. Fishermen at Karachi considered sea snakes practically harmless and were amused at the caution we observed in handling them. Malcolm Smith, a British herpetologist and physician who served many years as Court Physician to the King of Siam, wrote in his classic monograph of the sea snakes, "I have travelled considerably among the fisherfolk who live along the Gulf of Siam where sea snakes abound, and there is hardly a village that cannot tell you of its fatalities." [22] This also seems the case in Malaya and Vietnam, but in the Philippines, Ryukyus, and islands of Oceania fatalities are quite unusual despite the fact that here thousands of sea snakes are captured for food and for their skins.

Latin America

Latin America is second to Asia in numbers of snakebite accidents and deaths. Here, too, the scope of the problem is obfuscated by sketchy reporting. Mexico records about 200 snakebite fatalities annually, most of them in the states of Veracruz and Oaxaca, which contain considerable areas of tropical lowland and a fairly high population density. Costa

Rica, a small nation justly proud of the adequacy of its medical facilities, reports 25 to 35 fatal snakebites annually. Colombia and Venezuela each report 150 to 200. In Brazil, where the Instituto Butantan has encouraged the reporting of bites, there were about 2,000 fatalities annually at the time of the 1954 World Health Organization survey;[23] this number is now appreciably lower.

In 1957 I tabulated information on 104 recent snakebites treated at the Hospital San Juan de Dios in San José, Costa Rica. The average Costa Rican snakebite victim is a young man 16 to 25 years old working on a banana, coffee, or cacao plantation. He is bitten on the foot while at work; nearly all bites occur during the hours of daylight. As might be expected in a tropical country with rainfall fairly evenly distributed throughout the year, there is no marked seasonal incidence in bites.

In at least 33 of the cases the snake involved was *Bothrops atrox,* locally called terciopelo. Known under many Spanish and Portuguese names, this big pit viper ranges from southern Tamaulipas in Mexico to Misiones Province in Argentina. In English-language publications it is often referred to as fer-de-lance, although this name is more correctly applied to a related species confined to Martinique in the West Indies. Under any name, *Bothrops atrox* probably is responsible for more deaths than any other American reptile. It is often plentiful on plantations. A collection of 10,690 snake heads from Panama submitted for identification included more than 800 examples of this species.[24] In Costa Rica, young of this species, with yellow or ashy tails, are given a name different from that used for the adults; hence it was possible to determine that 13 of the 33 bites were inflicted by snakes probably less than 6 months old.

Twenty-one bites in my Costa Rican series were attributed to the eyelash viper, an arboreal species easily recognized by the row of pointed scales above each eye. This snake is plentiful in banana groves and occasionally reaches the United States in bunches of bananas. With this species also, more than a third of the bites were inflicted by young snakes. Although the eyelash viper is not considered especially dangerous, there was one death, the victim being a 60-year-old man.

Although at least fifteen species of poisonous snakes inhabit Costa Rica, these two accounted for over half the bites in my series. Eight bites were presumably inflicted by nonpoisonous snakes and 5 by snakes whose local Spanish names could not definitely be associated with any particular species. Nine bites were ascribed to the *"lora,"* a name applied to a green arboreal pit viper but also used for nonpoisonous green tree snakes of the genus *Leptophis.* Four bites were caused by the small pit vipers locally known as *tobobas* or *tamagas*; these are not generally thought to be dangerous and probably some persons bitten by them do not seek hospitalization. Four bites with one fatality were chalked up to coral snakes, which are represented in Costa Rica by four species. The remaining 20 were inflicted by unidentified snakes. In 7 there were definite signs of poisoning suggesting bites by pit vipers of the genus *Bothrops.* There were no bites by the bushmaster, largest of all pit vipers, and no physician on the staff of the hospital could recall treating a bite by this snake. Plantation owners and others with whom I talked said persons bitten by bushmasters do not live long enough to reach hospitals. This may be at least partially true, but I suspect that the bushmaster, an uncommon snake mostly restricted to undisturbed jungle, does not often attack anyone. Also, there were no bites by the tropical rattlesnake. In Costa Rica this dangerous species is restricted to Guanacaste Province, which is somewhat remote from San José.

Brazil is inhabited by no less than sixteen species of *Bothrops* pit vipers and twelve species of coral snakes as well as the bushmaster and tropical rattlesnake. In the rather densely populated region around São Paulo, the rattlesnake and jararaca are by far the most important species making up about 83 per-cent of the 8,000 to 9,000 poisonous snakes received annually by the serpentarium at the Instituto Butantan. In northern Brazil the most important species are the ubiquitous *Bothrops atrox,* the jararacussu, a giant semiaquatic pit viper, the Amazon tree viper, and the rattlesnake. In Uruguay, Argentina, and southern Brazil, the urutu, or vibora de la cruz, the jararaca pintada, and the rattlesnake cause most of the bites. Coral snakes play no significant part in the over-all problem in South America be-cause they rarely bite anyone. However, the larger species, which may be 4 feet long, are unquestionably dangerous.

Africa

Although Africa has many species of dangerous snakes, the importance of snakebite as a medical problem seems to be slight, although this may be partly a matter of reporting. The former European colonies made no particular effort to determine the incidence of snakebites among the native populations, and even less information has been forthcoming from the new African nations. Egypt between 1944 and 1948 reported 26 to 46 deaths a year. South Africa has 300 to 440 snakebites an-nually with 10 to 15 deaths, and Kenya in the 1946–1950 period reported 404 to 564 cases annually with 5 to 12 fatal.[25] In the Sudan during a 17-year period, the British physician Dr. Norman Corkill recorded 390 cases, with 24 deaths.[26] Mortality for all of Africa is estimated not to exceed 1,000 a year.

In the Union of South Africa, the only region where much information on snakebite is available, seasonal fluctuation shows a temperate-zone pattern, with the highest incidence from December through April (the southern hemisphere summer and fall), with a peak in March, and the lowest from June through August. Older children (10 to 14 years) and adolescents suffer most of the bites. Boys herding cattle suffer a relatively large number of bites.[27]

Probably the most important African venomous snake is the puff adder, which ranges over most of the continent exclusive of rain forest and desert. Often common in agricultural and pasture land, it is a large snake with long fangs and an unpleasant disposition. Its even larger relative, the Gaboon viper, rarely figures in snakebite accidents. Surprisingly, Jean Doucet, a French herpetologist who worked in the Ivory Coast, wrote that at Adiopodoume, only 1 of 11 persons hospitalized after being bitten by Gaboon vipers was severely poisoned.[28] He did not mention the size of the snakes involved; perhaps most of the bites were by very young reptiles.

The famed cerastes, or horned viper, accounts for numerous bites in the arid lands of North Africa, but fatalities are infrequent. This cannot be said of the saw-scaled viper, which also is found over a wide area in the drier parts of Africa. A hospital in Togo reported 80 percent mortality among patients bitten by this snake.[29] The night adders, another widely distributed group, are responsible for a fairly large number of bites, but their weak venom makes them no great hazard to life. The mole vipers are said to be of some importance in the Sudan.

Africa is the home of five species of cobras as well as several cobralike snakes, such as the ringhals, water cobras, and tree cobras. But only the Egyptian cobra in the thickly populated Nile Valley approaches its Asian cogeners as a menace to human life. The spitting cobra and ringhals prefer to defend themselves by spraying venom and will bite only when this tactic fails to deter the enemy.

Deadly arboreal snakes are an African specialty. The boomslang, despite its dangerous bite, usually flees or threatens. Walter Rose, a South African herpetologist wrote, "Indeed it will stand considerable abuse . . . before it gives warning that its patience is becoming exhausted." [30] The boomslang and the bird snake, another dangerous African colubrid, inflate the throat until the forebody is at least twice its normal diameter, and the scales stand out in a surprising manner. The mambas, with four species inhabiting most of Africa south of the Sahara, are decidedly more dangerous than the boomslang, although most herpetologists with wide field experience in Africa have found them unaggressive. Mambas are remarkably alert and may well be the quickest of all snakes in general movements. This amazing speed is usually used for escape, but occasionally a suddenly disturbed or cornered mamba will bite with deadly effectiveness. The black mamba, second in length only to the king cobra among poisonous snakes, is not as important as a cause of bites as the two species of green mambas although in a recently reported series of seven cases the fatality rate was 100 percent.[31] Nowhere are mambas known to cause any significant loss of life. However, it should be remembered that the statistics for most of

Africa are usually based on hospital treatment of cases. With mamba and cobra bites, the outcome is likely to be decided within a few hours, often before transport of the victim to a hospital can be arranged, much less accomplished. Victims of viper bites with a prolonged course of illness are more likely to be hospitalized, but here statistics are biased in favor of more serious bites. Less serious ones are likely to be treated in villages.

Australia

One of Australia's numerous faunal peculiarities is the dominance of venomous snakes. Of the 130 or so native species, half are elapids and about 24 are sea snakes, with 6 rear-fanged colubrids thrown in for good measure. In spite of this large number, the continent reports only 5 to 10 snakebite deaths annually, more than half of them in Queensland. The rate is 0.07 fatalities per 100,000, a little higher than that of the United States.[32]

There has been no recent comprehensive study of snakebite in Australia. The existing information indicates that the situation among the nonaboriginal population is much the same as in the United States. Almost half the persons bitten are children under 10 or boys in their teens. Although some persons are bitten while working in sugarcane fields or at other agricultural activities, hikers, hunters, and others participating in outdoor recreation also are affected. A high proportion of the bites are "illegitimate." Seasonal incidence is highest in the southern hemisphere summer, November to April.[33] Little is known about snakebite among the aborigines, but it is believed to be infrequent. They are excellent outdoorsmen and are generally able to avoid snakes except when hunting them for food.

The several forms of the tiger snake and the Australian brown snake account for most of the fatal and serious bites. The latter snake is common in wheat- and rice-growing districts, while the tiger snakes inhabit coastal areas and mountains but generally avoid the deserts. Although these species are basically timid, they will sometimes put up a determined defense. The brown snake is particularly dangerous when aroused and will quickly follow one strike with another. The short, thick death adder is a third widely distributed deadly species, more common in the northern part of the country and in semiarid parts of the interior. The Australian blacksnake, which is plentiful in moist habitats throughout the country, is reported to cause more bites than any other Australian snake, but fatalities are most infrequent.

Largest and most formidable of Australia's poisonous snakes is the taipan, which has a rather spotty distribution in the northern part of the country. There is a well-documented account of a taipan's making an apparently unprovoked attack and fatally biting a woman walking home from the movies. In another, almost fatal bite, the snake's fangs pierced through a shoe and heavy sock.[34] In spite of its large fangs and occasionally ferocious behavior, the taipan is ordinarily shy and quick to escape. It ranks with the king cobra, black mamba, bushmaster, Gaboon viper, and eastern diamondback rattler among the giant deadly snakes of the world. Adults of any of these species have enough venom to kill several persons. All defend themselves vigorously under most circumstances, and some have been known to attack without provocation. Yet as a group it is doubtful if they account for 1 percent of fatal bites. The explanation is probably the relative rarity of contacts between these species and man. All of these snakes tend to retreat before agriculture and urbanization; they are referred to by German zoologists as *Kulturfliegern* (literally, "culture-fleers," animals that retreat from towns, farmlands, and human society). The king cobra, black mamba, and bushmaster have wide ranges but are generally uncommon. The taipan and eastern diamondback rattler have comparatively small ranges, for the most part in regions of low population density, although the eastern diamondback can adapt to suburbia and exists in fairly large numbers in the densely populated Tampa Bay area of Florida. The Gaboon viper characteristically inhabits tropical forests and seems to have an extraordinarily placid disposition. All these snakes are somewhat specialized feeders; rarely is suitable prey plentiful enough to allow them to establish dense populations.

7. Immunity to Snake Venoms

Quite as mysterious as the terrifying and baleful effects of snake venoms is the seemingly magical immunity some creatures enjoy. Nearly 2,000 years ago Pliny the Elder wrote, "The sting of the serpent is not aimed at the serpent." A nearly identical Indian proverb is probably of equal antiquity. There is a very widespread belief that creatures preying upon snakes either have immunity to their bites or know of some plant or mineral that serves as an antidote. The modern biological specialties of immunology and toxinology have not completely resolved these matters. Part of the problem is the difficulty of obtaining wild animals in sufficient numbers to investigate adequately the extent of their immunity and the factors responsible for it. Any scientist whose research budget has not been drastically curtailed can have a hundred virtually identical mice or guinea pigs delivered to him simply by picking up the phone. Getting a hundred mongooses, mussuranas, cangambas, or king snakes of similar size and weight is an entirely different matter. Consequently our information on the immunity of snakes and various other wild animals to reptile venoms depends heavily upon fragmentary and random observations.

In Snakes and Other Reptiles

Poisonous snakes probably have a high but not absolute immunity to their own venoms. Raymond Sanders, formerly of the University of Utah, worked with a good series of Great Basin rattlesnakes collected at a hibernating den in Utah and concluded that it would be practically impossible for one adult of this species to kill another with its venom, although it would be possible for an adult to kill a small, young snake.[1] This confirms the observations of many herpetologists and snake handlers who have seen rattlesnakes bite themselves and each other without serious consequences unless the fangs penetrated a vital organ, such as the heart or brain. Tales of rattlers "committing suicide" with their own fangs are probably based for the most part upon instances where mortally wounded snakes bit their own bodies in a frenzy of excitement and pain. However, there is a well-authenticated case of a diamondback rattler that bit its own tail and died 27 hours later with signs of venom poisoning.[2] There are several reports of rattlesnakes having been fatally bitten by cottonmouths. The cottonmouth eats a greater variety of food than most rattlesnake species do and not infrequently includes snakes in its diet. Copperheads are slightly more susceptible to the venom of their own species than to rattlesnake or cottonmouth venoms; their venom has comparatively high toxicity for several species of North American snakes, particularly the little ringneck snake, a favorite food of young copperheads.[3] To sum matters up, North American pit vipers have considerable resistance to one another's venoms. Except for the copperhead, the species tested have more immunity to their own venom than to venoms of other species.

Symptoms of poisoning observed in snakes seem to be much the same as those in warm-blooded animals, namely hemorrhages and necrosis around the site of the bite.

The same tendency seems to hold with vipers in other parts of the world. The fatal dose of European viper venom for the viper is about 100 milligrams, which is at least 10 times the quantity one of these snakes could eject in a normal bite and 400 times the fatal dose for a guinea pig. Puff adders will succumb to puff-adder venom, but it takes comparatively large doses. I have seen saw-scaled vipers die after being bitten by cage-mates of approximately equal size; hemorrhages were noted in the tissues of the dead reptiles. In one series of experiments, it was found that 1 cubic centimeter of blood serum from the European viper neutralized 52 mouse-lethal doses of venom from this species. Neutralization was highly specific; venoms of other vipers, including the closely related asp viper, were not counteracted. The antitoxic factor was found to be in the globulin fraction of viper serum.[4] Globulins are those serum proteins that contain antibodies or specific immune substances.

There is less information about immunity of elapid snakes. C. H. Kellaway, who was Director of Research for the Burroughs-Wellcome pharmaceutical company, reported that the tiger snake is 180,000 times as resistant as the guinea pig to tiger-snake venom, and its immunity to venoms of other Australian elapid snakes, such as the death adder, is extremely high; also it is 13,000 times as resistant as the guinea pig to Asian cobra venom. His experiments indicate this resistance is greater than can be accounted for by the antitoxic power of the snakes' serum. Enzymes or other tissue substances apparently neutralize some of the venom.[5] Sir Joseph Fayrer and his associates in

India observed that young cobras sometimes died after being bitten by adults. Cobra bites were sometimes fatal to kraits, and kraits' fatal to cobras, while 5 drops (a comparatively large dose) of Cape cobra venom killed a mamba. Thomas R. Fraser of Edinburgh, a pioneer worker on immunity to snake venoms, in 1896 observed that serum from a king cobra protected rabbits against a lethal dose of Indian-cobra venom.[6] I have seen Indian kraits bite each other without ill effect, but their bite killed nonpoisonous colubrid snakes. These kraits refused to attack saw-scaled vipers and actually seemed afraid of them. Coral-snake bites apparently are fatal to most kinds of snakes, including coral snakes themselves. There is an account of a spectacular battle between a Brazilian giant coral snake and a South American false coral snake (*Erythrolamprus* species), itself a rear-fanged snake-eating species. Quite appropriately both snakes died, each apparently from effects of the other's venom.[7]

King snakes, which in one form or another inhabit most of the southern two-thirds of the United States, have long been known to have immunity to venoms of pit vipers. Their reputation as the dauntless foe of rattlesnakes and other venomous species has been overstated at times, but they will eat poisonous snakes, especially young ones. Rattlesnakes evidently recognize king snakes as enemies and adopt an entirely different defense when confronted by one. Instead of coiling and striking, a rattler keeps its head and tail against the ground and raises the midsection of its body. As the king snake approaches, the elevated part of the rattler is slammed down violently in an effort to club the attacker.[8] The rattlesnake ordinarily does not bite until it has been encircled by the king snake's coils. King snakes' immunity seems to be adequate to protect them from bites of normal prey; however, they can be killed by massive injections of pit-viper venoms. V. B. Philpot, of the department of pharmacology, Tulane University, and R. G. Smith, a physician of Holly Springs, Mississippi, showed that a substance in king-snake serum accounts for at least part of these snakes' immunity. Serum after heating to remove an unidentified toxic factor neutralized about seven mouse-lethal doses of cottonmouth venom and somewhat less than this quantity of diamondback-rattlesnake venom. It was about as effective an antitoxin as the commercially produced antivenin with which it was compared.[9]

In the tropical Americas the king snake's role as protector of mankind against poisonous snakes is taken over by the mussurana, a rear-fanged colubrid that may reach a length of 7 feet. The adult is almost uniformly black, but the young are brilliant pink with a black head and yellow collar. One Madge and I found at night in a Costa Rican banana grove appeared surrealistic against its dark background. The mussurana is almost exclusively a snake eater. Adults feed chiefly upon terrestrial pit vipers of the genus *Bothrops,* probably because these vipers supply a lot of snake meat in one package. Like the king snake, the mussurana seems to have adequate immunity to protect it against naturally inflicted bites. It is said to have little or no immunity to coral-snake venom.

Gila monsters are unaffected by injections of their own venom sufficient to kill 45 guinea pigs; the limit of their tolerance has not been established. Gila-monster venom killed asp vipers at a dose slightly more than twice that fatal for mice and rabbits when compensated for body weight; garter snakes were considerably more resistant. The toxicity of gila-monster venom for mice is counteracted by the globulin fraction of the lizard's serum as well as by an extract of the liver.[10]

In Mammals and Birds

No mammalian enemy of poisonous snakes enjoys a greater reputation than the mongooses, of which there are more than a dozen species in Africa and southern Asia. Actually, there is no convincing evidence that any mongooses are predominantly snake eaters. The Indian species seem to be omnivorous predators that will eat snakes if they are plentiful in the mammal's territory but will quickly shift to rodents, birds, or frogs. They do not feed by choice on poisonous snakes, and there is reason to believe they avoid the larger vipers. Experimental work indicates that mongooses have greater resistance to cobra venoms than do guinea pigs and other laboratory animals but not enough to protect them from bites by adult cobras. Mongoose serum did not protect rabbits against cobra venom. The resistance of mongooses to viper venoms is no greater than that of other mammals.[11] In combat with snakes, mongooses rely upon agility to avoid being bitten.

The meerkat, a small South African predatory mammal that eats snakes frequently, is about twice as resistant as the mongoose to Cape-cobra venom but shows no special resistance to puff-adder venom.[12] In South America the cangamba, a close relative of the hog-nosed skunk of the southwestern United States, is considered an important enemy of poisonous snakes. Observers report that it attacks such dangerous snakes as the jararaca and disregards their bites, which do not affect it in the least.[13] Some degree of immunity has been reported for genets, small catlike

African carnivores, and also for domestic cats. In fact, carnivorous animals generally seem to have more resistance to snake venoms than do rodents and herbivores of comparable weight; one experimenter has reported, for example, that keeping rats on a meat diet slightly increased their resistance to snake venoms.[14] The physiological basis for this immunity is unknown.

Wild and domestic pigs frequently kill poisonous snakes and have probably played a significant part in eradicating rattlesnakes from numerous localities in the eastern and midwestern United States. The thick skin and layer of subcutaneous fat of pigs protect them by retarding absorption of venom. Experiments show they have no particular immunity to rattlesnake venom, and they have been known to die from naturally inflicted bites. South African pigs, perhaps of a different breed than those used by experimenters in the United States, were considerably more resistant than sheep to cobra and puff-adder venoms.[15]

Although several kinds of predatory birds occasionally feed upon poisonous snakes, none has been demonstrated to have any immunity to venom. They depend upon speed and suddenness of attack to cripple the snake and are protected by their feathers and leg scales. There are several accounts of battles between hawks and poisonous snakes that have ended in the death of both combatants.

In Man

Immunity to snakebite has been claimed at one time or another for almost every snake-charming tribe and ophiolatrous, or snake-worshiping, sect. This has variously been attributed to divine protection, spiritual strength, talismans and amulets, ointments and other skin applications, herbal decoctions, and substances derived from the snakes themselves. There is little doubt that venom itself has been used as an immunizing agent since ancient times; indeed it would be more remarkable had this not been used. Although these practices antedate modern immunotherapy by centuries, neither anthropologists nor immunologists have investigated them very thoroughly.

South Africa is the principal region where immunization by venom inoculation is practiced. The Zulus believe they can guard themselves against bites of snakes by this method, although its effect is not permanent. The procedure is carried out annually, usually in October. Those to be inoculated have a fragment of skin cut from the back of the left hand, and snake venom mixed with saliva is rubbed into the wound. It is said that no snake will go near anyone so treated. Moreover, if the shadow of an inoculated man touches that of a man not so protected, the latter falls to the ground overcome by poison transmitted through the shadow.[16]

In other parts of South Africa, bushmen drink venom, chew dried venom glands, or swallow pellets of paper soaked in venom to secure immunity. Swallowing dried venom glands was said by one native to produce an intoxication similar to that caused by marijuana, doubtless a pleasant concomitant of the immunization process. In 1886, a British physician practicing in South Africa wrote: "Having a month ago seen a native named Snellsteve, who is a snake poison drinker and snake collector, put his hand into a box containing two yellow cobras and several horn and night adders, in doing which he was severely bitten and has never suffered anything more than a little pain, I feel I can no longer refuse to believe in the efficacity of the snake virus itself as a remedy against snake poison." [17] Unfortunately, he did not record which species actually bit the redoubtable Snellsteve. Night adders have weak venom and short fangs. With any luck at all, their bite might be expected to produce nothing worse than "a little pain." Likewise, neither of the South African horned adders is considered highly dangerous.

Arthur Loveridge, a British herpetologist with much experience in Africa, told of a snake man who claimed to be immune to venom because he let the young of poisonous snakes bite him from time to time.[18] The Eisowy, a North African snake-charmer sect, were said to gain immunity by eating poisonous snakes alive.

From India come several reports of snake showmen who permitted themselves to be bitten by snakes that were later shown to be poisonous by allowing them to bite fowls. One snake demonstrated its power most convincingly by fatally biting an onlooker.[19] There is no record of how these showmen immunize themselves, if, indeed, they do so. Demonstrations of the sort described might be arranged by rapid sleight-of-hand substitution of an intact snake for one that had been defanged. A riskier but more convincing demonstration might be managed by milking a snake almost dry, allowing it to bite the showman briefly but sufficiently to draw blood, and finally applying its jaws to the chicken or other test animal and manually squeezing the last bit of venom from the glands.

Madame Frances Calderón de la Barca, who lived in Mexico during the 1830s, heard from "seven or eight respectable merchants" that natives near Tampico, Mexico, inoculated themselves with rattlesnake venom, using the fang of a snake to inject it into the tongue, arms, and other parts of the body. This not only immunized them but gave them power to call up snakes to kill or cure people at their bidding." [20]

Members of the snake-handling religious cults of the southern United States are often bitten by the rattlesnakes and copperheads used in their services. Two Kentucky members of such a cult claim to have been bitten 30 and 50 times respectively.[21] The development of some degree of immunity in these individuals would be less surprising than its absence. In spite of this, George Hensley, a Tennessee farmer and the founder of the cult, died of a rattlesnake bite, although he claimed to have survived about 400 earlier bites. Another cultist died after what was said to have been his eleventh bite.

In a Florida study, fourteen biologists, animal dealers, snake handlers, and herpetologists who had been bitten 2 to 12 times apiece by poisonous snakes were interviewed in detail. Nearly all their bites were inflicted by North American pit vipers and ranged in severity from mild to almost fatal. There was no evidence that the repeated bites conferred any immunity. For one subject, his tenth bite and fifth rattlesnake bite was the most serious one he sustained. Others reported severe fifth or sixth bites after earlier mild ones. Serum samples from these persons did not neutralize the effects of rattlesnake venom on animals. The unpredictable amount of venom injected in a natural bite and the long and irregular intervals between bites were thought to be the main reasons for failure of immunity to develop in these persons.[22]

Probably no living man has absorbed more snake venom than William E. Haast, Director of the Miami Serpentarium. Now nearly 60 years old, Mr. Haast has been bitten more than 100 times by a wide variety of snakes. More than half of his bites have

been inflicted by elapid snakes and the majority of these by cobras. In addition to bites, he has received several courses of injections with a mixture of cobra venoms. While he unquestionably
has considerable immunity against elapid venoms, he has had
some serious bites among his last 50 or so. This either indicates
considerably more diversity among elapid toxins than has here-
tofore been believed or shows that high levels of immunity are
difficult to attain by repeated naturally inflicted bites.

Modern experiments indicate that immunization of human
beings against snake venoms is possible but so difficult that it is
doubtful if the primitive methods used by the Zulus can be very
effective. One of the few men who has been scientifically immunized is an Australian herpetologist who received 24 injections of tiger-snake venom during a period of slightly more than
a year. Before he began immunization he had been bitten 9 times
by Australian poisonous snakes—perhaps he felt his luck was
running out. His first injection was 0.002 milligram of venom;
this was increased to 25 milligrams (an estimated 8 to 16 times
the lethal dose) by the twenty-fourth dose. Although he had no
serious trouble, the injections were often accompanied by pain
and swelling of the arm, occasionally by low fever and signs of
allergy. When he began immunization his blood contained 0.2
unit of tiger-snake antitoxin per milliliter, evidently the result
of his earlier bites. Two months after immunization, his antitoxin
level had risen to 5.2 units per milliliter, probably enough to
neutralize the bite of any tiger snake, but a year later it had
fallen to 0.5 unit. About halfway through the course of injections he was bitten by a young dugite, an Australian snake
whose venom is evidently quite different from that of the tiger
snake. He developed such definite signs of neurotoxic poisoning

as blurred vision and difficulty in breathing. A little more than a year after his last immunizing injection he was bitten on the hand by a 3-foot tiger snake. He had no symptoms of poisoning other than slight swelling of the bitten hand. The level of antitoxin in his blood rose sevenfold soon after the bite. This was interpreted as an anamnestic or recall response indicating he received an appreciable dose of venom.[23]

Antivenins

The first successful scientific attempt to immunize an animal against snake venom was reported in 1887 by Henry Sewall, a young professor of physiology at the University of Michigan. He used venom from the massasauga, still occasionally found near Ann Arbor. After determining that pigeons died after injection of 2/5 drop of glycerin-diluted venom but survived a dose of 1/5 drop, he injected a group of pigeons with gradually increasing doses. About 6 months later, one of these pigeons survived a dose of 3 drops of glycerin-venom mixture and another withstood 4 drops. Sewall's experiment not only showed that immunization against snake venom was possible; it was the cornerstone of all antitoxin therapy. Sewall himself was aware of the wider implications of his observations, for he wrote, "I have assumed an analogy between the venom of the poisonous serpent and the ptomaines produced under the influence of bacterial organisms. Both are the outcome of the activity of living protoplasm although chemically widely distinct. . . . If immunity from the fatal effects of snake-bite can be secured in an animal by repeated inoculation with doses of the poison too small to produce ill effects, we may suspect that the same sort of resistance against germ disease might follow inoculation of the appropriate ptomaine, provided it is through the products of their metabolism that bacteria produce their fatal effects." [24]

His message reached the bacteriologists of Europe. In 1890 Emil von Behring (1854–1917), a German bacteriologist and immunologist, developed antitoxin for diphtheria and shortly afterward Von Behring and Shibasaburo Kitasato (1856–1931), a Japanese bacteriologist, developed tetanus antitoxin. For almost a half-century, until it was supplanted by sulfa drugs and antibiotics, serum therapy was the principal treatment for microbial diseases. Although antitoxic serum is still used in the prevention and treatment of diphtheria, tetanus, and a few other diseases, snakebite is one of the few conditions where antitoxin is still the main material for specific treatment.

The first antitoxic serum for snakebite treatment was produced in 1895 at the Pasteur Institute in Paris under the direction of the French bacteriologist Albert Calmette (1863–1933) from the serum of horses immunized against cobra venom. The preliminary work was done by two French scientists, Cesaire Phisalix and Gabriel Bertrand working at that time (1893–94) at the Museum of Natural History in Paris and by Fraser in Edinburgh. It was Fraser who coined the name "antivenene" for this type of antitoxic serum; the spelling "antivenin" is usually used in America. In regions where snakebite was an important medical problem, other laboratories began to produce antiserum. In 1899 Dr. Vital Brazil took over a cowshed near São Paulo, Brazil, as his laboratory and two years later began producing antivenins for use in tropical America. He wrote, "It was amongst these very poor surroundings where discomfort disputed with inadequacy . . . that the first technical realizations of the Instituto Butantan were achieved." [25] During the next half-century this institute became one of the best-known centers for research on venomous animals. Joseph McFarland, Professor of Pathology and Bacteriology at the Medico-Chirurgical College of Philadelphia prepared an antiserum against rattlesnake venom about 1899, but it had little neutralizing power. In 1904, Simon Flexner, an American pathologist, and Hideyo Noguchi, a Japanese bacteriologist, both working in the University of Pennsylvania Medical School at the time, prepared a considerably better rattlesnake antivenin in rabbits. It apparently was never used to treat human victims of snakebite. A commercial product was not available in the United States until 1927. Today 30 laboratories in 24 nations produce antivenins.

In all laboratories the basic procedure is the same. Horses are injected with 1/10 to 1/100 of a lethal dose of venom. This is increased at intervals of a week or so until the horse is receiving several times the lethal dose without serious ill effects. This requires a minimum of 3 months. During this time the horse produces antibodies, proteins of the immune globulin type, that specifically neutralize the venom injected. At the end of the immunization period the horse is bled and the antibody-containing serum separated. If given periodic booster injections of venom, a horse will produce high levels of antibody for 6 or 7 years and may yield 700 liters (about 180 gallons) of blood. Modifications of the procedure include treatment of the venom to reduce its toxicity for the horse and increase its power to stimulate antibody production. Fractionation methods, such as the addition of ammonium sulfate followed by centrifugation or filtration, are often used to separate the antibody containing globulin from the crude serum. The final product may be lyoph-ilized to give it greater stability and shelf life.

Antivenins may be produced against venom of a single species of snake (monovalent) or against a mixture of venoms (polyvalent). Luckily it is not necessary to produce a separate antivenin for each species of snake. Tiger-snake antivenin not only neutralizes venoms of most Australian snakes but also is at least moderately effective in neutralizing cobra, krait, ringhals, black-mamba, desert-blacksnake, and sea-snake venoms.[26] An antivenin that neutralizes venoms of most New World pit vipers has been produced by using a mixture of three rattlesnake and one *Bothrops* venoms.[27] One of the challenges in antivenin re-search is finding combinations of venoms that will give the broadest spectrum of protective antibodies.

Unfortunately, the need for antivenins is usually greatest in countries least able to afford research into methods to improve them. It has proved difficult to make antivenins with a neutraliz-ing capacity comparable to that of most bacterial antitoxins. This means that the antivenin, a foreign protein, must be given in large amounts. Immunizing animals with purified toxins rather than with crude venom is a promising approach that is used on a limited scale at the Rogoff Institute in Israel.

A few experimental antivenins have been produced in animals other than horses, but these antivenins have no clear-cut advantage except for persons allergic to horse serum. It may be possible to concentrate the toxin-neutralizing antibodies to a greater degree and combine them with chemical antagonists to the components of venom not amenable to neutralization by anti-bodies.

There are no international standards of potency for anti-venins. Although at least thirteen laboratories manufacture mono-valent or polyvalent antivenins against cobra venom, there is no way, short of setting up expensive and time-consuming animal experiments, to compare the neutralizing powers of these serums. Most laboratories have intramural standards to insure that this year's product will be approximately the same as last year's, but methods differ considerably among the various manufacturers.

Like any foreign protein that is given by injection, an anti-venin has some unpleasant and dangerous side effects. Most fre-quent of these is serum sickness, a bout of fever, itching, hives, and sore joints that develops 6 to 10 days after the serum injec-tion. Certain individuals sensitized to horse protein by previous serum injections or merely by association with horses may react to antivenins produced in horses by the violent reaction known as anaphylactic shock. Soon, sometimes within seconds after the injection, the person may collapse and have great difficulty breathing. Often he will die unless promptly and skillfully treated. In Britain in 1959 a child was bitten by an adder, received an in-jection of antivenin, and died of anaphylactic shock. This led to a widespread feeling among British physicians that the treatment might be worse than the disease. About two years later another child was bitten, received no antivenin, and died from the effect of the bite. Deciding whether to use or not use antivenin can pose quite a dilemma to a physician. In our files is the case of a young biologist who was struck by a copperhead that he was transferring from a bag to a cage. The fangs inflicted more of a scratch than a puncture, and there was only slight local pain. At the insistence of his employer he sought treatment, received an injection of antivenin, and suffered a serum reaction that cost him several days in the hospital and a painful neuritis.

Snake venom itself can cause allergy. Some cases of sudden death following snakebite have been suspected to be actually anaphylactic shock. A physician and herpetologist wrote us concerning his experience with venom allergy: "As you know I had been bitten a number of times by the *adamanteus* [eastern diamondback rattler] after he was defanged. This didn't worry me, but I hadn't reckoned on the possibility of becoming sensitized. Three weeks ago, never mind how it happened, I got some *horridus* [timber rattler] venom under my skin. It was not enough to worry me, and I didn't give it any more thought until about 5–10 minutes later my eyes nearly swelled shut in addition to being plastered with exudate. I developed hives over most of my body, and my tongue became swollen. Frankly I still wouldn't have become panicky if the wheezing had not commenced. I took some pyribenzamine and a cc. of adrenalin at the first sign of trouble, but as it became more pronounced . . . I got 40 units of ACTH. With these measures the reaction began to subside, but the massive edema in my periorbital tissues remained for several days. . . . My present status is that I feel that the direct toxic effects of venom are of less menace to me than the allergic aspect. . . ."

Inoculation of venom under the skin is not necessary to produce an allergy. A technician in my laboratory evidently became sensitized to cobra venom by lyophilizing and weighing samples. Eventually she could not open a vial of dry cobra venom without developing symptoms of violent hay fever.

8. Treatment of Snakebite

On the evening of January 25, 1964, Gerald DeBray, director of the Hogle Zoo in Salt Lake City, Utah, was bitten on the arm by a puff adder. He was given immediate first aid and received an injection of antivenin within an hour after the bite. Within 3 hours all the facilities of a large modern medical center were available and were used during the next 28 hours in a vain attempt to save his life. In Africa, the homeland of the puff adder, hundreds of persons are bitten annually. Most of them are treated by their tribal medicine men, and most of them recover. Do the witch doctors of Africa know something Western science doesn't? The answer is a barely qualified no. It is just possible that among the thousands of folk remedies for snakebite is an undiscovered substance or mixture of substances that is more effective than anything now in use, but the odds are against it.

The unpredictable course of snakebite gives almost any remedy a chance to establish a name for itself. Even if it were used only for bites of such potentially deadly snakes as the puff adder, any treatment not seriously dangerous in itself would succeed in about two cases out of three. If it were used, as is usually the case, for treating bites by nonpoisonous snakes and snakes whose venoms are too weak to be lethal under ordinary circumstances, its rate of "cure" might be 90 percent or better. Dr. Findlay Russell of the University of Southern California School of Medicine, a leading authority on animal toxins, gained nationwide publicity while treating a young man with a severe tiger-snake bite. Consequently he received dozens of letters of advice on how to treat his patient. Many were apparently motivated by genuine altruism; other correspondents suggested "a splitting of fees" or a subsidy for their particular nostrum. Two letters indicate the range of remedies advocated:

> Dear Doctor:
> Please try this magic cure for snakebite.
> Sprinkle cold water on the face of the victim and shout in a commanding tone thrice: "Get up! It is the command of T. C. Ramachander Rao!"
> I hope this will cure the boy. It has cured thousands in India.

> Dear Doctor:
> Do you know about toad pee? This is the best cure for all snake bite. Catch a toad and squeeze his pee into the wound, then kill the toad and leave wound soaked with pee this will kill the snake bite. My grandfather used to be bit by lots of snakes and never died because of this treatment.

Dr. Russell pointed out that most of the remedies suggested by his correspondents can be traced to writings of Greek and Roman physicians and writers, such as Nicander (*fl.* 2nd century B.C.), Celsus (*fl.* 1st century A.D.) and Galen (130–200? A.D.).[1]

Antivenin is the only specific antidote for the lethal toxins of snake venoms; however, it must be of the proper kind and administered in adequate dosage. Failures can usually be ascribed to administration of the wrong type of antivenin or of too little too late. In some cases, however, antivenins are simply not powerful enough to neutralize a massive venom injection from a large snake. Antivenins are not very effective in counteracting the local destructive effects of venoms. Recently, a chemical known as ethylenediaminetetracetic acid, mercifully abbreviated to EDTA, has been shown to reduce local tissue damage by inactivating venom enzymes. To be effective it must be injected quite promptly after the bite. It does not counteract the lethal effect of the venom.[2]

The corticotropins (such as ACTH) and corticosteroids (for example, cortisone) are potent substances with multiple biological activities, among them the reduction of inflammation and counteraction of the effects of certain bacterial toxins. Some physicians have reported these drugs highly effective in snakebite therapy, but others have found them of little value except for treatment of allergic serum reactions. Animal experiments have also given somewhat contradictory results, although none has shown that corticosteroids or corticotropins can save animals from doses of venom much in excess of the LD_{50}. Because some symptoms of snakebite resemble those of poisoning by histamine and because some venoms liberate histamine from tissue, the antihistamine drugs have occasionally been used as snakebite treatment. Animal experiments indicate that these drugs actually seem to increase susceptibility to pit-viper venoms.

No snakebite remedy has had a more colorful history than alcohol. Celsus' suggested in *De Medicina* that strong wine with pepper was an antidote; but alcohol, usually in the form of straight whiskey, gained its greatest popularity in the United

States between 1830 and 1870. During the last months of the Civil War, a snakebitten Confederate soldier was given a gallon of whiskey, then worth $450 in the inflated currency of the Confederacy; this was over the protest of a quartermaster officer who felt the remedy was worth more than the man. In his classical work on rattlesnakes, the late L. M. Klauber, a San Diego engineer who was also one of the world's leading herpetologists, states: "The rattler, more than any other cause, made the High Plains country a hard-liquor area. . . . One who had applied the precepts of safety first by imbibing freely was immune to rattlesnake bite until the effects had worn off. So the cure was taken as a safety measure against a possible encounter with the affliction." [3] A corollary of the immunity idea was that enough whiskey would not only save the man but kill the snake.

Two other tenets of whiskey therapy were that a person who has been bitten will not become intoxicated, regardless of the amount of alcohol administered, until the venom has been neutralized and that any continuation or increase in the symptoms of venom poisoning is an indication for more alcohol. Not surprisingly, the doses recommended were large. One physician, writing in a leading medical journal of the day, prescribed a half-pint of bourbon every five minutes until a quart had been taken.[4] Another physician administered a quart of brandy and a gallon and a half of whiskey over a 36-hour period. He reported in all seriousness that his patient was seen after recovery looking for another rattlesnake to bite him.[5] These reports represent informed medical opinion of the day, not folk medicine or humor.

By the turn of the century most of the medical profession had lost faith in the curative properties of whiskey, although its use as a folk remedy lingered much longer. It underwent an understandable upsurge of popularity during Prohibition. Today medical opinion condemns the use of alcohol for treatment of snakebite as strongly as it endorsed it a century ago. Certainly the large doses of liquor formerly prescribed imposed an additional burden on the liver, kidneys, and circulatory system struggling to cope with the trauma of snakebite. On the other hand, there is no evidence from animal experiments of a lethal synergism between snake venom and alcohol in small doses. It is usually said that alcohol is bad for the snakebite victim because it speeds up circulation and hastens absorption of venom. But anxiety and fear also increase heart rate and raise blood pressure, and this effect can be countered by the tranquilizing and vasodilating effect of a small dose of whiskey or brandy, especially in those accustomed to using alcohol.

One of the most widely used antidotes for venom was potassium permanganate, apparently first introduced by De Lacerda in 1881.[6] For the next half-century it was a standard item in snakebite first-aid kits. In a weak solution it makes a harmless antiseptic wet dressing. Unfortunately, some instructions for its use recommended liberal injection of the solution into tissues around the bite or the rubbing of crystals into incisions. Used in this manner, permanganate can be terribly destructive. Furthermore, it has no neutralizing action on venom in the tissues, although De Lacerda was correct in his observation that it destroys venom in the test tube.

With the possible exception of EDTA, already mentioned, none of the hundreds of materials that have been used locally for snakebite treatment has proved of any real benefit. In southern Indiana where Madge and I grew up, opinion was divided between those who advised soaking the bitten part in kerosine and those who advocated clapping the split body of a freshly killed chicken onto the bite. The first of these hurt like blazes; the second, although messy, was harmless enough unless you got an infection. Since most of the bites were by copperheads or by totally innocuous snakes, both treatments could boast an impressive number of cures.

Newspapers occasionally carry stories of intrepid individuals who have chopped off fingers or toes that have been bitten by snakes, or blasted the envenomed digit to shreds with a gun. For someone bitten by a very dangerous snake under circumstances such that antivenin and medical aid could not be obtained for hours, this drastic form of first aid might be life-saving. It must be done quickly, however. Animal experiments show that a sheep or a dog can absorb a lethal dose of elapid venoms within a minute. Viper venoms are absorbed more slowly. At best, this treatment adds the pain and shock of a severe wound to the effects of whatever venom is absorbed. Another radical measure is excision or cutting out of the area around the bite. This will save the lives of experimental animals if done promptly, but again, the procedure is highly traumatic, and even a skilled surgeon might have trouble deciding how large an area to excise.

In the United States, directions for first-aid management of snakebite usually recommend placing a ligature between the bite and the rest of the body, making incisions around the bite and sucking material from these incisions with a mechanical device or, in an emergency, with the mouth. Sucking a poisoned bite or sore is so widespread a practice among primitive peoples that one is tempted to call it instinctive. Experiments on animals and bioassay of fluids (the determination of the presence or strength of a substance by the use of tissue or a living animal) extracted from human cases of snakebite indicate that an appreciable amount of rattlesnake or cottonmouth venom can be extracted from incisions around the site of injection. Gennaro found that slightly over half of the radioisotope-tagged rattlesnake venom he injected into dogs could be removed by suction, providing the venom was injected into subcutaneous tissue rather than muscle and suction was begun within 3 minutes. But even with a delay of 2 hours, enough venom could be removed to make the procedure worthwhile.[7] Using suction by mouth is more hazardous to the bitten person than to the one doing the sucking, for it provides a good opportunity for dangerous bacteria to enter the wound. Despite the melancholy "Ballad of Springfield Mountain," in which the heroine dies in a vain attempt to save her lover by sucking the venom from his bitten heel, the danger of absorbing poison through cavities in the teeth or sores in the mouth seems to be remote.

The incision-and-suction treatment is almost unanimously condemned by physicians in Latin America and is not generally popular with those who have had experience treating snakebites in Africa and southern Asia. This difference in opinion partly reflects variation in the snakes involved. Cobras and other elapids are important in Africa and Asia, and their venoms are very rapidly absorbed and would not easily be removed by suction. The big *Bothrops* pit vipers of tropical America and the *Bitis* vipers of Africa have proportionally longer and straighter fangs than rattlesnakes, so perhaps there is greater chance of their injecting venom into the muscle where it cannot be sucked out. It is also possible that natives of these lands have a little less subcutaneous insulation than the average North American. Venoms of North

American snakes do not damage the blood-clotting mechanism as severely as do those of some vipers of Asia, Africa, and Latin America. In Pakistan I saw two hospitalized patients who had been bitten by saw-scaled vipers and had had the bites incised as a first-aid measure. Bleeding from these incisions was quite alarming and almost impossible to check; it probably contributed to the death of one of these individuals. Finally, infection of incisions is, for a variety of reasons, more likely to occur in the tropics.

A specialized sort of suction treatment is the snakestone; it has been used in almost every part of the world where dangerous reptiles are found. Many of these stones are bezoars, concretions found in the stomachs of goats and other ruminants; others are bits of calcined deer horn or bone, kidney or bladder stones, porous minerals, and semiprecious stones of several types. Under the name of madstones, they were used in the rural United States until quite recent times and were believed effective against bites by rabid dogs, scorpion stings, and all other kinds of venomous wounds. The best stones commanded such a high price that they were sometimes bought communally, each shareholder being entitled to use of the stone as required. In use, the stone is applied to the wound for a prescribed period, sometimes as long as it will adhere spontaneously, during which it draws out the poison. It is then regenerated by boiling in milk or by some other treatment. Needless to say, the amount of venom removed by such a stone would be minuscule. In West Pakistan, snakestones seem to be used more for their magical than their physical properties, for many of the most prized ones are not at all absorptive. We once captured a large but nonvenomous black royal snake before the surprised eyes of two Baluch goatherds. As we were showing them the snake, they saw a large lapis lazuli ring on Madge's hand. It was clear from their gestures and conversation that they considered this the secret of our power over snakes.

Cryotherapy, the treatment of venomous bites by application of cold, was proposed in 1906 by C. W. R. Crum for the treatment of copperhead bites and a little later for snakebites on parts of the body where absorption of venom could not be retarded by a ligature. In 1953–54 it received a great deal of attention as a result of publications by Herbert L. Stahnke of the Poisonous Animals Research Laboratory at Arizona State University.[8] The purpose of chilling is to retard absorption of venom and inhibit its local enzymatic action. Applied as ice packs, ice-water immersion, ethyl-chloride spray, and in other ways, cryotherapy has been used to treat snakebite in the United States for more than a decade. It has engendered a good deal of acrimonious discussion and remains controversial. Some physicians, especially those working closely with Dr. Stahnke, have obtained good results; others consider the treatment ineffective or harmful. Sometimes injury by cold seems to have been substituted for or added to injury by the venom.

Much of the reduction in snakebite mortality in the past quarter-century can be ascribed to better supportive treatment instead of to more effective antidotes for venom. Blood transfusions, antibiotics, better methods for detecting and treating shock, all have contributed. Respirators and artificial kidneys have been used occasionally to treat patients suffering from severe snakebites. As improved technology allows more and more vital functions to be taken over temporarily by mechanical devices, the victim of serious venom poisoning will have a correspondingly better chance for recovery.

9. Uses of Snake Venom

Concerning the use of snake venom in the healing arts, Laurence M. Klauber comments: "There is something peculiarly fascinating in the conversion of a dangerous creature such as a rattlesnake—and the essence of that danger, the venom—into a cure for disease. . . . The venom treatments began on a plane of folklore, as in Europe, where viper venom had been so used; but later some really scientific work was undertaken in an endeavor to cure afflictions with these exceedingly powerful toxins. It was expected that the results would parallel the important contributions of vegetable poisons to medicine, but in this they have proved a disappointing failure." [1]

The failure has not been for want of trying. In the Western world, at least, the homeopaths have made the most extensive use of reptile venoms. A British homeopathic physician, J. W. Hayward, in 1882 wrote a monograph of more than 200 pages on crotalus (rattlesnake venom), including indications for its use in at least fifty diseases and conditions. The venom, much diluted, was usually administered by mouth but was occasionally injected or used as a lotion or wet compress.[2] As late as 1925, crotalus was described as "one of the homeopath's most treasured drugs." Other reptile venoms used in homeopathic medicine included naja (cobra venom), lachesis (venom of the pit vipers now referred to the genus *Bothrops*), elaps (coral-snake venom), and heloderma (gila-monster venom). All but the last are listed in the 1938 edition of the homeopathic pharmacopoeia.

As for the uses of venom in regular (allopathic) medical practice, Findlay E. Russell and Richard S. Scharffenberg's *Bibliography of Snake Venoms and Venomous Snakes* lists almost 400 articles on this topic that have appeared in medical journals between 1900 and 1964.[3] About three-fourths of these fall into three general categories: treatment of hemorrhagic conditions, treatment of epilepsy, and relief of severe and intractable pain.

Snake venoms unquestionably affect blood coagulation, greatly speeding it up in some instances, inhibiting it in others, and sometimes producing the same end effect by different mechanisms. Likewise, the human body has a complicated system of safeguards against abnormal bleeding, and any of the components of this elaborate mechanism may singly or in combination be faulty. There are several kinds of hemorrhagic disorders, and some of them, such as thrombocytopenia (shortage of blood platelets, microscopic structures essential for the first stage of clotting), may be caused by dozens of substances and conditions. The complexity of both the remedy and the disorder probably explains the inconsistent results that have been obtained. Cottonmouth venom was used with some success for treatment of certain types of purpura, uterine hemorrhages, severe nose bleeds, and bleeding after tonsillectomy or tooth extraction. However, in 1940 a commercial preparation of this venom was found unacceptable by the American Medical Association Council on Pharmacy and Chemistry because the improvement produced was transient, and painful swelling often occurred at the injection site.[4] Russell's viper venom has been used in similar manner in Europe and India, and a preparation of it is currently produced by a British drug company. In 1962, bothropothrombin, a preparation from venom of the jararaca, was reported to have benefited 98 percent of a group of 1,300 patients with selected hemorrhagic disorders. The effects were palliative rather than curative.[5] This is one of the few favorable reports from the past decade. At present it is the general consensus that snake venoms can do nothing in therapy of hemorrhagic conditions that cannot be accomplished better and more safely by other means.

British workers, however, have recently prepared a highly effective anticoagulant from the venom of the Malay pit viper. The idea of using this venom therapeutically was conceived by II. Alistair Reid, who observed during his service in Penang, a city on an island off the northwest coast of Malaya, that blood of patients bitten by this snake had its clotting power impaired for as long as 26 days after the bite if they were not treated with specific antivenin. In spite of this, their general health remained surprisingly good, and they did not suffer from spontaneous bleeding. He writes of one of his early patients, "In 1958 a Malay woman walked three miles from her village to the Sungei Patani District Hospital. . . . She was eight months pregnant and had a swollen leg; she also had completely nonclotting blood. . . . She had been bitten on the foot a week previously by an *ular kapak bodoh,* the Malay name for the 'stupid snake' with which all rural folks in that area are familiar. . . . Two weeks after the bite both her leg and clotting had returned to normal. Two weeks later she was delivered without trouble of a healthy boy." [6]

The anticoagulant fraction of Malay-pit-viper venom, known as Arvin, has proved of considerable value in treating patients with venous thrombosis or abnormal clots in their veins. Not only does arvin prevent new clots from forming; it may also help dissolve existing clots. It promises to be useful in treating coronary occlusion and in cardiac surgery. Its action is prompt and lasts longer than that of other anticoagulant drugs. It has a wide margin of safety, and the effects of an overdose can promptly be reversed by antivenin.[7]

Epilepsy, particularly as the term was used at the turn of the century, includes several conditions and diseases characterized by recurrent convulsive seizures. Sometimes these may be secondary to injury, tumors, or infections; sometimes they are of psychogenic origin; and many fall into the group often called idiopathic, where the cause remains essentially unknown. For a short time early in the twentieth century, rattlesnake venom enjoyed a certain popularity in the treatment of epilepsy. The rationale of its use was based on a case report of an epileptic who remained free of attacks for two years after he had been bitten by a snake. Although a few physicians reported good results, many found the treatment of no value, and one death resulted apparently from injection of a bacterially contaminated venom solution. The treatment had been virtually abandoned in the United States by 1930. A few experiments in other countries with other venoms were not encouraging. Epilepsy, like cancer, is a disease that carries an aura of mystery and arouses a strong, emotional reaction in most persons. Also like cancer, it is sometimes confused with less serious conditions and may undergo spontaneous and unpredictable remissions or, rarely, even permanent arrest. Any drug or treatment, especially one in itself somewhat bizarre, can quite by accident gain an unwarranted reputation for effectiveness either through use in incorrectly diagnosed cases or when its use is coincidentally followed by a particularly striking remission.

The use of venoms for relief of pain evidently originated with Adolph Monaelesser, a New York physician who did most of his investigative work in Paris. His original idea came from observation of a leper whose symptoms improved markedly after he had been bitten by a spider. In 1933 Monaelesser reported cobra venom was a very effective analgesic, and it was rather widely used during the next two decades.[8] The venom was chiefly employed in palliating the symptoms of persons with inoperable cancer but was used in some other painful conditions such as migraine, angina pectoris, and the neuralgias of late syphilis. Cobra venom is said to be safer and more prolonged in action than morphine and does not have a narcotic's potential for addiction. Not all reports of its use have been encouraging, however. Frequently when it is used in doses sufficient to relieve the pain, unpleasant side effects, such as double vision and nausea, are almost as troublesome as the pain. Even the degree of pain relief is quite variable and may be little better than that achieved by aspirin. Although two commercial preparations of dilute cobra venom are available and presumably still used, it has been largely superseded by other analgesics. Cobra and probably other elapid venoms unquestionably can influence pain perception; eventually it may be possible to modify the toxin so that its analgesic property can be separated from its undesirable effects.

Leprosy is one of the first diseases to have been treated by the flesh and venom of snakes. According to one account, frugal

Greek peasants who found a viper drowned in their jug of
wine gave the wine to a leper, reasoning that his lot could
hardly be worsened if the drink killed him. He was promptly
cured, and viper flesh, marinated or otherwise, became a popular
remedy. Moses ben Maimon (Maimonides), Jewish court physician to Saladin, the Sultan of Egypt and Syria, in the twelfth century, used snake venom in treating leprosy and cancer.[9] References to the treatment of leprosy with snake venom appear in
medical journals up to about 1940; however in the more recent
ones it was used primarily for its pain-relieving property. The
association of snakes with the cure of leprosy and other skin
diseases is a natural enough one. Wounds of snakes and skin
infections often seem to improve almost magically after shedding,
and early physicians reasoned it should be possible to transfer
this useful property to their patients through the flesh, skin, or
venom of the reptile.

While snake venoms have not been conspicuously successful
in curing disturbances of blood clotting, they have been of
value in helping to understand the complex clotting mechanism.
Russell's viper venom is used in some of the methods for determining the quantity of prothrombin in the blood. Prothrombin
is a substance essential for the second stage of blood clotting and
is decreased in vitamin K deficiency, liver diseases, and some
other conditions.

Studies on the hemolytic, or red-blood-cell-dissolving, property of cobra venom spawned four interesting diagnostic procedures during the first half of this century. In 1908 Albert
Calmette, whose name is associated with the first successful
antivenin, reported that cobra-venom hemolysis was activated
by serum from persons with tuberculosis.[10] At about the same

time, other investigators reported that the opposite effect, in-hibition of hemolysis, was produced by the serum of psychotics, particularly those with schizophrenia.[11] This was the basis of the Much-Holzmann test for schizophrenia rather widely used in the years just before World War I. Eventually it was found that positive reactions to both these tests were shown by many normal persons or persons with unrelated diseases. Fervid proponents of the Much-Holzmann test maintained that these people either would become insane or had insane relatives. It was difficult to argue with such reasoning, but eventually the test was abandoned.

A third test, known as the Weil reaction, was based on the observation that red blood cells of persons with early syphilis were abnormally susceptible to cobra-venom lysis, while those of persons in the late stages of syphilis were abnormally resistant. This test was extensively used in Europe during the World War I period. It was about as reliable as the original version of the now standard Wassermann test and a good deal easier to per-form.[12] Eventually it was superseded by simpler and more de-pendable tests. In 1950 Madge bought our first sample of cobra venom from a man who was trying unsuccessfully to revive in-terest in the Weil reaction.

In 1952 two physicians, H. Lehndorff and M. J. Giannini, at New York Medical College proposed a cobra-venom test for pregnancy. They observed that serum from pregnant women specifically activated the venom's hemolysis of red blood cells of horses.[13] There was little effort to follow up this lead, for other pregnancy tests using less exotic materials were available.

All these reactions seem to depend upon abnormally high or low concentrations of certain lipids in the serum and blood cells during pregnancy and some disease states. These lipids are the substrate upon which the venom acts. But not all cobra venoms are alike, and, in most species, at least two hemolysins are involved. When the composition of venoms and the chemistry of their action are better known, some of the more readily available ones may become useful reagents in the clinical diagnostic laboratory.

Today, snake venoms have become tools of the biochemist and molecular biologist. An excellent source of enzymes, venoms are used by the biochemist to break down large, complicated nucleides into simple, more readily identified components, and to start and stop reactions in which living cells synthesize new materials. As chemical scalpels they can dissect structures too small for the finest knife or needle. The American biochemist Alton Meister of the National Cancer Institute wrote: "Although we are at a loss to know how L-amino acid oxidase may be useful to the snake, there are several ways in which the oxidase has been put to use by man in the biochemical laboratory. . . . More than thirty keto acids have been prepared by this method including many . . . not previously available." [14]

Snake and bee venoms are the richest known sources of the enzyme phospholipase A. This enzyme affects the membranes surrounding cells and subcellular particles. It has been used by investigators studying the physiology and ultramicroscopic structure of membranes. Two of our colleagues, Frank Padgett and Alvin S. Levine, have found that treating Rauscher virus, which causes leukemia in mice, with cobra or krait venom for varying periods of time peels the virus particle somewhat as an onion is peeled. The technique has yielded important information on how this virus is constructed, and they are using it to examine the structure of other viruses.[15]

10. Snakes and Human Violence

From the fourth century B.C., when Macedonian legionnaires came home from India with tales of snakes with eyes as large as shields, to today's marine corporal back from Vietnam with the story of a snake that will drop a man to the ground six paces after he has been bitten, snakes have been prominent in the annals of military campaigns. Although no military force in modern times has suffered appreciable casualties from snakebite, the mere presence of snakes has sometimes affected the efficiency of small units. I saw repairs on a battle-damaged warship in Philippine waters halted temporarily because a sea snake had been reported in a flooded compartment.

The Punic Wars (*c.* 264–146 B.C.) and Egyptian campaigns brought the Romans into contact with the northern fringe of Africa's rich serpent fauna. The mythical creature, the basilisk, with its deadly stare and poisonous breath may have been based on highly embroidered accounts of encounters with spitting cobras. The asp of classical antiquity was probably the Egyptian cobra, and Hypnale, the snake whose bite caused stupor, may have been a cobra or the desert blacksnake, another species with strongly neurotoxic venom. The Greek historian Diodorus Siculus, who traveled in Egypt from 60 to 57 B.C., reported that the sands of the Theban desert spontaneously generated serpents.

It must have seemed so a few years earlier to Cato's army. Cerastes, the common venomous snake of the region, buries its
coils under sand so that only its eyes and the tip of the snout
are visible. From this position it may strike with deadly accuracy
and must have been a serious hazard to sandaled Roman soldiers.
At this time the horned viper enjoyed the protection of ancient
Egyptian gods and was sacred to Jupiter as well, so little was
done to discourage its proliferation.[1]

The Carthaginians are reported to have defeated a Roman
expeditionary force in the third century B.C. by catapulting pots
of live snakes into their ships. In the crowded quarters of a
war galley this could be disastrous. It appears to be the only
instance where snakes played a decisive role in a military en-
gagement, although the tactic was occasionally tried by the
Saracens and others until the invention of gunpowder made it
obsolete. We have recently heard of snakes being left as living
booby traps along trails or in underground bunkers in Vietnam.
In the absence of detailed reports, it is more likely, however, that
the snakes may have chosen these sites voluntarily.

Probably the greatest number of snakebites suffered by U. S.
forces during combat operations over a short period of time
occurred during the campaign on Okinawa and some of the
other Ryukyu Islands during World War II. Almost all bites
were ascribed to the habu, which is plentiful on many of the
islands. Although one marine was struck in the face by a
large snake,[2] there were no fatalities; this record can probably
be attributed to good luck and good medical care. No figures
are available on the incidence of snakebites during the Vietnam
war, although an unofficial figure of 5 to 10 deaths annually
among U.S. troops has been given.[3]

The English writers Ramona and Desmond Morris (Mr. Morris is Curator of mammals at the London Zoo), in their book, *Men and Snakes,* give several instances of the use of snakes in torture and judicial execution.[4] Death by snakebite was often punishment for a particularly heinous offense—for example, parricide—during the time of the Mogul emperor, Jahangir (1569–1627). However, in ancient Egypt, death by this means was reserved for political prisoners who were entitled to a more honorable and less painful exit than the common criminal.

Snakes are occasionally used to harass unwanted individuals. During the summers of 1964 and 1965, civil-rights workers in Mississippi occasionally found that cottonmouths and other reptiles had been put into their cars. Practical jokes with live or dead snakes are commonplace in camps, barracks, and country schools. Some have had unfortunate and even tragic consequences. A Texas cowhand is said to have killed another cowboy who put a small rattlesnake with its mouth sewed shut into his boot.[5] Steven Anderson, a herpetologist with the California Academy of Sciences, while on an expedition in Iran, collected a nonpoisonous cliff racer with its mouth similarly secured. He adds, "This is fairly common practice, a snake with the mouth sewn shut being placed in someone's house or bed. This is considered a good joke on both the snake and the unsuspecting householder." [6] Such pranks were not viewed so lightly in Mogul India, the culprit being heavily fined and required to remove the snake with his own hands.

Snakes have been used as instruments of murder, although well-authenticated instances are few. Snakes are too secretive, too timid, and too anxious to avoid encounters with man to lend themselves to such plots; moreover, they are quite as likely to bite the would-be murderer as the chosen victim. Finally, the unpredictable results of a naturally inflicted bite are more likely to leave a living victim than a corpse. A Californian who sought to kill his wife by rattlesnake bite found the reptile unequal to the task and eventually drowned the unfortunate woman.[7] Administration of snake venom by force or by subterfuge would be a possible means of homicide, but there is no known instance of this.

Cleopatra remains history's most famous snakebite suicide. It is reasonable to think that the reptile she employed was the Egyptian cobra, for it was venerated in ancient Egypt, and its bite would provide a prompt and reasonably painless demise. The cerastes, another snake well known to the Egyptians of that time, is scarcely deadly enough to have been a good choice, and the saw-scaled viper would never be selected by anyone seeking a quick and easy escape from life's problems. Occasional suicide attempts employing snakes are reported in the press, one of the more recent ones being that of a Florida snake collector who succumbed to the venom of a cobra he deliberately provoked into biting him. A bacteriology professor chose a more scientific variant on the theme by injecting himself with a lethal dose of venom.

The use of poisoned arrows and darts is a tactic man has borrowed from the serpent and the scorpion, and, not surprisingly, venomous creatures themselves are often used to supply the poison. A 1941 symposium pointed out that arrow poisons are most extensively used in tropical Africa, southeast Asia, and northern South America, although at one time or another they have been used in nearly every part of the world. Some of the most effective poisons, such as curare of the South American

Indians and ipoh of the Semang of Malaya, are of plant origin, but snake venoms or the pulped heads of snakes were used by many American Indian tribes as an ingredient of arrow poison. The venom was often obtained by causing the snake to bite the liver of a deer or other animal. This was allowed to putrefy and sometimes mixed with spiders, ants, poison-ivy leaves, and other substances of real or presumed toxicity. The Bushmen of Namaqualand, a region of Southwest Africa, extract a resin from the root of the plant *Buphane toxicaria* and place it on a stone. The stone is then put into the mouth of a snake, usually the ringhals, and venom forced out to mix with the resin. The resulting gum is used to coat arrows and spears. In another African technique, the head of a puff adder is brewed with beetles, resin, and leaves of various plants. In East Bengal, arrows are poisoned by tieing to them bits of wadding soaked in cobra venom.[8] This is one of the few instances in which venom is the sole or major ingredient of an arrow poison and one of the few where it might be expected to be quite effective. In most of the mixtures it is highly diluted, sometimes with substances that would tend to inactivate it. In other cases, heating or putrefaction would destroy the venom's activity.

While many arrow poisons derived from plants contain substances of undoubted pharmacological activity, most of those derived from animals probably exert their principal effect by inducing gas gangrene, tetanus, and other severe infections. Spores of tetanus and gas-gangrene bacteria abound in decaying animal matter. It is interesting and significant that among many tribes arrows treated with the rapidly acting plant poisons are used only for hunting, while those treated with animal poisons are used in war. The latter would act too slowly to bring down game, but if they caused death in a particularly painful and horrifying way through infection, this would strike fear into an enemy. Sir Walter Raleigh (1552–1618) in *The Discovery of the Empire of Guiana* wrote: "The Aroras . . . are a very valiant or rather desperate people and have the most strong poison on their arrows. . . . For besides the mortality of the wound they make, the party shot endureth the most insufferable torment in the world and abideth a most ugly and lamentable death, sometimes dying stark mad, sometimes their bowels breaking out of their bellies which are presently discolored as black as pitch and so unsavory as no man can endure to cure or to attend them." [9]

11. The Hun-Khun and the Basilisk

While we were living in Pakistan I rashly granted an interview to one of Karachi's English-language newspapers on the subject of Pakistan's reptiles. During the following month or so a number of readers, via letters to the editor or personal communications, pointed out certain lacunae in my knowledge. About half of these were concerned because I had omitted the hun-khun from my discussion. One correspondent, a public official in a small city of Sind, expressed himself thus:

"In your paper dated 17th March 1962 you have published very interesting news regarding poisonous and nonpoisonous snakes. . . . This opinion, however, does not tally with our own experience. . . . The most deadly snake is supposed to be 'Hunkhun' [literally meaning 'strike and take,' 'taking' here referring politely to the dead body of the victim], a lizard-like snake which breaks up on being struck, each drop of its body fluid proving as deadly as its bite. It is therefore killed only by striking it with a 'dhinghar' which means a dry branch of a tree with all its twigs to cover up the breaking up bits completely.

"It is requested that this snake which does not belong to the Viper class may be identified and given its scientific name. . . . Obtaining of this specimen is very essential to make the public aware of this most dangerous snake."[1]

Another writer provided this description: "Hunkhun has a pointed, snout-like face with bright, beady eyes and it sits up on fore-legs, making an acute angle with earth. Hunkhun does not bite like ordinary snakes, but it strikes with the paw or scratches with it, and this is fatal. Each drop of its body's fluid coming out on being treaded upon proves fatal. It is therefore killed with a branch of tree to provide full cover for each bit of it."

A third correspondent with some background in zoology offered additional ideas: "Hun Khun is a slow moving lizard, often called a fat-tailed lizard because of its swollen tail. Natives describe it to be the deadliest creature and thus consider it more dangerous than Cobra. . . . But a zoologist will never believe in the existence of any more poisonous lizards besides Heloderma of Mexico. Well, if these lizards are non-poisonous, then why are they given bad names? I think this question is for the Herpetologists to answer. As regards Hun Khun it is also stated that it is killed either by pressing it under a bush or by burying it under a heap of mud to avoid rupturing its body, thereby spurting blood on the onlookers and causing their death. This shows that poison glands are also present on the skin. Dissection of the body will disclose the poisonous nature of this lizard." [2]

Actually, Madge and I had first heard of the hun-khun about six months after our arrival in Pakistan. The story was told around a campfire near the Indus by Pir Fazal Haq, one of Sind's hereditary saints. About two months later I encountered the creature itself on a desert road near Karachi. It is better known to herpetologists as the fat-tailed gecko (*Eublepharis macularius*) and is rather large as lizards of the gecko family go, exceptional specimens reaching a length of about 1 foot. As is true of all geckos, the tail breaks and regenerates easily. But in this species, the regenerated part becomes very bulbous, occasionally growing almost as large as the head. Strictly nocturnal and less active than most lizards, the hun-khun conducts a spirited defense when cornered. Rising high on its legs, it arches its back and waves its tail about rather like a scorpion preparing to sting. It opens its mouth and makes a noise like air going out of a small balloon. Anything within range of its jaws is likely to be bitten with some force, and rough handling makes the lizard excrete a clear, unpleasant-smelling fluid from its vent. Although it is a worthy antagonist for a creature near its size (I saw one battle a 3-foot sand snake to a draw), the bite of the hun-khun is completely nonvenomous, and I could find no indication that the skin or body fluids are toxic on contact.

In northern India a close relative of the hun-khun *Eublepharis hardwickei* is known as bis-cobra, implying that it has the killing power of twenty cobras. Among the great sand dunes of northern Baluchistan, a part of northwestern West Pakistan, where *Eublepharis* does not occur, the hun-khun stories are associated with another large gecko, the pop-eyed *Teratoscincus scincus,* whose defensive behavior is similar to that of the fat-tailed gecko except that *Teratoscincus* undulates its tail in a peculiar manner which produces a faint hissing sound, apparently by rubbing together of the large scales on the upper side of the tail.

This largely undeserved reputation follows geckos around the world. John Stephenson, a nineteenth-century English physician and writer on the medical properties of animals and minerals, writes that an East Indian gecko is used by natives of Java to poison their arrows, and adds, "The venom of this hideous reptile is so dangerous that if the part affected be not immediately excised or burnt, death will ensue in a few hours. Its urine is also said to be one of the most corrosive poisons; and its blood and saliva are regarded as equally deadly." [3]

Geckos of the genus *Coleonyx,* New World relatives of *Eublepharis,* are greatly feared in Mexico and the southwestern United States. When we went to the Big Bend region of Texas, our Spanish-American neighbors warned us of a dangerous little thin-skinned lizard that lived under rocks and stung like a scorpion. We had no trouble recognizing from this description the Texas banded gecko. Its relatives in the deserts of Arizona and southern California are often thought to be young gila monsters. In the province of Entre Ríos, Argentina, another small gecko, *Homonota darwini,* is believed one of the most poisonous of reptiles.

It is difficult to understand why certain geckos have acquired such a lurid reputation. Not only are they incapable of causing any injury worse than a strong pinch, but also most of the stories of their deadly powers have originated in lands where there are no poisonous lizards of any sort. Part of the answer may be in their appearance and defense displays that make them look as if they ought to be dangerous. Moreover, the most-feared species seem to be creatures that are not often encountered by the ordinary person. Although they may actually be common, their secretive and nocturnal habits keep them from achieving a degree of familiarity that breeds any logical understanding.

Other lizards occasionally share with geckos the onus of being malignant and dangerous creatures. Many rural folk throughout the southeastern United States fear "scorpions," the red-headed males of the broad-headed and five-lined skinks. And to add confusion to error, true scorpions are called "stinging lizards" in some sections of the South. Gerald Durrell, a British naturalist who has written highly entertaining accounts of his quests for unusual animals, found that his native African collectors flatly refused to capture specimens of the colorful grass skink they knew as que-fong-goo. It was considered so venomous that to touch it was fatal. He eventually obtained specimens by providing the hunters with boric-acid powder as an infallible protection against the lizards' poison.[4]

Many European beliefs concerning geckos and other lizards are adumbrated by Pliny the Elder's remarks concerning the salamander: "Of all venomous beasts there are not any so hurtful and dangerous . . . the Salamander can destroy whole nations at one time if they do not take heed and provide to prevent them. . . . If he climbs a tree, its fruit will be deadly with cold poison. If he touch a piece of wood later used to bake bread, the loaf will be deadly. . . . The wild boars in Pamphylia that have eaten Salamanders become venomous and whoever chance to eat of their flesh are sure to die of it. . . . Water or wine in which a Salamander has been drowned is deadly; even a single drop will kill a man . . . a bit of his spittle or moisture touching the foot causes the body hair to fall out." [5] But the creature was not without utility. In Rome a gutted salamander in honey was taken to incite lust.

Most puissant of the poisonous creatures described by the ancients was the basilisk. It was said to wear a golden crown to mark its sovereignty over other reptiles, and its breath and glance could scorch plants, split rocks, and kill all creatures but the weasel. If a man on horseback struck a basilisk with his spear, the reptile's poison traveled up the weapon, slaying both horse and rider. The best defense against the basilisk was a mirror that deflected the fatal glance back into the creature's own eyes. In early accounts the basilisk is depicted as a snake—perhaps based on the spitting cobra whose jets of venom can indeed do harm at a distance. Later, during the Middle Ages, a somewhat similar creature, the cockatrice, enters the legends. It was usually depicted as quadripedal with the feet of a bird and a serpent's tail terminating in a barbed sting. The cockatrice was generally thought to hatch from an egg laid by an aged rooster and brooded by snakes or toads, but in some places it was considered the offspring of the unnatural congress of chickens with ducks. If a cockatrice heard a cock crow, the cockatrice would die. Travelers in regions where these reptiles were reputed to occur carried roosters for protection.[6]

The first Spanish explorers to encounter the genuinely venomous Mexican beaded lizard, in about 1577, attributed to it the basilisklike property of deadly breath, a characteristic still occasionally credited to the closely related gila monster.[7] It is not altogether clear whether these beliefs originated with the Spaniards or other Europeans or were held by the pre-Columbian Indians.

Venomous breath is also attributed to the nonpoisonous hog-nosed snake, a common species in many parts of the central and eastern United States. An account of the region toward the western end of Lake Erie, published in 1793, states: "Of the venomous serpents which infest this water, the hissing snake is the most remarkable. . . . When you approach it, it flattens itself in a moment, and its spots, which are of various colours, become visibly brighter through rage; at the same time it blows from its mouth, with great force, a subtile wind . . . if drawn in with the breath of the unwary traveler, it will infallably bring a decline, that in a few months must prove mortal. No remedy has yet been found to counteract its baneful influence." [8]

While this chapter was in preparation, I was asked to see a woman who developed a rash on her forearm a few hours after she had killed a hog-nosed snake. She seemed quite relieved to learn that the rash had not come from venom sprayed at her by the reptile but appeared to be an early case of poison ivy.

Although there are at least as many species of lizards as there are of snakes, the only known venomous lizards remain the two species of helodermas, or beaded lizards, confined to a relatively small part of Mexico and the southwestern United States. It seems unlikely that additional species remain to be found in the few poorly explored sections of the globe, but rumors persist. In valleys of the Swiss and Austrian Alps there is said to be a stocky lizard known as *stollwurm* or *tatzelwurm* to which peasants ascribe many of the traits of the basilisk. No known European lizard or salamander could provide the basis for these stories, and the only bit of objective evidence for the animal's existence is a photograph taken in 1934, which might be a hoax. However, one zoologist took the stories seriously enough to propose the name *Heloderma europaeum* for the reported creature.[9] Until about 1950, some herpetologists almost wistfully hoped the very rare crocodile lizard (*Lanthonotus*) of Borneo might be venomous, since it is in some ways similar to the helodermas. Their hope was dashed when living specimens of this odd reptile became available for study. Charles M. Bogert, Curator of Reptiles at the American Museum of Natural History, whose anatomical study in collaboration with S. B. McDowell, an American herpetologist now at the Museum of Comparative Zoology, Harvard University, fairly conclusively demonstrated that *Lanthonotus* was not venomous, may have felt some regret; Bogert promulgated an elaborate spoof "proving" that the "swamp adder" encountered by Sherlock Holmes in "The Adventure of the Speckled Band" was a hybrid between a cobra and a gila monster.[10]

12. Snake Cults and Snake Charmers

The Cobra Exalted

Throughout India a symbolic equation of snake and phallus is specific and ubiquitous. The rearing stance and spread hood of an alert cobra, suggesting phallic tumescence, make this snake a natural symbol for human virility. It is considered to be a manifestation of the pre-Vedic fertility god, Siva, first and oldest of the Indian trinity. Siva is sometimes called Mahadev, king of serpents, and his altars, with the phalliform lingam set in its female counterpart, the yoni, are guarded by carved stone cobras, while living snakes are encouraged to live in his temples. Siva is described as having a girdle of cobras, earrings of cobras, a sacrificial cord of cobras, and an outer garment of cobra skins.[1]

Traditionally cobras are descended from the Nagas, serpent gods of Bharat, or ancient India. Their worship has been traced to prehistoric Dravidian times before the Aryan invasion of the subcontinent in about 1600 B.C. The Nagas' power to inflict disproportionate physical damage or almost instantaneous death is explained in Hindu Vedas as paralleling the energy of creation or fire. Remnants of ancient snake-worshiping clans persist in the tribal areas of West Pakistan and in the small principalities that border Pakistan and India along their Himalayan frontier. In such places, the Nagas retain much of their influence, and vil-

131

lage people solicit their help in times of famine and plague. Nagas guard 'hot springs and volcanoes and make precious gems by blowing on gold deep in the earth; astral Nagas manifest themselves as lightning. When angered, they blow their noxious breath across the land to harry man with plagues of malaria, called in India "snake-wind disease." Other indications of Naga displeasure include earthquakes, tidal waves, volcanic eruptions, and crop failures caused by drought.[2]

Every fine garden in Nagpur and along the Malabar Coast has a wild corner set aside as a *vishattum kavu* (poison shrine) where cobras are worshiped. Failure to respect such a shrine may result in leprosy, barrenness in women, death in childbirth and of children, sore eyes, itch, and too many snakes in the garden. The Naga-panchami, or festival of snakes, is particularly popular here. It is held on the fifth day of the first half of the lunar month of Sravana (July 20). During this time, snake charmers enjoy a brief prosperity through selling cobras to the merrymakers who release them as an act of religious merit. An enterprising snake man can catch and resell the same reptile many times. Temporary shrines are set up featuring the cobra in its role as the fertility god Siva. Figures of cobras, and live snakes as well, are carried in processions.[3]

Each September in the Punjab region of northwestern India and adjoining West Pakistan, the snake is worshiped by all castes and religions. During a nine-day festival in honor of Gugga, the patron of the snake tribes, the people make snakes of dough and paint them red and black. These they carry in winnowing baskets to each house in the village, collecting tribute of cloth and food and promising bountiful crops and fertile brides. Afterward, the celebrants bury the snakes, and the women leave

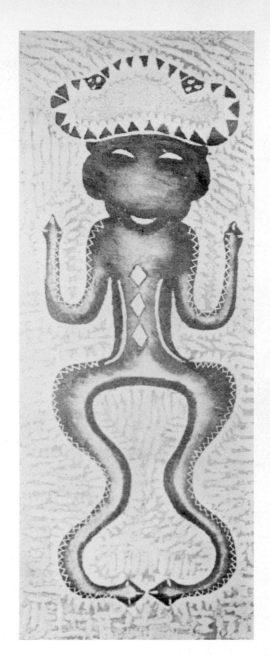

A contemporary painting
of a tribal totem of the
Paiwan people of Taiwan.
The distinctive pattern of
the "snake of a hundred
designs" appears in the
headpiece and the
ophiomorphic arms and
legs. (ALLAN ROBERTS)

Coatlicue, the Aztec "mother of the gods." This pre-Columbian
sacredotal stone figure of the goddess entwined with snakes
is more than 8 feet high; it is now in the National Archeological
Museum, Mexico City. (COURTESY SMITHSONIAN INSTITUTION)

(*Above*) The kerykeion or winged staff
of Hermes, messenger of the gods in
Greek mythology, is often confused with the
caduceus or serpent-entwined staff carried
by Asklepios, god of medicine (*below*).
The figure at Asklepios' left is
Telesphorus, the spirit of convalescence.
(ROMAN INTAGLIOS, COURTESY INDIANA
UNIVERSITY MUSEUM OF ART)

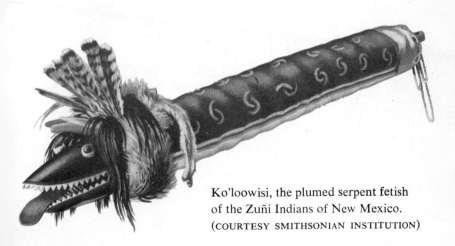

Ko'loowisi, the plumed serpent fetish
of the Zuñi Indians of New Mexico.
(COURTESY SMITHSONIAN INSTITUTION)

In the Jogi tribe of West Pakistan, life revolves around the
capture and display of snakes. *(Left, top)* A Jogi father and
daughter: the elaborate jewelry represents family wealth and
status; *(left, bottom)* a hunter dangles newly captured cobras;
(above) the tribe's two best collectors inspect "hot" cobras
(fangs intact) destined for an antivenin-producing laboratory.

A service of a snake-handling cult in North Carolina, using copperheads and rattlesnakes. The rattles are in sharp focus, showing that the snakes are not rattling and are therefore comparatively calm. (H. F. PICKETT)

Rattlesnake skull with fangs
swung forward as in striking;
the reserve fangs and
solid teeth are also visible.
(COURTESY JOHN TASHJIAN)

The timber rattlesnake, once common over much of the eastern
United States, was probably the first rattlesnake encountered
by the English colonists. (WILLIAM OATES)

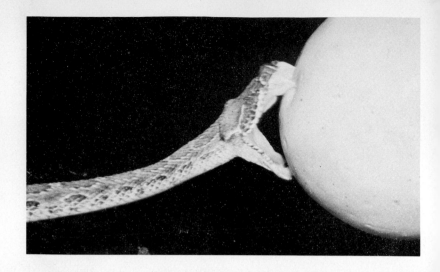

High-speed photographs of a rattlesnake striking a latex bulb:
(above) with a stabbing motion; *(below)* with strike
terminating in a strong bite.

(VAN RIPER; COURTESY UNIVERSITY OF COLORADO MUSEUM)

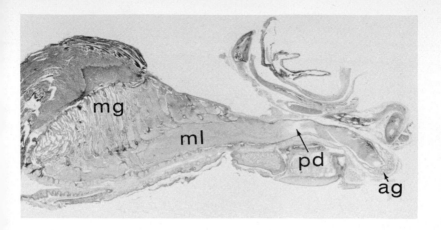

Longitudinal section of a rattlesnake venom gland, magnified
18 times. Tubules of the main venom gland *(mg)* empty into a
reservoir *(ml)* continuous with the duct *(pd)* leading to the fang;
tissue of the accessory gland *(ag)* surrounds the duct just
before it enters the fang. (COURTESY DR. HERBERT ROSENBERG,
FROM A HISTOLOGICAL PREPARATION BY DR. ELAZAR KOCHVA)

Extracting venom from an eyelash viper, a snake of rain-forest
areas from southern Mexico to northern South America. Ordinarily
venom is collected in a small vial; the large receptacle shown
was used for purposes of photography. (ALLAN ROBERTS)

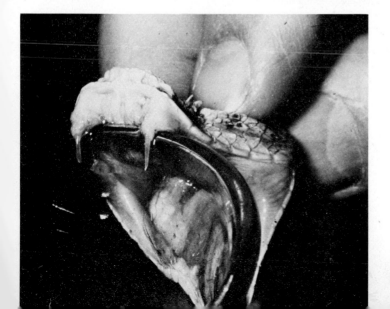

(Above) A young Mexican beaded lizard collected near Manzanillo on the west coast of Mexico. This species and its close relative the gila monster *(below)* are the only venomous lizards known; both are slow and relatively inoffensive. The gila monster is one of the distinctive animals of the southwestern United States; the one shown is feeding on nestling birds. (ALLAN ROBERTS)

The terciopelo, a big pit viper known by a number of different Spanish and Portuguese names and often called "fer-de-lance" in English literature, causes most of the snakebite deaths in Central America and northern South America. The young specimen shown was collected in eastern Mexico.

The secretive copperhead, whose patterns blend with the forest floor, has been able to survive in suburban areas where larger snakes have been killed off; it occurs from southern New England to western Texas. Its bite, though painful, is rarely fatal.

Russell's viper, a common dangerous snake of cultivated land
in much of India and Burma, was named for Dr. Patrick Russell,
whose classic pioneer work on Indian snakes and their venoms
was published around 1800.

Characteristic defensive pose of the saw-scaled viper: the
air-filled loops of the body are rubbed together, and the rough
scales on the sides help to produce a sizzling sound. Seldom more
than 2 feet long, this is one of the world's deadliest snakes;
it is found in dry regions of North Africa and southwestern Asia.

Largest of the Asian vipers, the Okinawa habu
is chiefly responsible for the high incidence of snakebites
in the Ryukyu Islands. (NEW YORK ZOOLOGICAL SOCIETY)

Found from Morocco to the Cape of Good Hope, the puff adder is
the best-known of the heavy-bodied African vipers, the leading
cause of snakebites in Africa, and the subject of many folktales
and myths. (NEW YORK ZOOLOGICAL SOCIETY)

This Asian cobra, collected near Bangkok, shows a monocle mark
on its hood instead of the more common spectacle mark. Abundant
in densely populated regions and with highly toxic venom, this
species, in spite of its rather timid disposition, is credited
with a relatively large number of fatal bites. A traditional
enemy of cobras and other venomous reptiles is the Indian mongoose,
but the pet mongoose shown below proved to be afraid of snakes.

The Indian krait, a vividly marked nocturnal snake of southern Asia, bites infrequently, but its venom is potently neurotoxic and a high percentage of its victims die.

Common in coastal waters from the Persian Gulf to the Sea of Japan, the annulated sea snake reaches a length of about 6 feet and has the flat tail characteristic of its whole family.

Extraordinarily large scales
mark the green mamba *(above)*,
a slim and deadly tree snake of
West Africa. Shown in its
characteristic rearing stance,
the king cobra *(right)* is the
largest of the venomous snakes;
it is found in forests and
grasslands in southern Asia,
Indonesia, and the Philippines.
(NEW YORK ZOOLOGICAL
SOCIETY PHOTOS)

offerings of curds on the grave. Failure to carry out this ritual may bring fever and sour the milk.[4]

Hindu women who want children leave offerings of milk, curds, saffron, and honey near a cobra's hiding place. In Mysore, Bombay, and the Kathiawar Peninsula, all of which lie along the western edge of the Indian peninsula on the Arabian Sea, a childless woman suspends a *nagakal,* a cobra carved in stone, in a well for six months. If she conceives, she arranges a shrine for the sculpture under a pipal tree. Earth from such shrines is considered a specific for leprosy.[5]

Royal houses in India often trace their lineage to one or more serpent ancestors. The rajas of Nagpur claimed to be descendants of a Naga who fell in love with and wed the lovely daughter of a guru, or teacher. Although he turned himself into a handsome prince in order to win his bride, she puzzled about his forked tongue and bitterly complained about his foul breath. She plagued him so unceasingly that he suddenly resumed his cobra form and plunged into the palace pool, a display of male temper that brought on premature labor for his bride. She died in childbirth and the royal infant was found on the grass beside the pool guarded by a huge cobra. The dynasty so founded adopted a crest showing a cobra with a human face, and Nagpur noblemen wore their turbans coiled like a snake with the head poised over the brow.[6] The seal of the maharajas of Orissa, a province southwest of Calcutta on the Bay of Bengal, also shows a cobra with a human face and ruling houses of Manipur and Kashmir claimed cobra antecedents.

According to legend, Kashmir was once covered by a lake. Vishnu pierced the mountain wall to allow the waters to drain away and appointed the Naga Karakota to guard the beautiful fertile valley. Karakota fathered the first royal prince of Kashmir, after which he retired to a sacred spring. He continued over the centuries to benefit the people with his benign wisdom, making Kashmir the most desirable spot on earth. In about 1592, when a Naga chieftain from Kashmir appeared in Delhi to pay his respects to the Emperor Akbar, a five-headed cobra suddenly sprang from the visitor's turban. Akbar was sufficiently impressed to give him a set of royal drums for his tribal shrine. Later the Mogul Emperor Jahangir erected a splendid pavilion over Karakota's sacred spring.[7]

The Chinese pilgrim Hiuen Tsiang, who visited the Swat River valley in the western Himalayas in 649 A.D., first recorded an ancient legend antedating the Aryan invasion. A Naga maiden, daughter of the great cobra who guarded the Swat River, fell in love with a prince who was afraid of snakes. To overcome his prejudices she turned herself into a superbly beautiful woman and they were wed. The marriage began auspiciously, but each night, as the princess drifted off to sleep, nine cobras emerged from the top of her head and waved about. This apparition made her husband nervous, and he feared for his manhood. One night, driven to desperation, he seized his sword and sliced off the offending heads. This solved his immediate problem; but his sons and all their offspring from that time on suffered from severe migraine.[8] Much later, the princess's Naga father, Apala, was converted by the Buddha. Before Apala's conversion he had habitually oppressed the people with floods and landslides, but after harkening to the teaching of the Holy One he agreed to seek tranquility and to confine such disasters to once every twelve years; a minimal outlet for his aggressions. The royal family founded by Apala's daughter collected relics of Buddha and housed them in a huge stupa, a sacred edifice built to house a holy relic, near Udigram. In 1962 we visited this shrine. It was being used to store hay.

Nagas played an important role in the life drama of Gautama Siddhartha (563–483 B.C.), the Indian prince who later became the Buddha. They convened in the garden of his mother, Queen Maya, and assisted her in his birth. When no hot water was available to bathe the prince, they handily caused a hot spring to gush forth.

Possibly the gentlest story ever told about a snake concerns the cobra, Muchilinda, who spread his hood to protect Buddha from the sun while he meditated in the desert. Grateful to the animal whose kindly concern had saved him from heat stroke, Buddha laid his hand on the serpent's still-spread hood and blessed him, leaving behind the familiar spectacle mark.[9]

When Buddha first arrived on the west bank of the Ganges, a welcoming committee of Nagas formed a bridge of their hoods to provide a dry crossing for him. There were, however, too many Nagas for just one bridge, so they formed four bridges. Buddha courteously became four Buddhas who crossed the river simultaneously so that none might feel slighted. After resting in the deer park in Benares, Buddha won his most spectacular convert. He expounded the Law to the great Naga Elapattra, whose five monstrous heads and hoods hovered over the park, while his tail terminated in Taxila, some 700 miles to the northwest.[10]

In spite of the Nagas' readiness to see the light, Buddhists generally considered them inferior beings who were reincarnated as cobras in the wheel of life because of an evil karma, or action. Even the mighty Elapattra was believed to be an unfortunate soul doomed to Nagahood for uprooting a cardamum tree.[11]

According to Plutarch, Alexander the Great was fathered
by Ammon (an Egyptian version of Zeus) in the form of a great
serpent.[12] Alexander may have found his reptile paternity an
advantage when he invaded India in 326 B.C. At Taxila in the
Punjab, the legendary home of the Naga Elapattra, he found the
maharaja keeping two great cobras as family totems. The
maharaja promptly became Alexander's ally. The priests of Taxila
had been expecting a miraculous return of Buddha and were
quick to recognize in the person of the Macedonian prince their
reincarnated lord. We were told by a Pakistani archaeologist that
in those areas occupied by Greek troops, notably the Malakand
Agency and Swat, sculptors of the Greco-Indian school regularly
gave their Buddha figures the face of Alexander.

According to Hindu legend, in the beginning, Brahma appointed the world serpent Shesha lord over all poisonous and
fanged creatures. But Shesha longed to abnegate evil and to em-
brace wisdom, and he begged the god for some enduring task
to amend his life. Brahma gave Shesha the world to guard, and
the great snake coiled around the earth to protect it from malignant influences. While fulfilling this task, Shesha won enlighten-
ment through meditation.[13] In the fourth century A.D., he appeared in Benares in the person of the famous grammarian,
Patanjali. During the bright half of the month of Sravana, a Naga
festival, Patanjali and his fellow grammarians assembled to
discuss virtue near an ancient well sacred to Shesha. *The Yoga
Aphorisms of Patanjali,* a classic guide for students of yoga, were
expounded and compiled at these meetings. Shesha's well may be
seen in Benares today. It has forty steps leading down into a circular depression to a stone door covered with carved cobras. This
is said to lead to Patala, the reptile netherworld.[14]

Hindus accord Shesha a primary role in their creation story. Once while Vishnu slept on Shesha's coils, the universe dissolved into a nebulous cosmic sea. Gods and demons importuned Shesha to lend them his avatar, or other manifestation, Vasuki, so that they might create the world. Shesha complied and also furnished them Mount Mandara for a churning stock. They looped Vasuki around the mountain and began to pull him back and forth so as to bring about the world as butter is churned. Eighty-eight gods hauled at his head and ninety-two demons pulled on his tail. After a thousand years of uncomfortable friction, Vasuki lost his patience and bit wildly at the rocks, releasing floods of venom that threatened to engulf the nascent world. The churners cried for help, and Siva appeared and drank off the poison before it could do any harm.[15] A beautiful rendition of this story is carved on the colonnades of the great temple at Angkor Wat, which was built in the twelfth century by Surya-varman II, one of the last Hindu kings to rule Cambodia.

In the Cambodian version of this story, a second churning brought about ambrosia to insure immortality to the gods and demons. Vishnu's sacred bird, the eagle Garuda, raided Indra's house and stole the precious liquor. He let a few drops fall on some sharp grass. Cobras found the drops and greedily licked them up, gaining for themselves eternal life but cutting their tongues so that they were ever afterward forked.[16]

Khmer monarchs of Cambodia, who ruled from the ninth to the twelfth century, A.D., claimed descent from a Naga princess who wedded an exiled Indian prince. Her cobra father swallowed the waters that covered Cambodia and gave her the country for her dowry. According to a thirteenth-century Chinese writer, Jayavarman VII, the king of Cambodia, was obliged to spend part of every night in a golden tower in Angkor Thom where he copulated with a nine-headed cobra. After this, he was free to visit his wives and concubines. Should the cobra not appear, the king would die; if the king failed in his obligation for a single night, the country was doomed.[17]

In parts of Malaya and Indonesia, the sluggish and phlegmatic Wagler's pit viper is believed to be a reincarnation of a former raja. As befits its station, it is considered too indolent to hunt for its meals, and a small bird comes periodically to feed it. It is encouraged to live near houses, for its presence is said to bring good luck. Many of these vipers are kept in a temple on Penang Island. They are fed on eggs and handled freely. Despite the snakes' generally good disposition, visitors to the temple are occasionally bitten but no fatalities have been reported.[18]

As in ancient India, volcanoes in old Japan were said to be guarded by supernatural venomous snakes. These serpents sometimes took advantage of warriors who were away from their village by assuming a man's form and sleeping with his wife. From such liaisons whole villages claimed descent. In each generation a few children were born with dry, scaly skin (probably congenital ichthyosis), considered evidence of their reptile antecedents. The Ainu, Japan's aboriginal people, believed that the first snake was a god who became enamored of the fire goddess. When she descended to the earth, the god followed as a flash of lightning that became a serpent.[19]

The mythic proclivity of snakes to assume human form in order to do harm is widespread in Asian folklore. The Ifuyao head hunters of the Philippines say that the cobra is a kind of were-snake. It transforms itself into a tempting female in order to enslave the souls of men and hasten their death. Such possession can be recognized by the onset of a heavy, damp, depressed feeling.[20] Bedouins of the Arabian peninsula believe that the *haia soda,* or desert blacksnake, can call with the voice of a young woman and lure men to their death. This same reptile can also appear as a she camel full with milk, and when a thirsty wanderer approaches, the snake returns to its true form and bites him.[21]

The Snake Charmers of Sind

It is uncertain whether the snake-charming performance so well known in southern Asia and northern Africa originated in Egypt or in India, or whether it borrowed something from both regions. Snakes clearly were important in the religion of ancient Egypt, and India's serpent worship goes far back in time and deep into the culture of the land. The snake charmer has been part of the Western world's image of India since the days of the first European trading companies, and today this stereotype is inclined to make the Western-educated native of the subcontinent a bit testy when questioned about snakes and snake charming.

While the details and perhaps the basic philosophy of snake charming vary from Morocco across the breadth of southern Asia, display of the cobra is common to all. It is hard to imagine a type of snake better suited for this sort of exploitation. Cobras are large enough to be impressive, unquestionably dangerous, and unmistakable because of their spectacular rearing stance with spread hood. Cobras respond to visual cues to a greater degree than do most venomous snakes, and they sway their entire elevated forebody in response to movement. Although probably no more intelligent than other snakes, they give an impression of alertness that is lacking in many. Finally, their defensive strike is a comparatively slow, sweeping movement easily evaded by an alert individual. Snake charmers of India and surrounding regions usually use one of the varieties of the Asian cobra, and North African snake charmers usually employ the Egyptian cobra.

One of the most spectacular demonstrations of Oriental snake charming is seen in parts of Burma. The snakes used are freshly captured king cobras, sometimes 10 feet long. These snakes are sacred to two powerful mountain spirit gods and guard their shrines. The snake charmers are frequently, but not invariably, young women. The ceremony is held in a public place in the village and is a mixture of entertainment and religious ritual. After preliminary prayers and music, the snake baskets are opened and the snakes are teased until they rear and strike repeatedly at the performers who deftly elude them. At the climax of the display, the leading performer kisses one of the snakes on the top of its head as it rears poised to strike. After this, the snakes are returned to their baskets and eventually released in accordance with the snake charmers' promise to the gods.[22] I have seen color slides of what appears to be a similar ceremony held near Chittagong in East Pakistan close to the Burmese border.

Most of what we know of snake charmers in Asia was learned from the Jogi tribe living near Tatta in Sind, West Pakistan. Tatta lies near the western edge of the Indus delta. During its days of greatness in the fourteenth and fifteenth centuries, it stood on the banks of the river, and the first Europeans to visit it described it as a city larger than London. In those times, according to Sindhi legend, a huge snake lay with its head beneath the wall of Tatta and its tail beneath the wall of Delhi. The Jogis predicted that as long as the snake lay in this position Sind had nothing to fear. They recommended that an iron stake be driven through its head to fix it in place. This was done, but the ruler, Jam Tamachi, was skeptical. He pulled up the stake, which was found covered with blood. At this moment the snake turned, leaving its tail where its head had been, and the power of Sind was forever lost.[23] The Indus shifted its course, and Tatta today is a crumbling shell of a town with only the great mosque of Shah Jahan and the thousands of stone tombs on Makli Ridge testifying to its vanished glory.

But Tatta and the nearby river town of Pir Patho are still the hub of the Jogi world. The Jogis move their encampment about within a 20-mile circle, shifting in response to floods, fluctuations in the snake population, and the whims of unfriendly police magistrates. The life of the tribe revolves about the capture and display of snakes. They also collect animals of other sorts for teaching laboratories, scientists, and animal dealers. Jogis do not farm or fish, nor do they keep domestic animals other than a few chickens and dogs. Most marriages are evidently within the tribe, and strong family resemblances are apparent. Young women of the village are sequestered from the eyes of strange males, but they do not observe strict purdah and are not veiled. Old women may be sent into the towns and cities to beg and may carry snakes with them to attract attention. Jogis show a great deal of affection for their younger children, and the youngsters themselves are generally plump and healthy-looking. Since Pakistan is a Moslem nation, the tribe finds it discreet to profess nominal allegiance to the creed of Muhammad, but they are not overly conscientious in observing its rituals and taboos.

Jogi men customarily wear turbans, long shirts reaching to the knees, and saronglike lower garments under their shirts.

Traditionally, the shirt is red with yellow stripes and the turban orange or ocher, but today a number of variations are seen. Formerly the men wore necklaces of amber and agate beads and pierced their ears for great hoops of amber; these ornaments are now likely to be made of plastic. Jogi women wear voluminous trousers of brilliantly striped fabric under bright red shirts ornamented with mirrors and embroidery. They cover their heads with wide cotton scarfs, hand-blocked in blue and red designs. Their jewelry, which reflects the family status and prosperity, includes massive silver anklets, bangles, necklaces, gold nose rings, and as many silver earrings as can be piled on.

Equipment for the snake show includes a *bheen,* reed baskets and clay pots to hold the snakes, and elaborately embroidered bags for carrying these articles. The *bheen* consists of two wooden flutes fitted with bamboo reeds and cemented with beeswax into the bottle section of a gourd. It may be decorated with bits of silver and glass and hung with a swag of netted colored beads. A chip of mirror is often set in the end to catch and hold the snakes' attention. The player uses his cheeks as bellows and blows into the neck of the gourd. Basic tones are sustained on the two stops of the left flute, while the melody is played on the eight stops of the right. Melodies are in minor keys, and the tone is resonant and piercing with the strong beat common to most Indian *ragas.* To Western ears, Jogi renditions of British marches sound eerily like the pipers of a Scottish regiment. The snake baskets are constructed of reeds snugly bound with goatskin thongs and reinforced with split withes, twigs or branches. Geometric designs in ocher and black may be painted on the sides. The bags for carrying the equipment are decorated with small mirrors held in place with bright-colored floss. The designs on the bag are characteristic for each tribe.

While some Jogis live more or less permanently in cities such as Karachi and Hyderabad, most of them prefer to commute from their villages. In the cities they post themselves near hotels and railroad stations where they can readily draw a crowd, or they wander through the better-class residential areas, playing their flutes as they go.

The performance may be simple or elaborate and is usually held in the open air. When two Jogis work together, one usually plays the flute while his partner handles the snakes. As the show begins, the performer blows into the snake basket, then raps it smartly against the ground. He lifts the lid, and the cobra, thoroughly aroused, rises to perhaps a third of its length with its hood widely spread. The snake man now begins to play his flute, swaying his body from side to side as he plays. The snake also sways, following the man's movements rather than the music. It is easy to distract the reptile by waving a hand near its head. A cooperative snake may rear up half its length and continue its weaving movements as long as the performer wishes. Sometimes the snake will strike, hissing loudly as it does so; often the Jogi lifts it from the basket and drapes it around his neck and shoulders. Sometimes he may exhibit a second or third cobra or may show other kinds of snakes with the cobra or alone. The saw-scaled viper is often used; its peculiar crablike movement and vicious striking make it an interesting attraction. Pythons are used, although they are not particularly common in Sind. They contribute little to the action, but their size makes them fine attention getters. Such large harmless snakes as the dhaman and royal snake are frequently found in snake charmers' baskets. They put up an impressive fight, and few of the audience know that they are not dangerous. The Indian sand boa with its plump, stubby tail is often billed as a two-headed snake. The tail may be mutilated to simulate eyes and a mouth.

Cobras used in shows are almost always rendered harmless by breaking off their fangs and cauterizing the sockets or by sewing the mouth shut. This severely limits the life of a cobra but is doubtless a wise precaution. We recall watching one sidewalk snake show where a monkey-wallah and his simian companion were waiting in the wings hoping to profit from an audience already on the spot. Suddenly the monkey darted into the circle of spectators, seized the cobra by the tail, and neatly flipped it into the crowd. There was instant pandemonium, but the defanged snake could hurt no one. Curiously enough, the vipers, in many respects more dangerous than the cobras, are often left in possession of their fangs and so are very young cobras.

A cobra-mongoose combat may be part of the snake charmer's performance. Rarely does either principal have any heart for this affair, and it usually develops into a real farce with the cobra doing its best to escape and the mongoose either sulking or going into an hysterical screaming fit. Eventually the animals may be goaded into a fight of sorts, but the promoter seldom allows them to do real damage to each other. Sometimes, if the crowd is sufficiently bloodthirsty and prosperous-looking, the mongoose may be allowed to kill the cobra, or a harmless snake which has been substituted for it. The audience is expected to repay the snake man handsomely for the loss of his snake.

Jogis have a reputation for knowing magic, both black and white, and augment their income by selling various charms. Most potent is the small gold crown of a Vasing Nag, a hundred-year-old white cobra. Another is best described by quoting from a letter we received from a magistrate in a Sindhi town: "Some cobras . . . are supposed to possess a 'mun,' a dark brown substance that shines on a dark night and instantly heals snakebite, provides an antidote for all poisons, and attracts wealth and good luck. Some Jogees used to offer such 'muns' for sale in old days when we had not yet absorbed much of Lord Macauley's English." We would only add that they still do. Magic healing stones to be applied to snakebites are a standard item in a Jogi's pack. Most of those we examined were rough cabochons of heat-treated agate; some were enteroliths, or bezoar stones. Some Jogi charms and nostrums insure sexual potency or fertility and can have unexpected results. One woman came to a Karachi hospital with the story that a Jogi had given her snake eggs to be swallowed to cure her barrenness. She now complained that the eggs had hatched and filled her stomach with snakes.

A snake charmer expects to pick up occasional fees for ridding a house or compound of snakes. If there are no resident reptiles, he is not above planting a snake or two on the premises and catching it before the amazed eyes of the householder; however, the snake does not always feel obligated to cooperate in this deception and often hides itself well enough to avoid capture. Also, as every herpetologist knows, no container in which snakes can be easily carried is really escape-proof, and the Jogi's reed baskets and little clay pots are no exception. It will never be known how many small, disjunct populations of Indian snakes and how many records of species far from their expected range have originated from such escapes. Some herpetologists believe that the difficulty in constructing any satisfactory classification scheme for the cobras of Asia may be due in part to generations of snake charmers who have carried the snakes from one region to another.

We spent enough time in the field with Jogis to learn something of their methods. They use no technique unknown to Western collectors, nor do they rely to any extent upon charms and magic. They are particularly skillful at tracking reptiles to burrows and other hiding places and digging them out. The better collectors can pick up an incredibly faint trail. Much of the time, however, they wander about, investigating likely habitats and watching for reptiles moving or resting in the open. We introduced the tribe to night collecting, a technique they had previously used very little. We supplied them with a Petromax lantern, and the investment paid off in a markedly increased catch of rare nocturnal lizards and small desert snakes. The Jogis' real secret weapons in collecting are time and endurance. Investment of enough man-hours will eventually produce specimens, and a hunting party may spend days in the field living under conditions the average Westerner would find unbearable.

The Jogi collector usually carries his flute on field trips. It is his badge of office and may insure him safety in regions where strangers are not particularly welcome; also, he enjoys music when the day's work is done. Once when a big snake escaped under a rock ledge, we asked our Jogi companion if he would play on his flute and lure it out; we got a very disdainful look as our answer.

Jogis handle poisonous snakes in a casual and insouciant manner but have considerable ability to judge the snakes' temperament and probable reactions. Nevertheless, they are bitten occasionally. They claim no immunity to snake venom, and the concept of immunization with repeated small doses of venom seemed to be completely strange to them; yet they do rely heavily on various secret remedies that they would not share with us. Although they frequently sought our help in cases of dysentery, chills, sore eyes, or other illnesses, when Laung, the chief of the tribe, was bitten by a cobra and lay almost completely paralyzed, they were not at all interested in our offer to treat him with anti-venin. During the fourteen months that we were closely associated with them, the tribe lost one man from a cobra bite and two others were seriously bitten. On the other hand, several bites that were trivial occurred.

To a Jogi, death from the bite of a cobra means that the bitten man has violated his oath to Gogol Vir, patron of all snakes. However this is not necessarily true of death following the bite of a *khupper* (a large saw-scaled viper), for this snake is an outlaw and not subject to Gogol Vir. According to legend, the khupper lay hidden above the door in Gogol Vir's house near Tatta and bit him on the head. Before the saint died he instructed his son to cook and eat his flesh so that his magic powers might be passed on, but no sooner had the son prepared this dish than seven hungry thieves stole it. Feasting on it, they became masters of magic and gained ascendance over snakes.[24]

We often felt that this account of the occupation and charac-ter of the tribe's founders was absolutely correct. The Jogis were such flamboyant charlatans and such mendacious rogues that it was impossible to deal with them any length of time without be-coming unspeakably annoyed. Yet the very outrageousness of their chicanery helped anger to evaporate quickly. As we de-

veloped more mutual respect, flagrant attempts to cheat us became fewer. The hospitality they showed us seemed free and
spontaneous, although they spoke not a word of our language, and
we very little of theirs. They had no difficulty in accepting us as
fellow snake hunters, and eventually most of them seemed to feel
we were friends as well.

13. Myths from Africa and the Middle East

In Egyptian mythology, the first snakebite predated creation. As Ra, the sun god, busied himself with making the earth, he stepped on a snake that had been sent at the order of the goddess Isis. His "case history" appears in the Ebers' Papyrus, compiled about 1550 B.C., as follows:

"Ra wailed, 'I have been stung by a serpent which I could not see. This is not the same as fire; it is not the same as water. But still I am as cold as water and then again as hot as fire. All my body sweats, and I tremble. My eyesight is not steady, and I cannot see, for the sweat pours over my face in spite of the summer's pleasant air.' " [1]

A modern physician would say that the visual disturbance, sweating and trembling, along with the failure to mention swelling or abnormal bleeding, point to poisoning by a snake with neurotoxic venom, probably the Egyptian cobra. Ra's suffering was so intense that he determined to protect gods and men in the future by drawing up a treaty with the serpent tribe. As this soon proved not to be respected by the snakes, he gave earthdwellers a magic word, *hekau*, to ward off snakes.[2]

The first to get this word became the earliest-known snake shamans, the Psylli of North Africa, whose history goes back to at least 1500 B.C. Pliny the Elder described them as people who smelled bad, an observation we have occasionally made about snake charmers. He said, "These men had naturally in their bodies that which like a deadly bane and poison would kill all serpents, for the very air and scent that breathed from them was able to stupefy and strike them stark dead." [3] Psylli men checked the legitimacy of their children by exposing newborn babies to "the most fell and cruel serpents," trusting the tribal effluvium to protect its own. Psylli monopolized the international trade in poisons and antidotes. Augustus Caesar is said to have summoned them to treat Cleopatra, where they scored a resounding therapeutic failure.

During the great Islamic conversions in North Africa in the twelfth century A.D. many Psylli became dervishes or Moslem mendicants. When enthusiastic pilgrims readied themselves for the journey to Mecca, the Psylli danced among the camels of the departing caravans, "with live snakes around their arms and necks, having their faces in contortions like the insane. They sometimes tear at the snakes with their teeth. People press forward to touch them, especially the women want to touch their foaming mouths with their hands." [4] As late as 1900, Saadeyeh dervishes commemorated the birth of the Prophet Abraham by partially swallowing live snakes in order to absorb the reptilian magic. The snakes' mouths were secured with silver rings or sewed with silk cord to prevent them from biting. [5] After their conversion to Islam, Psylli substituted chants from the Koran for the old incantations to Ra. Each tribe and family passes the efficacious phrases on to the next generation as a closely guarded secret.

Psylli have long earned their living by ridding houses of snakes. Napoleon is reported to have summoned one of them to evict a cobra from his headquarters during his campaign in Egypt. While undertaking such a mission, the dervish assumes an air of great mystery and chants: "I adjure you, by God, if ye be above or if ye be below, that ye come forth! If ye be obedient, come forth; if ye be not obedient, die! die! die!" [6] With proper timing and an apprehensive audience, this can be a dramatic performance. If a snake appears, the dervish obviously has beckoned it; if not, the recalcitrant reptile has doubtless been slain by the magic incantation. Either way, the snake man wins.

When handling cobras, North African snake charmers some-times stretch the reptile out on the ground and press or rap it sharply on the head. This seems to immobilize the snake, and it remains inert and stiff for several minutes. This may be the "secret art" known to Aaron and the magicians of Egypt whereby rods became serpents.

The French naturalist André Villiers reports that the snake charmers of West Africa use highly effective herbal preparations to discourage snakes from biting them. They prepare a pulp of such plants as *Euphorbia hirta* and *Ageratum conizoides* and rub this over their bodies. They then stroke the snakes and put a little of the pulp in their mouths. This seems to induce tetany of the jaw muscles and inflammation of the venom glands. After such treatment, cobras, mambas, and puff adders can evidently be handled with impunity. [7]

These snake charmers also do a thriving business in amulets, or *gris-gris,* to prevent snakebites. A popular one in Senegal is the *lar,* a sausage-shaped bit of wood bound with colored cloth, with tufts of horsehair protruding from the wrappings. One or more of these are strapped to the calf of the leg. [8]

Snakes were all-important in the theology of ancient Egypt,

possibly because the Nile's yearly flood flushed them out in great
numbers and suggested a direct connection between the reptiles
and the fertility bestowed by the inundation. The Nile itself was
pictured as originating in a great cave where its guardian spirit,
a serpent, controlled the level of its waters.

Both the cobra and the cerastes were venerated, and both appear in the architecture, painted friezes, and papyri of nearly
every district and dynasty. The cobra as a symbol of vitality and
benevolence was incorporated into Egypt's royal crown, and a
hieroglyph of two spitting cobras signified Upper and Lower
Egypt. The widely prevalent but wholly erroneous belief that
snakes milk cows may have originated in Egypt, where the cobra,
as a symbol of life, was nourished by the cow goddess, Hathor.[9]

Other gods in the Egyptian pantheon had serpent counter-
parts or familiars. Ra wore a cobra on his crown. The hawk-
headed god Horus was sometimes shown holding cobras in his
hands. He was called "stopper of snakes," and his image was commonly carried as a charm against snakebite. Thoth, god of speech
and letters and judge of men's souls for their journey into the
hereafter, was sometimes shown as a snake. The Egyptian concept
of the universe included a cosmic serpent, Sati, who cradled the
earth in his coils to protect it from malignant forces. The four
corners of Egypt's paradise were guarded by fire-breathing
cobras that are possibly prototypes of the cherubim in Genesis.
The Underworld was ruled by Apop, a huge snake who embodied
darkness and evil. Nightly he battled with Ra as the sun god's
chariot passed through his domain, and each dawn signified that
Ra had once again triumphed.

Egyptians saw an eclipse as a battle between Apop and Ra
in which the dark serpent temporarily succeeded in engulfing the

sun god. Priests in Ra's temples at Thebes and Heliopolis assisted their deity in this emergency by burning drawings of Apop
and dismembering wax images of the serpent with flint knives
and melting them in the sacred fire.[10] Their incantations seem to
echo in the first two verses of the sixty-eighth Psalm:

> Let God arise, let his enemies be scattered: let them also
> that hate him flee before him.
> As smoke is driven away, so drive them away: as wax
> melteth before the fire, so let the wicked perish in the
> presence of god!

It is difficult to accept as merely coincidental the fact that a
popular charm against vipers in England and northern Europe
is to draw a circle on the ground around the snake, make a cross
inside, and recite these two verses.[11]

Before going to bed, Egyptians often made a circle around
their cots with a stick or an engraved ivory wand to ward off
snakes and scorpions. This custom has its counterpart in the
American West where the cowboy keeps rattlesnakes away by
coiling his horsehair lariat around his sleeping bag.

Perhaps because the snakes defaulted on their agreement
with Ra, ancient Egyptians attached a singularly terrible significance to death from snakebite. The body of the victim was
considered virulently profaned, and the "pure spirit of the eternal"
would not inhabit it. Even mummies were provided with amulets
against post-mortem bites. The guilty snake also suffered, for
the earth refused it sanctuary, and it could not return to its hole.[12]

Throughout the Middle East, Semitic peoples worshiped
snakes, although the relation of ophiolatry in Chaldea and surrounding regions to that of Egypt is not well understood. Among

the Israelites, Moses and Aaron were snake shamans who com-
peted successfully with Pharaoh's priests. Moses led his people
from Egypt under the aegis of Nehushtan, a brazen serpent set
on a pole. Subsequently, over a span of 500 years, the Hebrews
transmogrified their ancient snake gods into devils. In 701 B.C.
the religious reformer Hezekiah "broke into pieces the bronze
serpent that Moses had made" (II Kings, 18:4).

A legend as to why snakes are venomous comes from
Palestine. In the days when Adam dwelt happily in Paradise, the
Devil scratched about the hedgerows of Eden's perimeter trying
to break in, while the vigilant cherubim repeatedly drove him
away. He called to the animals inside for help, but none would
heed him. At last the snake, tempted by a promise of the sweetest
food in the world, agreed to smuggle him in. The Devil concealed
himself in the snake's hollow tooth and invaded Paradise. Immediately the snake demanded his reward and asked what the
sweetest food might be. The Devil replied that it was human
blood. Adam objected on the grounds that no one had ever
tasted human blood and challenged the Devil to prove his state-
ment. So he dispatched the mosquito to collect blood samples
from all creatures. When her mission was accomplished, the
mosquito flew back and met Adam's friend the swallow. The
swallow asked, "Which was the sweetest?" The mosquito opened
her mouth to say, "Human blood," but the swallow seized her
tongue and bit it off so that the sound was perverted to "Frog."
The snake who had seen and heard all this struck at the swallow
and pulled some of the feathers from her tail, leaving it forked
like his tongue. The Archangel Michael intervened and drove
the snake from Eden, carrying forever in his teeth the Devil's

evil sweat. But thanks to the swallow, snakes to this day prefer frogs to all other food.[13]

Black Africa has been the home of many snake cults, but they are rarely based on the worship or manipulation of venomous reptiles. Most cults center about the python, whose impressive size and relatively docile temperament make it an appropriate deity. Eighteenth-century accounts from slave traders and early missionaries describe python worship in Dahomey, where each village housed its living god in a circular clay temple. The snakes were credited with control of the water supply, the earth's productivity, and man's fertility. Priests fed them with small game and mediated communication between the people and their god, and priestesses entertained them with songs and dancing. In orgiastic rituals, the priests often worked themselves into frenzies, falling into trances and speaking in unknown tongues.[14]

Dahomey and Uganda python cults, unwittingly transplanted to Haiti by French slavers, formed the nucleus of the voodoo religion once widely prevalent among West Indian Negroes and occasionally seen in other slave-holding sections of the Americas. Snake handling and the use of snakes as surrogate phalli by female votaries were a part of voodoo ritual. The snakes used were always of nonpoisonous species.[15]

In many parts of tribal Africa, the natives believe that their ancestors haunt old hunting grounds in the form of snakes. Nigerian hunters importune their help by putting eggs and milk on an anthill. If a snake emerges, the hunt will be successful.[16]

On the island of Fernando Po, West Africa, the people consider the cobra their guardian deity, with the power to confer blessings, grant requests and, if angered, to inflict illness, curses, and death. In an annual ceremony, a cobra skin is hung in the public square of each village to invoke the god's protection, and the children born that year are brought to touch its tail.[17]

In Kiziba, west of Lake Victoria, if a woman accidentally kills a snake with her mattock, she hurries to the snake priest with the offending tool and a propitiatory offering of two strings of cowries and an ox hide. The priest ceremoniously wraps the snake in the hide and buries it. The next day he purifies the village with a compound of earth, water, and leopard guts. Each woman dips her hoe into this mixture and spins it so that the liquid flies off. This appeases the spirit of the slain serpent, everyone breathes easier, and the women may return to their fields.[18] If hunters among the Efik of Nigeria accidentally kill a poisonous snake, they put its body across a path until the new moon shines. If this is not done, the hunters themselves may be bitten.[19]

A ritual for gaining control over snakes comes from the Hausa people living along the northern border of Nigeria. It requires that a man cut off the head of a black snake and in the head put the seed of a ramma plant. He then buries the head in a grave exactly seven days old. For three consecutive nights he must water the grave; then the ramma seedling will appear. After seven more days he takes fat saved from the body of the snake and goes to the grave at midnight. There he strips naked, lies down, and rubs the snake fat on the plant. A djin in the form of a man with a big head will appear and with him another djin in the form of a big snake. These will try to frighten the suppliant, but he must not be dissuaded by them. When the ramma plant has grown to a length of about 4 feet, the man again goes to the grave at midnight. He strips, pulls up the plant, and winds it around his waist as a girdle. Thereafter the girdle will turn into a snake when the owner wishes.[20]

In Senegal it is believed that the puff adder has, at the base of its tail, a ball of grease with magic properties. This gives the snake a particular aversion to human excrement, and it will leap over ten houses to avoid contact with this substance. If a man touches a puff adder with a stick that has been smeared with human excrement, the snake becomes enraged and will pursue its tormentor for hours, even though he flees on horseback. As the story is told today, if a man tries to escape in an automobile, the snake will still catch him and deal him a mortal blow.[21]

14. European Snake Worship and Myths

The Snake-Haired Mother of the Winged Horse

In pre-classical Greece (certainly as early as 3000 B.C.), before the gods achieved Olympus, many of them were snake deities. Zeus himself was an old chthonic serpent god, a fertility daimon, or spirit, known as Zeus Meilichios.[1] In this guise he cohabited with Semele, daughter of the earth mother, Demeter. Semele bore Dionysus who became the divine patron of crops and vines. Women of his cults plaited snakes into their hair, wound them around their bodies, and sometimes, in orgiastic frenzy, tore them to pieces with their teeth. In an initiation to the Dionysian mysteries, a snake was let down between the candidate's breasts and taken away below from between her thighs to express sexual and mystic union with the god.[2]

According to Greek legend, Cecrops, an Egyptian, founded the city of Athens about 1556 B.C. He was a wise, tolerant leader who gave his people laws and taught them to cultivate the olive. When dissension broke out over whether the city's patron deity should be Athene or the sea god, Poseidon, Cecrops democratically put the matter to popular vote. Women outnumbered the men by one, and they chose Athene, goddess of wisdom. A statue of the goddess with her serpent familiar was erected on the

Acropolis, and a living snake was kept near her shrine as the guardian spirit of the city. After fifty years of peaceful reign, Cecrops died. He had been a model ruler in all respects except for one disturbing feature. From the waist down, he had the form of a serpent.[3]

Poseidon did not forget that the virgin goddess had bested him. One day he surprised Medusa, then a lovely girl, praying at Athene's shrine. He raped her and ran away. Athene was furious at this desecration of her temple, and, since the real culprit had escaped, she turned her hapless votary into a monster. Medusa's hair became a cluster of vipers, her hands turned to brass, her body became sheathed in scales, and her teeth were like the tusks of a wild boar. To look upon her meant instant death.

Not content with what she had done, Athene incited the hero Perseus to kill Medusa. She gave him her sacred shield so that he could safely look at Medusa's reflection in it and decapitate her as she slept. As Athene watched, Perseus cut off the monster's head. Medusa's dying shrieks so delighted the goddess that she invented the flute on the spot so that their shrill tones might not be lost.[4]

As Perseus tucked the head into his pouch, a marvelous winged horse rose from Medusa's body. The hero mounted the horse and flew off toward Africa, while drops of blood seeping through the pouch fell to earth and bred a race of especially virulent vipers. Meanwhile, Athene collected the rest of Medusa's blood from the headless corpse. Later, when Apollo brought his son Asklepios to Athens to receive her blessing, the goddess gave the boy Medusa's blood. When he became the divine practitioner of the medical arts, he healed the sick with blood from Medusa's left side and induced euthanasia with blood from her right side.[5] His special province was human reproduction, and women who wanted children left offerings at his shrines. Other women importuned him to arrange trysts for them with dead heroes who were thought to visit sleeping women in the form of snakes and occasionally father their children.[6]

Temples to Asklepios were built throughout all of Europe that was under Greek influence. They served as both sanatoriums and hospitals. Sleep was the keystone of Asklepian therapy and was induced by warm baths, massage, hypnosis, and soothing drugs. Snakes were kept in the temples and fed milk by Hygieia, daughter of Asklepios. They restored sight by touching the eyes of the blind with their tongues.[7]

In his human form, Asklepios carried as his emblem the caduceus, a staff entwined with a single snake. Modern herpetologists have identified the snake of Asklepios with a nonpoisonous constricting snake similar to the rat snakes of the United States. Widely distributed in southern Europe, it is found in small, separated colonies in the northern part of the continent. These colonies may have descended from snakes kept in Asklepian temples.

Hermes, messenger of the gods and protector of travelers, also was originally a fertility spirit in the form of a snake. His emblem was the kerykeion, a staff tipped with bowed snakes and often confused today with the caduceus. With this he summoned forth souls to renewed life, caused trees to blossom, plants to bear fruit, and animals to produce young.[8]

Milk Mothers and the Golden Viper

The custom of keeping house snakes to guard the family's fortunes was surprisingly widespread in Europe and may have been based on snakes' real utility as predators on mice. In 1435, Jerome of Prague, reporting on his missionary work in Lithuania, said every householder in that country had his own serpent, "to which he gave food and did sacrifice." [9] The nearby Letts reared and worshiped house snakes that were embodiments of their ancestors and also fertility symbols. The snakes were protected by the goddess Brehkina and were known as *peena maates,* or milk mothers. They were fed milk and sprinkled with beer on special occasions.[10] Even today, peasants in parts of Greece pour milk through a hole in the floor called the "snake's door." [11]

Milk is almost universally considered a favorite food of snakes, and beliefs that the reptiles steal it from cows or nursing mothers are found in folklore of southern Europe, India, the United States, and Latin America. The custom of offering milk to snakes is equally widespread. Snakes have no way to obtain milk from natural sources, and herpetologists have repeatedly observed that snakes have no interest in fresh milk unless they are extremely thirsty. There is, however, an intriguing observation that the odor of milk in an early stage of spoilage attracts rattlesnakes, and they may even drink it in small amounts.[12] Since raw milk spoils rapidly in hot weather, a saucer placed near a snake's hiding place might, in fact, occasionally tempt the reptile out.

Every well-appointed Roman household had at least one guardian snake. Pliny the Elder commented, "We destroy their eggs, else they would multiply too fast." [13] Serpent worship was rare, although at Lanuvium, 16 miles south of Rome, priestesses attended a huge snake in a cave. Young women were sometimes taken to this shrine to check their virginity; it was regarded as established if the snake ate their offerings.[14]

Pliny wrote that the Marsi, who lived near Rome, had a natural immunity to snake poison. He credits this to their being descended from the sorceress Circe.[15] The Marsi were snake handlers, and the custom has not yet died out in their territory. Each year near the first of August, young men from the village of Cocullo hunt snakes in the bare, rocky hills of the surrounding countryside. On August 4, they drape a figure of St. Dominic with serpents and carry it through the village. Local historians claim the custom commemorates the occasion when St. Dominic, on his grand walking tour from Rome to Toulouse, stopped in Cocullo in 1218 and saved the people from a plague of vipers by making the snakes harmless.[16]

In the seventh century, the Lombards of northern Italy, although nominally Christian, clung to their old superstitions and worshiped a holy tree and the image of a golden viper. Their priest, Barbatus, was not able to stamp out these heathenish practices. Finally, when King Ramuald was away, Barbatus begged Queen Theodorada to get him the image of the snake. She protested that to do so would mean her death, but he persevered and eventually obtained it. As soon as the golden viper was in his hands, he melted it and delivered the gold to a goldsmith to be made into a plate and chalice. When the king returned, Barbatus served the Eucharist to him from the new utensils and confessed that he had destroyed the snake.[17] Here the story ends abruptly, like an episode in a television serial. No further mention is made of ophiolatry among the Lombards. However, the Visconti family of Lombardy has a device on their arms showing a snake with a child in its mouth. Tradition has it that this was adapted during the Crusades from the shield of a conquered Moslem, but it may just be the last remaining token of the Lombardy serpent cult.

St. Patrick and the Druids

There is evidence dating from the first century B.C. to suggest that Druid sects used snakes in their rites. The poet Lucan saw a Druidic grove of sacred oaks entwined with snakes. Carvings of snakes have been found on monoliths in Scotland.[18] At Carnac in Brittany a sinuous course of huge stones almost 8 miles long suggests an enormous snake. It is associated with a neolithic ceremonial center. The name Carnac is derived from Cairn-hac, which means "serpent's hill." [19] A large Bronze Age communal grave at Newgrange, Ireland, now being excavated, has yielded pictographs of coiled snakes.[20]

As late as 1900, snakes were being sacrificed in Midsummer Eve fire festivals of Druidic origin. The British anthropologist Sir James G. Frazer describes such a ceremony at Luchon in the Pyrenees. A hollow column of strong wickerwork was constructed, interlaced with foliage, and raised to a height of about 60 feet. Its base was banked with shrubs and flowers and filled with combustibles. At sunset, a grand procession, chanting hymns, marched to the column and encircled it. When the fire was lit, as many live snakes as could be gathered were thrown into the column by men and boys who danced wildly about it. To avoid the flames, the snakes wriggled up the wickerwork to the top and, lashing out vainly in all directions, finally dropped into the fire while the celebrants cheered.[21]

There is a long-standing antipathy between snakes and the Irish. Among other beliefs, Irishmen are said to be able to immobilize vipers by drawing a circle around them; washing a viper bite with milk of an Irish cow will cure it; a variety of blue stone found on Irish beaches heals snakebite; and Irish air is so pure that no snake can survive in it.

Late in the fourth century when St. Patrick introduced Christianity into Ireland, he met formidable opposition from the Druid priests. They were so obstinate and antagonistic that, in spite of his kindly disposition, he cursed the land, turning it into dreary bogs, cursed the rivers so that the fish died, and cursed the women's cooking pots so that they never boiled. He aimed an especially virulent curse at the Druids themselves, and the earth promptly opened and swallowed them. Finishing off in good style, he drove out the snakes by beating on a drum. At one crucial point, he knocked a hole in the drumhead, but an angel immediately appeared and mended it.[22] The snakes Patrick drove from Ireland may have been effigies, or possibly even real reptiles kept by the Druid cult, though there is no definite evidence for this.

Ireland is far from paradise from a snake's viewpoint, being entirely too damp, misty, and cool. Nevertheless some species could doubtless survive there, and perhaps some day a chance introduction will end the Emerald Isle's claim to snakelessness. In fact, it has been tried. In 1831 James Cleland, an Irish gentleman, bought six harmless snakes in the Covent Garden market in London. Returning to Ireland, he released the reptiles in his garden at Rath-gael in County Down. About a week later, one of them was killed about 3 miles away. The man who killed it thought it a kind of eel, but it was identified by Dr. J. L.

Drummond, a celebrated Irish naturalist. The realization that a "rale, living sarpint" had been killed very near the burial place of St. Patrick caused incredible consternation. One clergyman preached a sermon in which he considered it a sign that the end of the world was near. Another insisted that it foretold the coming of an epidemic of cholera. Rewards were posted for the destruction of other snakes found in the vicinity, and three more were killed. The last two were never found. For a long time the country folk seethed with indignation, and Mr. Cleland wisely divorced himself from the whole shebang.[23]

A Hell of Cold Venom

Although only the European viper and the grass snake reach the Gulf of Bothnia, Baltic mythology swarms with snakes, mostly venomous and unpleasant. The Judeo-Christian hell contrasts strongly with the Norse version of what awaits oath breakers and murderers after death. Whereas desert tribes could imagine nothing worse than being confined in a hotter place, the Baltic people felt that the ultimate horror was some-place colder. To them, hell is a dark, icy hall composed of snakes' bodies. The serpent heads all look inward, and cold venom constantly drips from their jaws to form a poisonous river flowing down the center of the hall. In this terrible river, the damned are forced to wade and swim forever.[24]

Numerous petroglyphs of crested serpents have been found at Romove and Upsala, Sweden, traditional centers for the cult of Odin. The accompanying runes are not clearly understood, but it is possible that ophiolatry was part of the rites celebrated by votaries of the northern gods.[25]

Snakes figure in the *Prose Edda,* a Norse version of the origin and end of the world. In this saga, the ash tree Yggdrasil fills the universe. Its topmost branches overshadow Asgard, the home of the gods. Its leaves are fresh and green, but deep in the earth a dragon, helped by a mass of vipers, constantly gnaws at its root. The Norns, or fates, water the tree daily. Sitting in its shade, they weave the web of life. Near the tree's top, a rainbow forms a bridge from Asgard to earth. Around the earth a great serpent lies coiled with his tail in his mouth. This is the Midgard Snake who waits under the sea for the hour of doom.

As evil prevails and good vanishes from the earth, a bitter winter will set in, and for three seasons the world will be sheathed in ice. Then powerful wolves, fat from the flesh and bones of adulterers and murderers, will deluge the earth with blood and slaver from their jaws. The sun will grow dim, the frightened stars will fall, and the gods will prepare themselves to die.

At this moment, the dragon and his vipers will sever Yggdrasil's root, and the terrible Midgard Snake, roused by the commotion, will twist his way to land. Thor, god of thunder, will meet him and strike him a mortal blow with his hammer, but Thor himself will die, drowned in floods of venom from the monster's mouth. The rainbow bridge will collapse as the gods ride to battle. Raging flames curling about the world tree will consume the palaces of Asgard, destroy all life on earth, and make the oceans seethe until the blackened land sinks below the boiling waters.[26]

15. The Belled Vipers of America

The remarkable parallelism between snake myths of the Americas and those of the Old World suggests that man's ideas about snakes were already deeply embedded in his mind when he crossed the Bering land bridge and began to populate the Western Hemisphere. The basic themes are the same or very similar. They include cosmic serpents, snakes that control rain and guard the water supply, snakes as lightning and rainbows, snakes as familiars of fertility deities and symbols of vitality and everlasting life, phallic snakes, and snakes as ancestors and tribal totems. The way of the serpent is the same, only the species change. The roles assigned to vipers and cobras in the Old World are all given to a single type of New World reptile, the rattlesnake.

North American Indians respected all snakes but reserved their veneration and worship for the rattlesnake, the most dangerous venomous snake on the continent. No Indian willingly killed a rattler, but if it became necessary to do so, he was careful to ask the snake's pardon for fear another rattler would quickly come to revenge its death. Tribal sachems and medicine men might safely dispatch a rattlesnake if they took care to dispose of the reptile's remains with proper respect. Otherwise torrential rains would cause floods and drive the tribe from its encampment.[1]

Rattlesnakes figured prominently in Indian magic and medicine. Powdered rattles were commonly administered to women in labor to facilitate a rapid and easy delivery; sometimes snake skins were bound around the belly for the same purpose. Rattlesnake fat or oil was widely used for treating sore muscles and joints, and the powdered flesh was given to those with fever. Fangs were used for scarification, either for treatment of illness or in ceremonies such as the green corn dance of the Seminole. Among the Pomo of California, a magic poison was made from the blood of four rattlesnakes mixed with pulped spiders, bees, ants, and scorpions. This was dripped onto an effigy of the victim or smeared on an arrow that was shot over his house. Eyes removed from a rattlesnake while it was blind prior to shedding its skin were rubbed on abalone shell. The treated shell was then used to flash light into the eyes of an enemy, causing him to become blind like the snake.[2]

The Algonquin people credited Gee-chee Manito-ah, the Great Spirit, with creating the first serpent. One day while hunting, Manito-ah became annoyed with his penis because it kept getting in his way. He wrung it off and flung it into the bushes where it turned into the rattlesnake. Understandably, the Algonquins called it the king of serpents and used its figure in their picture writing as a symbol of life.[3]

The association of rattlesnakes and rain was common across North America. The Shawnees heard thunder as the voice of a celestial rattlesnake, and the Sioux saw lightning as a rattler striking its prey. Micmac tribesmen saw the black clouds of an approaching storm as seven flying rattlesnakes coiling about one another, crying in the thunder as they crashed across the sky and appearing in streaks of lightning as they dived toward the earth.[4] The Shoshone in Idaho and Wyoming believed the firmament was a dome of ice against which a huge serpent lay coiled. As he moved, his scales abraded the ice and it fell to earth. It fell as rain in summer and as snow in winter, and when the snake was angry, it fell as hail. Sometimes the snake showed himself in the sky as a rainbow.[5]

Kickapoo territory in Michigan and Wisconsin was heavily infested with rattlesnakes that were held sacred because of their control over rain. One Kickapoo legend says that there was once a beautiful girl who was Rattlesnake's younger sister. Whoever he bit, she healed with her gentle touch, until finally he lost his patience and killed her. Manito-ah turned her into the arrow-leaved violet whose healing leaves the Kickapoos used as an antidote for snakebite.[6]

In the southwestern desert region of the United States, where rainfall is always a serious concern, the Sia implore the rattlesnakes to intercede with the cloud rulers to water the earth and help it bear abundant crops.[7]

The best-known American Indian snake ceremony is that celebrated each year by the Hopi of Arizona to insure fertility and produce rain. The festival lasts nine days, although the best-known part of it, the snake dance, lasts less than an hour. On the first day there is a snake hunt, and the priest admonishes the hunters, "If you find a rattlesnake anywhere, pray to it— may it be raining soon! The crops will thrive, and our children will thrive." [8]

Hunters collect both rattlers and harmless snakes such as the bull snake and return with them to the kiva, or lodge room,

of the snake fraternity, where priests put the reptiles in clay
pots. The hunt may continue for as many as four days; meanwhile the snake priests make whips and wands of eagle feathers
which the dancers will use to control the snakes. At noon on
the ninth day, the snakes are ceremoniously washed and allowed
to crawl about the kiva for a few hours. After this the priests
put the snakes into bags and carry them to the kisi, a temporary
shrine constructed near the dancing space. In front of the shrine
is a hollow covered with a board. This represents the entrance
to the underworld where the gods live who control the rains.

At sundown, the snake priests emerge from their kiva and
approach the dancing space. As each passes the kisi, he stamps
on the board, which gives forth a hollow sound to advise the
gods that the dance is about to begin. Priests of the antelope
fraternity line up near the shrine to set the rhythm for the dance,
but only the snake priests dance. As each dancer passes the
kisi, a priest hands him a snake, which he puts in his mouth. An
assistant, or hugger, diverts the reptile's attention with a feather
whip, while a second helper, the gatherer, follows behind to
pick up the snake when the dancer is finished with it. Each trio
moves about the circle with a slow shuffle until all the snakes
have been danced with. Then the priests draw a circle on the
ground with corn meal and pile the snakes inside this ring.
Women scatter more sacred meal on them. Finally priests pick
up the reptiles and run down the paths leading away from the
ceremonial site. They release the snakes, first instructing them
to carry prayers for rain to the underworld gods.[9]

The insouciant manner in which Hopis handle the rattlesnakes has caused speculation as to whether the snakes are
drugged, defanged, or milked of their venom prior to the dance.

In 1932, Charles Bogert and a companion collected one of the rattlers used in the dance at Shongopovi soon after it had been released at a shrine about a hundred yards from the mesa where the dance was held. He found that not only the functional fangs but also the reserve fangs had been removed. He sent the specimen to Laurence M. Klauber, who commented in part: "This had been done with a knife as indicated by cuts rather than tears, and on the whole it was rather neatly done if you forget the snake's feeling in the matter. . . . Offhand, it doesn't seem to me that the underworld gods would be disposed to send too much rainfall in return for so damaged a Western Union messenger." [10]

In 1954 a New Mexico college student brought to the Bronx Zoo a defanged rattlesnake he had picked up after the Hopi snake dance at Walpi. He had had the snake for almost two years, and the fangs had not regenerated. However the Hopis do not always remove the fangs from their snakes. Specimens collected in 1883 and sent to the U.S. National Museum were found to have their mouths undamaged. Klauber saw rattlers with apparently intact fangs used in a 1931 ceremony.[11]

Hopis are inclined to downgrade their neighbors, the Zuñis, because the latter know nothing of the snake-dance mysteries, but Zuñis have a mysterious snake of their own, an archaic fetish made of deerskin stretched on cottonwood hoops, crowned with eagle feathers, and fitted with fearsome teeth and a long red tongue. This is Ko'loowisi, the plumed serpent, who plays a climactic role in initiating Zuñi boys into tribal fraternities. Only those initiated may dance in the dancing place of heaven.

Priests masked and dressed as gods begin the initiation rites by telling the Zuñi history myth, the saga of a long migration.

They say that in the beginning the Zuñis passed through a soot-dark world over a place where the water had receded. They crossed a moss world and a mud world, stumbling over one another in the darkness. Finally they saw the sun and, taking heart, turned toward the center of the earth, making camp at a long series of springs and arriving at last at the house of Ko'loowisi.

After the priests have told the myth several times, they conduct a rabbit hunt. The first rabbit taken is a sacrifice to insure early puberty and many children for Zuñi girls.

On the last day of the ritual, priests, warriors, and seed gatherers, with much ceremony, carry the effigy of Ko'loowisi before the initiates. One priest blows a conch to make it seem as though the snake is continually roaring. Water from sacred springs has been secretly poured into the body of the fetish so that each initiate may receive a bowl of water from the serpent's mouth. The boys carry these bowls home to share the magic liquid with their families and to sprinkle on next year's seed corn to insure its germination.[12]

Another southwestern Indian tribe, the Pima, include in one of their legends a clinically accurate account of death from rattlesnake bite. Pimas never tell this story in summer for fear of angering some passing rattler but reserve it for winter evenings when the snakes are safely hibernating.

As the Pima tell it, when Elder Brother, whose business it was to control life, first visited earth, he found the four tribes of men and all the animals living together in one great house. Rattlesnake was there and was known as Soft Child. Everyone liked to hear him rattle, and he got little rest because the other animals continually prodded and scratched him. At last he went to Elder Brother and complained that no one would let him alone. Elder Brother plucked a hair from his own chin and cut it into little pieces. These he fitted into Soft Child's mouth and said, "Now when anyone torments you, bite him!"

That evening as Soft Child lay basking in the doorway in the setting sun, Rabbit came and scratched him as he had often done before. So Soft Child bit Rabbit as Elder Brother had instructed him to do. Rabbit scratched the snake again and was again bitten. Then he ran about the great house telling everyone that Soft Child had bitten him twice.

By the time the moon rose, Rabbit began to feel hot and ill. He called for cool sand to lie upon to ease his fever, but this brought him no relief. He begged for low bushes to cover him and cooling breezes to ease his pain. These were quickly found, but they gave him no comfort. Rabbit's fever mounted, and his tortured body swelled and blackened. By the time the moon set, he found peace in death. And everyone was angry because Elder Brother had put death in Soft Child's mouth.[13]

The rattlesnake's association with rain and fertility continues southward into Middle America. Huichol Indians in Jalisco, Mexico, believe that a mythical red rattlesnake brings rain, creates flowers, and takes special care of children.[14] The Opata of Mexico equate the rattlesnake's strike with a thunderbolt, and the Toltec thunder god holds a golden serpent representing lightning.[15]

In the cities of the highly developed Mayan (300–900 A.D.) and Aztec (1325–1517 A.D.) civilizations, numerous figures of feathered rattlesnakes and carvings of the snakes on temple walls indicate that the species was highly respected and credited with supernatural powers. If not actually worshiped, it was at times considered a manifestation of one of the gods. The recurrent feathered-serpent motif is not so fanciful to anyone who has seen a big Central American rattlesnake that has just cast its skin. The large scales are highly keeled or ridged and have a striking velvety sheen; the resemblance to the plumage of a bird is evident.

Stone sculptures of plumed and feathered serpents at Chichen Itzá and Uxmal on the Yucatán peninsula are believed to represent the Mayan culture hero Kukulcan, who united his people in a peaceful confederation and taught them the arts of husbandry and medicine.[16]

The Aztecs worshiped a similar hero, Quetzalcoatl, whose name means "quetzal bird" plus "snake." In Aztec cosmogony, heaven and Quetzalcoatl were created on the first day. Quetzalcoatl controlled the sun and the seasons and was credited with inventing the Aztec calendar. He was the patron of human reproduction and devised the Aztec marriage ceremonies. When women found that they were pregnant, they addressed prayers of gratitude to him. Paradoxically, Quetzalcoatl's priests practiced celibacy and mortified their flesh, piercing their tongues and penes with thorns of the maguey plant.[17]

When his work was finished, Quetzalcoatl set sail on the eastern sea in a boat made of snake skins. The Aztecs were looking for his return when the Spaniards arrived in 1519. Sentries watching for him sighted the Spanish ships sailing westward and hastened to inform Montezuma that Quetzalcoatl was coming. The invaders were greeted with gifts that included a snake mask set with turquoise.[18]

Among the wonders of the Aztec capital at the time of the Spanish invasion were the zoological gardens of Montezuma.

Like all proper zoos, it had a snake house. Bernal Díaz del
Castillo (1498–1560), in his well-known account of the conquest of Mexico describes it: "They have in that cursed house
many vipers and poisonous snakes which carry on their tails
things that sound like bells. These are the worst vipers of all,
and they keep them in jars and great pottery vessels with many
feathers. There they lay their eggs and rear their young, and
they give them to eat the bodies of Indians who have been
sacrificed." [19]

The snake with the bells, or, as another early traveler
described it, the serpent with the castanets in its tail, became
notorious in Europe as a formidable reptile who preferred to
be left alone but, if provoked, courteously warned that it would
strike. It quickly became a symbol for colonial America. Several
rattlesnake flags were carried by rebel contingents during the
American Revolution. The two best-known are the Navy jack
showing a rattlesnake stretched diagonally across thirteen al-
ternating red and white stripes, and the Gadsen flag with a
coiled rattler on a yellow field. Both include the motto, "DON'T
TREAD ON ME!"

European immigrants to North America tended to in-
corporate rattlesnakes into snake stories from their homelands
with the result that contemporary folklore about rattlers may
sometimes be traced to the Talmud, Greek mythology, Pliny,
or the Eddic myths. We once saw a cross-cultural snake heraldry
nicely illustrated on the façade of a Texas hospital. The carved
serpent twined around the staff of Asklepios bore a splendid set
of rattles.

16. Snakes in the Space Age

Carnivals and Snake Shows

The snake show was part of every carnival or circus that toured the midland United States during the 1920s and 1930s. Generally speaking, there were two types of shows. One featured a statuesque female who draped herself with large, good-natured snakes. Indian pythons were particular favorites, but boa constrictors and large indigo snakes were occasionally used. Unless the lady chose to inject something of her own personality into the performance, it was about as exciting as watching ice melt. The onlookers assumed the snakes were hypnotized or doped; actually they were simply unusually tractable individuals of normally docile species.

A second type of show made use of a motley collection of smaller snakes confined in a canvas enclosure. Rattlesnakes were regularly used in these shows but other venomous species very rarely, although the audience was led to believe otherwise. Sometimes large lizards, such as iguanas, monitors, or gila monsters, were exhibited. It was the job of the barker outside the tent to persuade the spectators that the reptiles on display were of unparalleled ferocity and deadliness. I recall one barker who intoned in a voice reminiscent of the late W. C. Fields, "Killers from the jungles of the Amazon . . . from the great peninsula of India . . . they feed on the warm blood of the living!"

A man in the pit with the snakes had the job of keeping things stirred up and convincing the audience that he was exerting superhuman control over a mob of reptiles ravening for his blood. Nearly all the rattlesnakes and other venomous species used in pit shows were "fixed"—that is, their fangs had been surgically removed by the animal dealer. My brother and I once tried to sell a cottonmouth to a carnival showman; he quickly lost interest when he found the snake was "hot"—that is, in possession of an intact venom apparatus. Nevertheless, by accident or poor surgical technique, an unaltered venomous snake occasionally did get into a pit show. As a junior medical student I saw a showman in serious condition from the bite of a rattlesnake he had been handling. Occasionally a carnival would introduce a specialty act, such as a combat between a rattlesnake and a king snake or between snakes and cats, dogs or rats. These acts usually bombed, the animals being less bloodthirsty than those who came to watch. For those of more jaded taste, there was the geek. I saw just one of these humanoids. He picked up a foot-long garter snake from a box, let it slip through his fingers for a minute or two, then bit it behind the head and swallowed it.

Today the traveling snake show, along with its parent circus or carnival, has almost vanished from the American scene. It was succeeded by the reptile exhibit that caters to the traveler. Roadside snake shows began with the growth of automobile travel and reached their zenith in the decade following World War II. They were most numerous in the southern and southwestern states where reptiles could be maintained outdoors most of the year, and a good variety of local species was available.

Within recent years, changes in public taste and the growth of high speed, nonstop travel on freeways and turnpikes have caused a decline in the popularity of these attractions; however, a number still seem to be prospering in those areas that have a large influx of tourists. Some roadside snake exhibits play up the sensational and dramatic in the same way as the old tent shows, and others are merely fronts for various activities, legal or otherwise. Many, however, make a genuine attempt to maintain an exhibit combining education with entertainment. Some of the largest are operated by or employ personnel with scientific training, and they have made noteworthy contributions to herpetology. The Miami Serpentarium maintains one of the largest collections of poisonous snakes in the world and processes and supplies much of the snake venom used for research in the United States. Ross Allen's Reptile Institute at Silver Springs, Florida, has published many scientific papers dealing with reptiles and amphibians of the southeastern United States, British Honduras, and the West Indies. Some of the smaller exhibits have concentrated on displays of interesting local species and have added significantly to knowledge of reptile habits and distribution patterns. Other exhibitors have provided useful tips on keeping rare and delicate species of reptiles in captivity.

Rattler Roundups

Hunting poisonous snakes for sport has long been popular in parts of the United States, for it combines elements of excitement and risk with the virtuous feeling of performing a public service. Rattlesnake hunts were held in New England as early as 1680 and were a regular practice during colonial days.[1] Hunting is quite easy in places where large numbers of snakes congregate for hibernation. Rattlesnake dens may be found in most states. The late Raymond Ditmars, long-time curator of reptiles at the Bronx Zoo and the first American herpetologist to write extensively for the general public, wrote exciting accounts of collecting timber rattlers and copperheads at dens within 50 miles of New York City. According to an 1855 account, rattlesnake hunting in the region of Lake George in upstate New York was a girls' sport, the huntresses killing as many as a hundred snakes a day by taking them by their tails and snapping them.[2] This is an exceedingly hazardous way to dispose of a heavy-bodied poisonous snake like a rattler, but perhaps country girls were more rugged in those days. A large rattlesnake den was once located in bluffs just north of Columbus, Ohio, but was destroyed by quarrying. Fangs can still be occasionally found by sifting debris from deep in crevices. My father told me that, during his boyhood, rattlesnakes were hunted at a den in Crawford County, Indiana, for their oil which was valued for treatment of rheumatism.

Some of the most famous snake dens in the Midwest are located along the Big Muddy River in extreme southern Illinois, although in recent years the numbers of snakes have been drastically reduced. Our good friend and companion on many field trips, Dr. Philip W. Smith of the Illinois Natural History Survey, visited these dens with his wife on October 1, 1942. They collected approximately 80 snakes, most of them timber rattlers and cottonmouths, with black racers, ribbon snakes, green snakes, and several other species present in smaller numbers.

These dens are noted for the variety of snakes that congregate there. In 1946 and 1947 my brother and I recorded 18 species from the area, and several additional ones have been found by others. Dens in the western states are more likely to harbor rattlesnakes in almost "pure culture" with other species uncommon.

In 1943 when Madge was taking flight training with other women pilots at Avenger Field near Sweetwater, Texas, there was a densely populated den of western diamondbacks in a red-clay gulch off the end of the main runway. When the late March sun tempted the huge rattlers to bask on the runway, trainees experienced serious cockpit trouble, and many of the girls pulled up their gear and took their planes around the pattern again.

Sweetwater is one of several small cities in the south and southwest that have found rattlesnake roundups a good way to obtain civic publicity, for they have more originality than a rodeo and more pizzazz than a dogwood festival. One of the oldest and best-known is held at Okeene, Oklahoma; it has been an annual event since 1940. According to recent information, thirty other communities now hold such festivities, about two-thirds of them in Texas and Florida.

Events of the celebration may include rattlesnake barbecues, demonstrations of snake milking, story-telling contests, and meetings of the "White Fang Club" whose membership is composed of hunters who have been bitten. Liquor is often imbibed freely and a rancher living near Okeene commented that the snake hunters are a greater nuisance than the snakes. The hunt itself is held on a mild spring day when the snakes are just emerging from their hibernating crevices or holes to bask in the sun. Hunters often work in pairs, one man raking the snakes out of their shelter with hook or tongs and the other pinning and bagging them. In 1954, 1,576 rattlers were reported to have been taken at the Okeene roundup, but recent bags have been less than 500. A catch of 150 to 200 rattlers is considered good for roundups in Florida and other southeastern states. Although the number of snakes captured has declined at most dens in recent years, the rattlesnake populations seem to hold up surprisingly well in the face of these depredations. This may be because comparatively few small rattlers are taken. The young snakes may be overlooked by the hunters or may emerge from hibernation later than adults. There is also some reason to think that many juvenile rattlers hibernate in other sites and do not go to the dens until they are sexually mature.

Some of the snakes captured at the roundups go to venom-processing laboratories; others are sold to exhibitors or animal dealers. Zoos often buy part of the catch, the largest and best specimens being put on exhibition while the others are killed and frozen to serve as food for king cobras and other snake-eating species. Towns that stage the roundups are in the ambivalent position of publicly sponsoring the eradication of dangerous creatures for the benefit of humanity, yet secretly hoping that the rattlesnakes will continue to propagate and bring the community an annual taste of excitement and a break in its routine.

Snake Handlers of the Bible Belt

One snake-handling exhibition in which spectators may be confident that no one has tampered with the snakes' venom apparatus is a grim test of Christian faith practiced by communicants of a few small church groups in the southeastern states.

This all began in 1909 in Grasshopper Valley, Tennessee, when a farmer, George Hensley, felt called to make a literal test of verses 17 and 18 in the sixteenth chapter of Mark, which read as follows:

> And these signs shall follow them that believe: In my name shall they cast out devils; they shall speak with new tongues;
> They shall take up serpents; and if they drink any deadly thing, it shall not hurt them; they shall lay hands on the sick and they shall recover.

Not being a man to shirk his duty to the Lord, Mr. Hensley quickly hunted out a large rattlesnake and found that he could manipulate it with apparent safety. After a few days, he demonstrated this ability in a service at Sale Creek church and exhorted others in the congregation to prove their faith by doing likewise. Handling rattlesnakes and copperheads became a part of the religious services in this and other small churches of the region.

About 1934 the practice had spread to adjoining Kentucky where independent Holy Roller sects adopted it and added it to their other customs of glossolalia ("speaking with tongues") and healing by prayer and the laying on of hands. These mountain regions were sufficiently removed from the mainstream of American life so that few beyond them knew of the cult. In 1938 a farmer who hated snakes and disapproved of his wife's handling them in church services had three members of the Pine Mountain Church of God arrested and brought to court in Harlan, Kentucky. They were acquitted, but the Associated Press picked up the story, and snake-handling sects have been making headlines ever since.[3] The most recent is August 20,

1968, when a lay minister of the Holiness Church of God in Jesus' Name in Big Stone Gap, Virginia, held two rattlesnakes against his temples, was bitten and died the next day.[4] Some members of the congregation were arrested; one was convicted (and another acquitted) by a Circuit Court of Appeals under a state law which forbids handling snakes "in such a manner as to endanger the life and health of another person." The convicted man announced his intention to appeal.

These snake-handling cults flourish in the repressive atmosphere of fundamentalist Protestantism, which forbids dancing, drinking, smoking, going to the theater, using cosmetics, and dressing immodestly. Members of these churches live at a subsistence level as hard-scrabble farmers, mill workers, miners, or domestics. They depend upon their church for social life, and in their search for identity, preferably a better identity than other people's, they look to their religion for some sign to set them apart. Snake handling, with its accompanying publicity and local police harassment, gives them a feeling of importance and reassures them that they are a chosen people.[5] As one of their preachers put it, "We're not ignorant! God's people are the wisest people in the world. There's people with money in the bank that does this."

Services at which the congregation plans to handle snakes may begin early in the day and continue long after sundown. Sometimes, in fine weather, the people will pack lunch baskets and set up a temporary place for worship at a picnic spot. Tamborines and guitars provide music, and services often begin with singing old revival hymns such as, "Jesus Is Getting Us Ready for the Great Day," "The Devil in a Box," and "Ring Them Bells of Love!" The cultists sway to the rhythm, clap their hands, and stomp their feet. Women often wheel in backwards circles, hands waving and eyes closed, moving in sudden jerks and spins in a manner like that of the whirling dervishes of Islam. Between hymns the preacher exhorts his flock to open their hearts to the Lord's anointing, while the people respond with phrases like "Thank God for Jesus!" and "Hallelujah to Glory!"

As the music continues, emotional responses proliferate, and tension rises high. The preacher passes among the congregation encouraging the members to pray; he assists women who become overzealous and faint in religious fervor. When a devotee is "about to break," the preacher may hand him a snake, or the man himself may plunge his hand into the snake box and pull one out. While the rest of the cultists shout, "It's the Power!" and "Thank you, Jesus!" all of the snakes are removed from the box and passed around. Some of the faithful wind the snakes around their necks; others may wear a rattler or copperhead like a crown. Women permit the snakes to crawl about their shoulders and breasts; sometimes they allow their babies and young children to touch the reptiles. At one meeting, the preacher shouted, "Let's everybody get closer to God and handle more and bigger snakes! There's no church on earth can handle snakes like we do!" [6]

After everyone who wishes to handle a snake has done so, attention begins to wander, and the snakes are returned to their box. Ordeals by fire may follow. Some members of the group apply blow torches to their feet or hold flaming pools of kerosine in their hands. It is reported that no visible damage to the skin results from these demonstrations unless the votary becomes frightened at some critical moment and breaks out of his self-hypnosis. Some especially zealous person may seek to show his perfect faith by drinking a massive dose of strychnine; results are rarely other than fatal.[7]

When the activities of these church groups became known, their services attracted hundreds of curious persons. They were tolerated and even welcomed so long as they did not offer to interfere with the meeting. However, as it became evident that children and others not capable of exercising independent judgment were running serious risks of being snakebitten, several state legislatures passed laws forbidding snake handling in religious services. Persecution set a final seal on the cultists' claim to be God's chosen people, and they have protested that these laws infringe upon their constitutional right to religious liberty. It is on this ground that the snake handler in Big Stone Gap based his appeal of the Circuit Court decision.

The only report of a Christian snake-handling ceremony well beyond the southern mountains comes from that hotbed of bizarre folkways, southern California. At a religious service in Long Beach in 1954, two persons were bitten, one fatally. The relationship of this group to those in the East is uncertain; it evidently disbanded soon afterward.[8]

It is somewhat puzzling that there are not more bites among the Appalachian snake handlers. All who have knowledge of the sect say that most of the snakes they handle are freshly captured and have not been tampered with in any way. Weston LaBarre, a Duke University anthropologist, who has written the definitive work on this sect, believes that the continual passing of the snakes from hand to hand during the services disturbs their normal defensive reflexes and makes them unwilling to bite.[9] This is supported by reports that many of the bites occur as the snakes are taken from the box in which they are kept and in which they would presumably be able to coil normally. Berthold Schwarz, a psychiatrist who has observed the snake-handling ceremonies, believes that some of the cultists can induce a state of cataplexy in the snakes and has a photograph that tends to support this idea.[10]

The timber rattlesnake, the species usually handled in the services, is one of the more mild-tempered rattlers; furthermore, when kept in captivity, it is curiously prone to spells of apathy when almost nothing short of severe injury will provoke it to strike. The copperhead, the other species commonly handled, has a more uncertain temper but is relatively docile. Its venom is comparatively weak, and its bite is probably not able to kill an adult under most circumstances.

Along the cult's southern boundary in Georgia and northern Florida, congregations sometimes handle the eastern diamond-back rattlesnake, in nearly every way a more dangerous snake than the timber rattler. It is bigger, has more venom, longer fangs, and a more irritable disposition. One of these snakes killed the sect's founder, George Hensley, who was bitten on July 24, 1955, during a service at Lester's Shed near Altha, Florida. He was 70 years old and claimed to have survived 400 previous bites.

The total number of bites among the snake handlers is unknown, for they refuse all aid other than prayer. Accepting the services of a doctor is considered an admission of weak faith. As a Kentucky coal miner said after being bitten, "I'm letting the Lord do my doctoring." In 1947 the parents of a young girl bitten during a church meeting refused medical assistance for her, insisting that "the Lord would heal her." [11] LaBarre recorded 20 fatalities during snake-handling religious services up to the autumn of 1961.[12] There have been at least two deaths since then.

17. How Snakes Acquired Charisma

⋙⋙⋙⋙⋙⋙⋙⋙⋙⋙⋙⋙⋙⋙⋙⋙⋙⋙⋙⋙⋙⋙⋙⋙⋙⋙⋙⋙⋙⋙⋙⋙⋙⋙⋙⋘

Some time near the beginning of the Pleistocene, when snakes were pretty much as they are today but man was not yet quite man, a curious association between the two had its beginnings. The primates that were to become men were indulging in a unique sort of cerebral activity. They were taking images that came into their brains by way of perfectly good mammalian sense organs, coloring them with emotions, and projecting them, somewhat distorted, upon a screen of inner consciousness. At the same time, they were gradually finding a way to tell each other about these inner images. Nearly everything in the environment of these protohumans must have been projected upon that screen, but some images persisted longer and got superimposed on others. The snake was one of these images. There is no good biological reason why this should be so. The relationship of snakes and man has come about because man is a maker of images and symbols, who found in the snake a peculiarly potent symbol. This in turn means that the snake as an animal has some characteristics that set it apart from other creatures in man's environment. One of these characteristics is the power of some snakes to inflict suffering and death in a singularly mysterious and terrifying manner.

Early man was not given to analysis; his thinking was prelogical, and the action of venom as a chemical agent was beyond his understanding. Furthermore, he was alarmed and confused by his encounters with snakes. Their body conformation puzzled him, and their ability to appear suddenly and just as suddenly to vanish frightened him. As man shared intensely emotional experiences within his immediate family group he began to build a mystic complex of ideas and beliefs that had little reality but which invested snakes with supernatural properties.

In his classic monograph, *Les Fonctions mentales dans les sociétés inferieures,* the French anthropologist Lucien Levy-Bruhl hypothesized that primitive man did not necessarily believe what he saw; rather, he saw what he believed. Often the actual object or animal hardly existed for him but only acted as a catalyst for the preconceptions, preperceptions, and pre-conclusions by means of which man saw anything that his senses could not readily define.[1] Protoman's confused and frightening experiences with snakes may have initiated his first impulses toward religion and ultimately influenced his ideas about death and immortality, his psychosexual body imagery, and possibly even his ambivalence toward the opposite sex.

Pleistocene hunters observed that when they beat an animal to death it bled profusely. The stuff of life seemed to be blood, and hungry hunters drank it eagerly, first for food and later to gain for themselves the virtues and magic qualities of their prey.[2] Snakes are fairly easy to hunt and kill and may have been an important source of food, as they still are for certain tribes in Africa and Australia.

However, in hunting snakes, early man encountered something not explainable in terms of his experiences with other game. Sometimes the snake struck first, and the hunter died from a wound so inconsequential that it bled hardly at all. Such a death did not seem to be in the natural order of things. Even more terrifying must have been the snakebite that caused bleeding from the victim's nose, mouth, eyes, and most significantly, his genitals. While such bites were not always fatal, they signified that some snakes possessed immensely powerful magic.

Men noticed very early that women regularly and mysteriously bled from their genitals in a manner that suggested they were snakebitten. However, women seemed to suffer few ill effects at such times, although they might reject males and wander off by themselves. Men suspected that their women might actually be consorting with snakes—perhaps sharing their magic secrets and practicing mystic rites of their own. They began to feel afraid of women and to develop a deep dread of menstrual blood. They imposed severe restrictions, sometimes confining girls at menarche in cages for periods of several years so as to control their supposed magic powers, or denying women the right to touch the earth and see the sky during their menstrual periods.[3]

Magic powers are widely attributed to women at such times. Peasants in Lebanon believe the shadow of a menstruating woman immobilizes snakes, causes flowers to wither, and trees to die. A Talmudic legend says if a menstruating woman passes between two men she thereby kills one of them. Pliny the Elder in his monumental *Natural History* says that the presence of a woman "in her courses" can sour wine, blight crops, cause fruit to fall prematurely, dim mirrors, blunt razors, rust iron, and cause mares to miscarry. Some of these beliefs are still current in the rural midwestern United States. Pliny also wrote that dogs that taste menstrual blood go mad and "if they bite anything afterwards they leave such a venom the wound is incurable." [4]

A mystical association between menstruous women and snakes is recorded in the folk literature of cultures widely separated in time and geography. The Argentine herpetologist Marcos Freiberg writes that an Indian tribe in northern Argentina believes that a menstruating woman can kill a snake instantly by stepping over it, and when she combs her hair she must quickly burn the combings before they turn into poisonous snakes.[5]

Semitic peoples of North Africa and the Middle East formerly explained menstruation as a supernatural wound caused by snakebite. In the same way, as late as 1900 the Chiriguanos Indians of southeastern Bolivia enclosed a girl at her first menstrual period in a hammock suspended from the roof of her parents' hut. She remained in the hammock three months while, at regular intervals, the older women of the tribe beat the threshold of the hut and the paths leading to it in order to drive away the snake that had bitten her.[6]

The Yuki Indians of California believe that the dangerous element in rattlesnake poison is menstrual blood, which they hold to be the deadliest of poisons. Navajo, Zuñi, and Hopi tribes of the American Southwest believe that the smell of a menstruous woman is so offensive to a rattlesnake that it will seek her out and bite her.[7] Contrariwise, Makusi women of Guiana are cautioned not to venture into the jungle while menstruating lest they be seduced by amorous serpents.[8] Italian and Greek peasants still warn their daughters at menarche not to wander about the vineyards for fear of attracting snakes.

In Australia the Gunwinggu tribe forbids any menstruating

woman to approach the tribal waterhole, and they caution her especially not to eat water plants and roots. Should the guardian snake of the pool see or smell her, he will first kill her and then abandon the site, depriving her people of precious water.[9] This tribe accords snakes a primary role in human reproduction, for it is the snakes who give the unborn child its soul. They say that a fetus must be built up by five or six ejaculations on successive days, the semen combining with menstrual blood and internally flowing breast milk to form the babe. However, the actual spirit of the child must be provided by the sacred snakes from a supply that they keep temporarily housed in fish, lizards, and tortoises.[10]

In 1965 Mary Woodward, an American collector of Australian art and ethnic material, recorded the creation story of the Liyagalawumirri people as told by Dawidi, an aborigine artist and story teller. The Wawilak sisters walked across the country to Arnheim Land, naming the sun, moon, stars, and all living things as they touched them with their yam-digging sticks. Finally they camped near Mirrimina, home of Yulungurr, the great python. The younger sister profaned his water hole with her menstrual blood, whereupon Yulungurr rose from the depths and swallowed the sisters and their children and kept on swallowing until he had ingested every living thing. Then he rose from the depopulated earth like a great rainbow. In heaven, in conversation with other great pythons, he was overcome by shame for losing his temper. He plunged back to earth and disgorged everything back into its place. The imprint of his fall is a huge triangular ceremonial ground still used by the Liyagalawumirri people.

A widespread belief showing man's mistrust of the female

is the sadistic fantasy of the vagina dentata, the woman who castrates the male during coitus by means of teeth set in her pudendum. In a version of this story from the Tsimshian and Kwakiutl Indian tribes of the northwest Pacific coast, the woman's vulva is a rattlesnake's mouth. Tribal heroes transform her into an ordinary woman by spitting on her genitals.[11]

A different association of snakes and female genitalia comes from the mythology of the Warrau, Akawai, and Makusi tribes of the Pomeroon River basin in Guiana. In this story, Alligator promised to give his daughter to the Sun. However, Alligator had no daughter, so he hastily sculptured a beautiful woman from a wild plum tree, lavishing care on her external charms but neglecting certain essential anatomical features, so that the Sun rejected her. Then a woodpecker was called, and, in return for being fed from the maiden's hand, the bird neatly pecked out the missing parts between her thighs. Alligator completed the project by pulling a snake from her vagina, after which the Sun gladly accepted her for his bride.[12]

An association of women and snakes continues to be strong in man's imagination. On October 20, 1968, a Toronto psychiatrist, Dr. Daniel Cappon, said that the outsized female bust that titillated thousands of girl-watchers on New York's Wall Street recently had the same hypnotic attraction as snakes have. Men are, he contended, fascinated and frightened by snakes and by women's breasts.[13]

Snakes are widely believed to control the fertility of man, his crops, and his domestic animals. This is doubtless because of snakes' physical shape and because large snakes are often found in or near water and thus associated with arable land. Magic rituals involving women with snakes in order to encourage fertility or celebrate successful harvests are widely known. They were customarily observed during the vernal equinox or near the end of summer. Often described as being barbarous and obscene, they were serious religious ceremonies considered essential for human welfare. In India, particularly in Nagpur and along the Malabar Coast, such rituals have persisted into modern times. During the yearly festival of the snakes women encouraged living cobras to penetrate their vaginas in a graphic simulation of the fertility god Siva's union with the mother goddess Shakti. In the 1880s a visitor to Nagpur said: "Rough pictures of snakes in all sorts of shapes and positions are sold and distributed, something after the manner of valentines. In the ones I have seen in days gone by, the position of the women with the snakes were of a most indecent description and left no doubt that, so far as the idea in these sketches was concerned, the cobra was regarded as a phallus." [14]

There are many other associations of mother goddesses with snakes. In Macedonia and classical Greece, snakes were sacred to Demeter. In festivals in her honor, celebrants carried living snakes and images made of paste in the shapes of snakes and phalli.[15] A recently deciphered Sumerian poem of about 4000 B.C. tells how a snake frustrated the goddess Inanna by coiling about the base of a tree which she had carefully cultivated and wished to cut for her couch. The snake could not be charmed away, but Gilgamesh, a prototype of Hercules, slew it.[16] The snake-and-tree motif appears again in Genesis, where Eve probably represents an early Semitic fertility goddess. Coatlicue, the Aztec mother of the gods, is shown with her head fashioned from two great rattlesnake heads and her skirt woven of snakes.[17] The Japanese goddess of connubial bliss, Benten, often manifested herself in the form of a sea snake. She is pictured as being accompanied by a white serpent with the head of an old man who acts as her messenger.[18]

Early man considered death an unnatural event brought about by violence or malignant influences.[19] He noticed that the snake, if left alone, seemed never to die but simply continued to shed its skin and renew its youth. Apparently the snakes who possessed the terrifying secret of sudden death also knew the secret of eternal life. Man wanted not to die, and he searched for some magic or religious formula to avert death. LeBarre suggests that man finally decided that the snake purchased enduring life by ritually sacrificing part of itself—namely, its cast skin. Man observed that his penis not only resembled a snake but had some magic powers of its own, so he excised his foreskin in an effort to emulate the snake and gain immortality.[20] This symbolic act did not win for him his immediate objective, but he was loath to surrender his expectations and eventually rationalized his failure by assuming that God's original plan had gone awry. Clearly He had meant that man should be immortal, but somewhere along the line a serious mistake had occurred, and the snake had cheated man of his birthright.

As to how this came about, mythology provides a variety of stories. The familiar account in Genesis is probably incomplete, for it does not explain what motivated the snake. Frazer, in *The Golden Bough*, concludes that, in the original story, the wily serpent tempts Eve in order to reserve for himself the fruit that conferred the blessing of immortality.[21] Several African tribal myths give a similar explanation of why man dies and snakes live forever. The Wapare people who live near Mount Kilimanjaro say that the snake tempted man to eat eggs, which were forbidden food. God punished man with a great famine, reducing his numbers to two, a young man and a young woman from whom all the generations of the earth are descended.[22] In the region bordering the southeastern shore of Lake Tanganyika, the Wafipa and Wabende tribes say that one day the high god Leza came to earth and asked all living creatures, "Who wishes not to die?" Unfortunately all men and all animals were asleep, except for the clever snake who had anticipated the god's visit. Only he was alert and ready to answer, "I wish never to die." And that is why snakes never die but must be killed. According to Frazer, almost identical stories to explain human mortality are told by the Dusuns of Borneo and the Todja-Toradjas of the Celebes.[23]

A Central American Indian myth shifts the blame to a woman. When the creator was finished with making the world, he was so pleased that he decided to grant all creatures eternal life, first experimenting with the snake and teaching it to rejuvenate itself by casting its skin. Soon he had enough snake skins to make a boat. As he set sail on the eastern sea, he called back to the assemblage on shore, "You will always be young like the snakes." But the woman could not believe her ears and shouted back in a disrespectful voice, "You don't say!" The angered god then testily replied, "You shall all die!" Only the experimental snake lives forever.[24]

When his attempts to win immortality proved unsuccessful, man tried yet another plan to induce the snakes to share their magic with him. He claimed them as kin, making them tribal ancestors. In many cases he chose large constricting snakes, boas and pythons, or, as in the case of the Caribe Indians of the Orinoco valley in Venezuela, the impressive anaconda.[25] However in Africa, India, parts of China and Japan, and North America, he chose venomous antecedents. Wherever the cobra occurs, it was often honored in this manner. In America the rattlesnake was widely respected as an ancestral totem, and many Indians addressed it as "grandfather." [26] In Taiwan the deadly "snake of a hundred designs" (*Agkistrodon acutus*) was adopted by the aboriginal Paiwan people as their maternal ancestor. They say that the first Paiwan chiefs sprang from the eggs of this snake.[27] From Australia comes the story of the "terribly great Wallunqua" of the Murchison Range waterhole. This serpent was 150 miles long and regularly went berserk, ravaging the countryside and urinating billabongs. Warramunga aborigines who claim him for a totemic ancestor are afraid to speak his name. They ritually kill his image to insure tribal increase.[28]

The Australian Aborigines have an appropriate name for the period during which their tribal myths and religious rites evolved. They call it "the dreaming," and say that in the beginning creation's "dreaming" lay in the belly of the fertility mother, Eingana, a rainbow snake.[29]

During man's "dreaming" he saw rivers, rainbows, and lightning as snakes, and snakes as gods, creators, and guardians of hell. Today a majority of the world's people do not see the snake as just an animal but still see it in terms of its ancient charisma. Snakes have been classified, dissected, and explained in terms of evolution and ecology. Their scales and teeth have been counted; their venoms detoxified, chromatographed and fractionated. Yet with all this, the snake remains today the one animal that man universally respects and fears, covertly loves, and intensely hates.

TABLES

REFERENCE NOTES

GLOSSARY

BIBLIOGRAPHY

Tables

~~~~~~

1. Geologic Time Chart of the Evolution of Snakes and Lizards

Period or Epoch	Duration (years before present)	Remarks
Recent	25,000	Reptiles reinvade formerly glaciated parts of Europe and North America
CENOZOIC ERA		
Pleistocene	25,000 to 2 million	Reptile faunas apparently similar to those existing today; northern faunas forced southward by glaciation
Pliocene	2 million to 12 million	Pit vipers present in North America early in this epoch; viper fossils in Europe
Miocene	12 million to 30 million	Major period of snake evolution. Elapids evidently developed early; vipers and pit vipers at least by middle of epoch
Oligocene	30 million to 40 million	Colubrids probably evolved. Oldest fossil of a venomous reptile (*Heloderma*)
Eocene	40 million to 60 million	Boas and pythons the dominant snakes; no fossil evidence of other modern snake families

201

1. Geologic Time Chart (continued)

Period or Epoch	Duration (years before present)	Remarks
Paleocene	60 million to 70 million	Evolution and radiation of boas and other primitive snakes
MESOZOIC ERA		
Cretaceous	70 million to 130 million	Earliest snake fossils from latter part of this period
Jurassic	130 million to 168 million	Lizards appear late in this period
Triassic	168 million to 200 million	Earliest modern reptiles (turtles and crocodiles)

2. Metric System Conversion Table

	Metric system	Approx. U.S. equivalents
meter (m)	1 meter	39.27 inches
centimeter (cm)	0.01 meter	0.39 inch
millimeter (mm)	0.001 meter	0.04 inch
kiloliter (kl)	1 cubic meter	1.31 cubic yards
liter (l)	1,000 cubic centimeters	0.91 quart; 1.06 liquid quarts
centiliter (cl)	10 cubic centimeters	0.61 cubic inch; 0.34 fluid ounce
milliliter (ml)	1 cubic centimeter	0.06 cubic inch; 0.27 fluid dram
gram (g)	1 cubic centimeter	0.035 ounce; 15.43 grains
milligram (mg)	1 cubic millimeter	0.015 grain

3. Scientific Names of Reptiles Mentioned in Text

Adder	*Vipera berus*
death	*Acanthophis antarcticus*
horn	*Bitis caudalis, B. cornuta*
horned puff	*Bitis caudalis*
night	*Causus* species
puff	*Bitis arietans*
Anaconda	*Eunectes murinus*
Beaded lizard, Mexican	*Heloderma horridum*
Bird snake	*Thelotornis kirtlandii*
Blacksnake	
Australian	*Pseudechis porphyriacus*
desert	*Walterinnesia aegyptia*
Black royal snake, *see* Royal snake	
Boa constrictor	*Constrictor constrictor*
Boomslang	*Dispholidus typus*
Brown snake, Australian	*Pseudonaja textilis*
Bushmaster	*Lachesis mutus*
Cat-eyed snake	*Leptodeira* species
Cerastes	*Cerastes cerastes*
Cliff racer, *see* Racer	
Cobra	
Asian	*Naja naja*
Cape	*Naja nivea*
Chinese	*Naja naja atra*
Egyptian	*Naja haje*
forest	*Naja melanoleuca*
Indian	*Naja naja naja*
king	*Ophiophagus hannah*
Philippine	*Naja naja philippinensis*
spitting	*Naja nigricollis*
tree	*Pseudohaje* species
water	*Boulengerina* species

3. Scientific Names of Reptiles Mentioned in Text (continued)

Copperhead	*Agkistrodon contortrix*
Coral snake	
Arizona, or Sonora	*Micruroides euryxanthus*
Brazilian giant	*Micrurus frontalis*
North American	*Micrurus fulvius*
Oriental	*Calliophis* species
slender	*Leptomicrurus* species
Cottonmouth	*Agkistrodon piscivorus*
Crocodile lizard	*Lanthanotus borneensis*
Cuatro narices	*Bothrops atrox*
Dhaman	*Ptyas mucosus*
Dugite	*Pseudonaja nuchalis*
Escorpion	*Heloderma horridum*
False coral snake, South American	*Erythrolamprus* species
Fer-de-lance	*Bothrops lanceolatus;*
	often applied to *B. atrox*
Gecko	
fat-tailed	*Eublepharis macularius*
Texas banded	*Coleonyx brevis*
Gila monster	*Heloderma suspectum*
Glass snake	*Ophisaurus* species
Grass snake	*Natrix natrix*
Green snake	*Opheodrys aestivus*
Habu	*Trimeresurus flavoviridis,*
	T. mucrosquamatus
Chinese	*Trimeresurus mucrosquamatus*
Okinawa	*Trimeresurus flavoviridis*
Hog-nosed snake	*Heterodon platyrhinos*
Hundred-pace snake, *see* Hyappoda	
Hyappoda	*Agkistrodon acutus*
Indigo snake	*Drymarchon corais*
Jararaca	*Bothrops jararaca*

Jararaca pintada	*Bothrops neuwiedi*
Jararacussu	*Bothrops jararacussu*
King snake	*Lampropeltis getulus*
Krait	
banded	*Bungarus fasciatus*
Indian	*Bungarus caeruleus*
many-banded	*Bungarus multicinctus*
sea	*Laticauda colubrina* or *L. laticauda*
Long-glanded snakes	*Maticora* species
Mamba	
black	*Dendroaspis polylepis*
green	*Dendroaspis angusticeps* or *D. viridis*
Massasauga, *see* Rattlesnake, Massasauga	
Mulga snake	*Pseudechis australis*
Mussurana	*Clelia clelia*
Pit viper	
Malay	*Agkistrodon rhodostoma*
Wagler's	*Trimeresurus wagleri*
Python, Indian	*Python molurus*
Racer	
black	*Coluber constrictor priapus*
cliff	*Coluber rhodorachis*
Rattlesnake	
Brazilian	*Crotalus durissus terrificus*
canebrake	*Crotalus horridus atricaudatus*
Central American	*Crotalus durissus durissus* and *C. d. tzabcan*
diamondback	*Crotalus adamanteus* and *C. atrox*
eastern diamondback	*Crotalus adamanteus*
Great Basin	*Crotalus viridis lutosus*
Massasauga	*Sistrurus catenatus*

3. Scientific Names of Reptiles Mentioned in Text (continued)

Mojave	*Crotalus scutulatus*
Pacific	*Crotalus viridis oreganus* and *C. v. helleri*
pigmy	*Sistrurus miliarius*
prairie	*Crotalus viridis viridis*
sidewinder	*Crotalus cerastes*
timber	*Crotalus horridus horridus*
tropical	*Crotalus durissus*
western diamondback	*Crotalus atrox*
Ribbon snake	*Thamnophis proximus*
Ringhals	*Hemachatus haemachatus*
Ringneck snake	*Diadophis punctatus*
River snake, Asian	*Enhydris plumbea*
Royal snake	*Sphalerosophis atriceps*
Salt-marsh snake, Indonesian	*Fordonia leucobalia*
Sand boa, Indian	*Eryx johni*
Sand fish	*Ophiomorus tridactylus*
Sand snake	*Psammophis schokari*
Sea snake	
annulate	*Hydrophis cyanocinctus*
beaked	*Enhydrina schistosa*
pelagic	*Pelamis platurus*
small-headed	*Microcephalophis gracilis*
Skink	
broad-headed	*Eumeces laticeps*
five-lined	*Eumeces fasciatus*
Snake of Asklepios	*Elaphe longissima*
Snake of a hundred designs	*Agkistrodon acutus*
Spotted night snakes	*Hypsiglena* species
Taipan	*Oxyuranus scutellatus*
Terciopelo	*Bothrops atrox*
Tiger snake	*Notechis scutatus*

Tree viper	
Amazon	*Bothrops bilineatus*
Popes'	*Trimeresurus popeorum*
white-lipped	*Trimeresurus albolabris*
Urutu	*Bothrops alternatus*
Vibora de la Cruz, *see* Urutu	
Viper	
asp	*Vipera aspis*
Chinese mountain	*Trimeresurus monticola*
European	*Vipera berus*
eyelash	*Bothrops schlegelii*
Gaboon	*Bitis gabonica*
hognose	*Bothrops nasutus*
horned	*Cerastes cerastes*
jumping	*Bothrops nummifer*
Levantine	*Vipera lebetina*
mole	*Atractaspis* species
Palestine	*Vipera xanthina palaestinae*
Palestine horned	*Pseudocerastes persicus fieldii*
Popes' tree,	
see Tree viper, Popes'	
Russell's	*Vipera russelli*
saw-scaled	*Echis carinatus*
Turkish	*Vipera xanthina xanthina*
white-lipped tree, *see* Tree viper	

4. Reptile Venoms: Yields and Toxicity

Arrangement is by taxonomic classification: lizards, colubrids, elapids, sea snakes, mole vipers, true vipers, pit vipers. Abbreviations (second column

Reptile	Average adult length (inches)	Distribution
LIZARDS		
Gila monster *Heloderma suspectum*	15–18 total; 10–12 body	Arizona (U.S.) and Sonora (Mexico); small areas in adjoining states
COLUBRIDS		
Boomslang *Dispholidus typus*	48–60	Savanna regions of Africa south of the Sahara
ELAPIDS		
Death adder *Acanthophis antarcticus*	18–24	Much of Australia and New Guinea; some nearby islands
Australian brown snake *Pseudonaja textilis*	60–70	Drier areas of Australia and eastern New Guinea
Tiger snake *Notechis scutatus*	50–65	Tasmania and southern half of Australia exclusive of desert
Australian blacksnake *Pseudechis porphyriacus*	60–75	Eastern and southern Australia
Indian krait *Bungarus caeruleus*	36–48	Most of India and Pakistan
Banded krait *Bungarus fasciatus*	50–65	India to southern China south through Malaysia and Indonesia

from right): I-P—intraperitoneal; I-V—intravenous; S-C—subcutaneous. A
list of principal sources is given at the end of the table.

Venom yield (milligrams) average adult specimens	Lethal dose (LD_{50}) in micrograms for 20-gram mouse	Estimated lethal dose for human adult
0.75 to 1.25 ml liquid secretion	80 s-c	Probably about half the yield from an adult lizard, but this quantity very rarely injected in natural bites
4–8	1.2 I-v 250 s-c	Very small, probably 5 mg or less
70–100	5 I-v 10 s-c	About 10 mg. Before development of anti-serum, about 50% of bites fatal
5–10	0.2 I-v 5 s-c	Very small, probably 2–3 mg
35–65	0.8 I-p 3.5 s-c	About 3 mg
30–50	10 I-v 40 s-c	Probably 40–50 mg. Bites are very rarely fatal
8–12	1.8 I-v 9 s-c	Very small, probably 2–3 mg. About 50% of bites fatal even with antivenin treatment
25–50	72 s-c	Difficult to estimate. Bites by this species are almost unknown

4. Reptile Venoms: Yields and Toxicity (*continued*)

Reptile	Average length	Distribution
Eastern green mamba *Dendroaspis angusticeps*	70–90	East Africa
Black mamba *Dendroaspis polylepis*	100–120	East and central Africa
Asian cobra *Naja naja*	45–65	Southern Asia from Iran to Taiwan, the Philippines, and Indonesia
Egyptian cobra *Naja haje*	60–70	Much of Africa, exclusive of rain forest and extreme desert; small areas in Saudi Arabia
Spitting cobra *Naja nigricollis*	60–70	Most of Africa except for the Sahara and southern tip
King cobra *Ophiophagus hannah*	90–150	Southeast Asia from India to the Philippines and Indonesia
Ringhals *Hemachatus haemachatus*	40–50	South Africa
Brazilian giant coral snake *Micrurus frontalis*	40–48	Southwest Brazil, Paraguay, adjacent Argentina, Bolivia, and Uruguay
North American coral snake *Micrurus fulvius*	23–32	Coastal North Carolina to west Texas (U.S.); northeast Mexico
Black-banded coral snake *Micrurus nigrocinctus*	25–37	Southern Mexico to northern Colombia

Venom yield	Lethal dose (mouse)	Estimated lethal dose for human adult
60–95	26 I-V 61 S-C	About 15 mg
	5 I-V 5.5 S-C	About 10–15 mg. Close to 100% fatality rate in untreated cases
150–200	3–8 I-V 4–8 I-P 3–9 S-C	About 15–20 mg
175–300	19 I-V 35 S-C	Probably a little less toxic than the venom of the Asian cobra
200–350	23 I-V 61 S-C	Lethal dose probably 40–50 mg
350–450	34 S-C	Probably slightly less toxic than the venom of the Asian cobra. Very few bites reported
80–120	22 I-V 52 S-C	Lethal dose probably 50–60 mg. These snakes usually "spit"; rarely bite
20–30	50 S-C	Apparently less toxic than venom of North American coral snake
3–5	20 I-P 26 S-C	Lethal dose probably 4–5 mg
	62 S-C	Apparently less toxic than venom of North American coral snake

4. Reptile Venoms: Yields and Toxicity (*continued*)

Reptile	Average length	Distribution
SEA SNAKES		
Erabu sea snake	36–50	China and Philippine seas to
Laticauda semifasciata		Fiji and Samoa
Annulated sea snake	54–66	Persian Gulf to Sea of Japan
Hydrophis cyanocinctus		and Java Sea
Beaked sea snake	36–50	South Asian waters from
Enhydrina schistosa		Arabian Sea to Coral Sea
Hardwicke's sea snake	25–30	Gulf of Siam to Coral Sea
Lapemis hardwickii		
MOLE VIPERS		
Northern mole viper	20–24	Savannas of north and west
Atractaspis microlepidota		Africa; southwest Saudi Arabia
TRUE VIPERS		
Rhombic night adder	22–28	Most of Africa south of the
Causus rhombeatus		Sahara
Puff adder	35–50	Africa, exclusive of rain forest
Bitis arietans		and extreme desert; parts of
		Arabian peninsula
Gaboon viper	50–60	Rain forest regions of tropical
Bitis gabonica		Africa
Cerastes; horned viper	20–25	Saharan region of Africa; parts
Cerastes cerastes		of Middle East; Arabian
		peninsula

Venom yield	Lethal dose (mouse)	Estimated lethal dose for human adult
2–3	10 s-c	No bites known. Not thought to be a dangerous species
5–9	7 i-v 4.8 i-p 13 s-c	Lethal dose probably about 4–5 mg
10–15	2.5 i-v 2.3 i-p 3.0 s-c	Lethal dose estimated as 1.5 mg
1.5–2	4 i-v 5.5 i-p	Lethal dose probably about 2 mg
5–10	90 s-c	Lethal dose probably about 10–12 mg
20–30	185 i-v 300 s-c	Not considered capable of inflicting a fatal bite on an adult
60–200	7 i-v 73 i-p 155 s-c	Lethal dose 90–100 mg
50–600	14 i-v 250 s-c	Generally considered somewhat more toxic than puff-adder venom
20–45	10 i-v 300 s-c	Lethal dose 40–50 mg. Fatal bites uncommon

4. Reptile Venoms: Yields and Toxicity (*continued*)

Reptile	Average length	Distribution
Saw-scaled viper *Echis carinatus*	16–22	Northern and western Africa to drier parts of India
European viper *Vipera berus*	19–24	Most of Europe and across northern Asia to North Korea
Levantine viper *Vipera lebetina*	30–45	Middle East and Russian Asia to Kashmir
Russell's viper *Vipera russelli*	40–50	West Pakistan to Taiwan
PIT VIPERS		
Malay pit viper *Agkistrodon rhodostoma*	23–32	Thailand to Vietnam, south to Java and Sumatra
Cottonmouth *Agkistrodon piscivorus*	30–45	Southern U.S. in lowlands to central Texas and southern Missouri
Copperhead *Agkistrodon contortrix*	24–36	Eastern U.S. to southeast Nebraska and western Texas
Terciopelo; fer-de-lance *Bothrops atrox*	45–70	Mexico to northern Argentina in moist lowlands
Urutu; vibora de la Cruz *Bothrops alternatus*	35–45	Southern Brazil, northern Argentina, Uruguay, Paraguay

Venom yield	Lethal dose (mouse)	Estimated lethal dose for human adult
20–35	24 I-V 131 S-C	Unusually toxic for man. Lethal dose may be as small as 3–5 mg
10–18	11 I-V 16 I-P 129 S-C	Lethal dose 20–25 mg
75–150	320 S-C	Lethal dose 70–75 mg
130–250	1.6 I-V 95 S-C	Lethal dose 65–70 mg
40–60	124 I-V 467 S-C	Lethal dose 50–60 mg. About 2% of bites are fatal
100–150	80 I-V 102 I-P 516 S-C	Lethal dose 100–150 mg
40–70	218 I-V 127 I-P 512 S-C	Lethal dose probably 100 mg or more. About 0.3% of bites are fatal
100–200	85 I-V 76 I-P 440 S-C	Lethal dose 50–60 mg
60–100	257 S-C	Lethal dose 50–60 mg. About 40% of bites by adult snakes believed potentially fatal if untreated

4. Reptile Venoms: Yields and Toxicity (*continued*)

Reptile	Average length	Distribution
Jararaca *Bothrops jararaca*	40–50	Southeastern Brazil, adjacent Argentina and Paraguay
Hognose viper *Bothrops nasuta*	16–23	Southern Mexico to northern South America
Eyelash viper *Bothrops schlegelii*	17–25	Guatemala to northern South America in forest
White-lipped tree viper *Trimeresurus albolabris*	16–25	Eastern Pakistan to southeastern China; south to Sunda Islands
Okinawa habu *Trimeresurus flavoviridis*	50–60	Larger islands of Ryukyu group
Wagler's pit viper *Trimeresurus wagleri*	30–35	Islands and peninsulas of southeastern Asia
Bushmaster *Lachesis mutus*	70–100	Southern Nicaragua to the Amazon Basin
Western diamondback rattlesnake *Crotalus atrox*	35–65	Southwestern U.S.—Arkansas to southern California; northern Mexico
Timber rattlesnake *Crotalus horridus*	35–55	Eastern U.S. to Minnesota and central Texas
Pacific rattlesnake *Crotalus viridis helleri*	30–48	Southern California exclusive of desert areas; Baja California (Mexico)

Venom yield	Lethal dose (mouse)	Estimated lethal dose for human adult
40–70	12–33 I-V 41–141 S-C	Lethal dose probably 40–50 mg. About 18% of bites by adult snakes believed potentially fatal if untreated
12–25	733 S-C	Not believed capable of inflicting a fatal bite on an adult
10–20	663 S-C	Probably more toxic for man than most *Bothrops* venoms
8–15	7.5 I-V 255 S-C	Not believed capable of inflicting a fatal bite on an adult
	85 I-V 546 S-C	Lethal dose believed to be comparatively large. About 3% of bites are fatal
65–90	15 I-V 71 I-P 92 S-C	No well-documented reports of fatal bites
300–500	738 S-C	Lethal dose believed to be large—probably 125–150 mg
200–300	62–84 I-V 54–168 I-P 150–385 S-C	Lethal dose believed to be about 100 mg
100–200	52–62 I-V 14–145 I-P 161–183 S-C	Lethal dose believed to be 75–100 mg
75–160	26 I-V 32 I-P 71 S-C	Lethal dose 50–70 mg

4. Reptile Venoms: Yields and Toxicity (continued)

Reptile	Average length	Distribution
Mojave rattlesnake *Crotalus scutulatus*	30–40	Western Texas to southern California; northern and central Mexico
Sidewinder *Crotalus cerastes*	18–25	Southwestern U.S. and northwestern Mexico in deserts
Brazilian rattlesnake *Crotalus durissus terrificus*	40–50	Southeastern Brazil; adjacent parts of Argentina and Paraguay
Massasauga rattlesnake *Sistrurus catenatus*	18–28	Great Lakes region (U.S.) southwest to eastern Arizona
Pigmy rattlesnake *Sistrurus miliarius*	15–22	Southeastern U.S. west to Missouri and eastern Texas

Principal Sources of Data

BELLUOMINI, HELIO. "Extraction and Quantities of Venom Obtained from Some Brazilian Snakes," in W. Bücherl, E. E. Buckley, and V. Deulofeu, eds., *Venomous Animals and Their Venoms* (New York: Academic Press, 1968), pp. 101–106.

BÜCHERL, WOLFGANG. "Über die Ermittlung von Durchschnitt und Höchst-Giftmengen bei den häufigsten Giftschlangen Sudamerikas," in Behringwerke Mitteilungen, *Die Giftschlangen der Erde* (Marburg/Lahn, West Germany: N. G. Elwert, 1963), pp. 94–114, tables 1–17.

CHRISTENSEN, POUL A. *South African Snake Venoms and Antivenoms* (Johannesburg: The South African Institute for Medical Research, 1953), pp. 4–10, tables 1–2.

———. "The Venoms of Central and South African Snakes," in Bücherl, Buckley, and Deulofeu, *op. cit.,* pp. 442–443, table 1.

Venom yield	Lethal dose (mouse)	Estimated lethal dose for human adult
50–90	4.2 I-V 4.6 I-P 6.2 S-C	Lethal dose small, probably 10–15 mg
25–35	52 I-V 110 S-C	Lethal dose probably 40–50 mg. Very few fatal cases known
20–40	2.5 I-V 8.5–12 S-C	Estimated lethal dose 10 mg. About 60% of bites by adult snakes presumed fatal if untreated
25–35	4.4 I-P 105 S-C	Estimated lethal dose 30–40 mg
20–30	485 S-C	Not believed capable of inflicting a fatal bite on an adult

FAIRLEY, N. H., and SPLATT, B. "Venom Yields in Australian Poisonous Snakes," *Medical Journal of Australia,* I (1929), 336–348.

KLAUBER, LAURENCE M. *Rattlesnakes* (Berkeley: University of California Press, 1956), II, 764–779, tables 11:2–11:8.

MINTON, SHERMAN A., JR. Unpublished data.

REID, H. A. "Sea-Snake Bite Research," *Transactions of the Royal Society of Tropical Medicine and Hygiene,* L (1956), 517–542.

SCHÖTTLER, W. H. A. "Toxicity of the Principal Snake Venoms of Brazil," *Journal of Tropical Medicine,* XXXI (1951), 489–499.

U.S. NAVY BUREAU OF MEDICINE AND SURGERY. *Poisonous Snakes of the World* (Washington, D.C.: Government Printing Office, 2nd ed., 1968), table 1.

5. Some Important Enzymes of Reptile Venoms

Distribution and Sources	*Biological Activity and Toxicity*

PROTEINASES

High in most pit vipers and vipers of genus *Bitis*. Small amounts probably in all reptile venoms. Good sources: puff adder, cottonmouth, hundred-pace snake, terciopelo	Break down proteins and aid snakes in digestion of their food. Largely responsible for the local necrosis and hemorrhage seen in snakebites and for the effects of the venom on blood clotting

HYALURONIDASE

Probably in all reptile venoms. Good sources: gila monster, Indian krait, Eastern diamondback rattlesnake, asp viper	Dissolves the gel surrounding normal tissue cells and fibers, thus speeding absorption of the toxic components of venom

L-AMINO ACID OXIDASE

Presence correlated with yellow color of venom; absent in sea snakes, some elapids, a few vipers, most very young snakes. Good sources: Levantine viper, cottonmouth, Chinese habu	A versatile enzyme attacking many different substances but without intrinsic toxicity. Presumed to be important in the digestive function of venom; may activate other venom components

CHOLINESTERASE

In all elapid venoms, questionable in sea snakes, none or only traces in vipers. Good sources: forest cobra, Indian krait, banded krait	Inactivates acetylcholine, a substance essential for nerve-impulse transmission. Not directly implicated in the neurotoxic action of venoms; function remains obscure

PHOSPHOLIPASE A

Probably in all reptile venoms.	Reacts with lecithin, a component of

5. Some Important Enzymes of Reptile Venoms (continued)

Distribution and Sources	*Biological Activity and Toxicity*
Good sources: horned puff adder, black mamba, spitting cobra, mulga snake, cottonmouth	cellular and intracellular membranes, to form substances that alter the permeability of these membranes and release histamine from tissues. May play a part in the production of hemorrhage and shock by venoms

RIBONUCLEASE

In all snake venoms tested. Good sources: Asian cobra, Russell's viper, Gaboon viper	Breaks down ribonucleic acid (RNA), the substance responsible for directing protein synthesis in cells. Role of ribonuclease in venom unknown

DEOXYRIBONUCLEASE

In all snake venoms tested. Good sources: forest cobra, Gaboon viper, eastern diamondback rattlesnake	Breaks down deoxyribonucleic acid (DNA), the hereditary material of the cell. Role of deoxyribonuclease in venom unknown

5'-NUCLEOTIDASE

In all snake venoms tested. Good sources: timber rattlesnake, terciopelo, Gaboon viper	Breaks down certain phosphorus-containing compounds (adenosine-5-phosphoric acid and inosine-5-phosphoric acid) essential for energy production in cells. Function in venom poisoning obscure

PHOSPHOMONESTERASE

In many elapid venoms, a few viper venoms. Good sources: Asian cobra, Egyptian cobra, Wagler's pit viper.	Breaks down certain phosphorus-containing compounds in cell nuclei. Role in venom poisoning obscure

5. Some Important Enzymes of Reptile Venoms (concluded)

Distribution and Sources   *Biological Activity and Toxicity*

PHOSPHODIESTERASE	
Probably in all reptile venoms. Good sources: terciopelo, Russell's viper, eastern diamondback rattlesnake, Egyptian cobra	Breaks down certain phosphorus-containing compounds in cell nuclei and may contribute to production of substances responsible for fall of blood pressure in venom poisoning
ADENOSINE TRIPHOSPHATASE	
Probably in all snake venoms. Good sources: Gaboon viper, Russell's viper, eastern diamondback rattlesnake	Destroys adenosine triphosphate (AIP), the main source of energy for chemical reactions in cells. May play a part in the production of shock and rapid immobilization of prey by venom

Note: Only a comparatively few reptile venoms have been thoroughly investigated with respect to their enzymes and other biochemical properties. Venoms of many species and even groups of species have received little or no study by biochemists. Helpful as an introduction to the field are:

BOQUET, PAUL. "Venins de Serpents: Ière Partie—Physio-pathologie de l'envenimation et Propriétés Biologiques des Venins," *Toxicon,* II (1964), 5–42; "IIème Partie—Constitution Chimique des Venins de Serpents et Immunité Antivenimeuse," *ibid.,* III (1966), 243–279.

RUSSELL, FINDLAY E. "Pharmacology of Animal Venoms," *Clinical Pharmacology and Therapeutics,* VIII (1967), 849–873.

SARKAR, N. K., and DEVI, ANIMA. "Enzymes in Snake Venoms," in W. Bücherl, E. E. Buckley, and V. Deulofeu, eds., *Venomous Animals and Their Venoms* (New York: Academic Press, 1968), pp. 167–227.

ZELLER, E. A. "Enzymes as Essential Components of Bacterial and Animal Toxins," in James B. Sumner and Karl Myrback, eds. *The Enzymes* (New York: Academic Press, 1951), I, 986–1013.

———. "Enzymes of Snake Venoms and Their Biological Significance," *Advances in Enzymology,* VIII (1948), 459–495.

Reference Notes

CHAPTER ONE: Evolution, Classification, Distribution

1. Carl Gans, "The Feeding Mechanism of Snakes and Its Possible Evolution," *American Zoologist,* I (1961), 217–227.

2. Angus Bellairs and Garth Underwood, "The Origin of Snakes," *Biological Reviews, Cambridge Philosophical Society,* XXVI (1951), 193–237.

3. Hymen Marx and George B. Rabb, "Relationships and Zoogeography of the Viperine Snakes (Family Viperidae), *Fieldiana Zoology,* XLIV (1965), 161–206.

4. Bayard H. Brattstrom, "Evolution of the Pit Vipers," *Transactions of the San Diego Society of Natural History,* XIII (1964), 185–268.

5. Charles W. Gilmore, "Fossil Lizards of North America," *Memoirs of the National Academy of Sciences,* XXII (1928), 1–201.

6. Aaron Taub, "Systematic Implications from the Labial Glands of the Colubridae," *Herpetologica,* XXIII (1967), 145–148.

7. Raymond B. Cowles, "Evidence of Venom in *Hypsiglena ochrorhynchus*," *Copeia,* No. 1 (1941), 4–6.

8. Charles M. Bogert, "Dentitional Phenomena in Cobras and Other Elapids with Notes on Adaptive Modifications of Fangs," *Bulletin of the American Museum of Natural History,* LXXXI (1943), 285–360.

9. Laurence M. Klauber, *Rattlesnakes* (2 vols. Berkeley, Calif.: University of California Press, 1956), I, 369–373.

10. *Ibid.,* I, 219–244.

11. Charles M. Bogert and Rafael Martin del Campo, "The Gila Mon-

ster and Its Allies," *Bulletin of the American Museum of Natural History,* CIX (1956), 151–154.

CHAPTER TWO: Venom Glands and Venom Secretion

1. Aaron M. Taub, "Ophidian Cephalic Glands," *Journal of Morphology,* CXVIII (1966), 529–542.
2. Carl Gans and Elazar Kochva, "The Accessory Gland in the Venom Apparatus of Viperid Snakes," *Toxicon,* III (1965), 61–63.
3. Elazar Kochva and Carl Gans, "The Venom Gland of *Vipera palaestinae* with Comments on the Glands of Some Other Viperines," *Acta Anatomica,* LXII (1965), 365–401.
4. Elazar Kochva and Carl Gans, "Histology and Histochemistry of the Venom Gland of Some Crotaline Snakes," *Copeia,* No. 3 (1966), 506–515.
5. Joseph F. Gennaro, A. H. Anton, and D. F. Sayre, "The Fine Structure of Pit Viper Venom and Additional Observations on the Role of Aromatic Amines in the Physiology of the Pit Viper," *Comparative Biochemistry and Physiology,* XXV (1968), 285–298.
6. Herbert I. Rosenberg, "Histology, Histochemistry and Emptying Mechanism of the Venom Glands of Some Elapid Snakes," *Journal of Morphology,* CXXIII (1967), 133–156.
7. Aaron M. Taub, "Comparative Histological Studies on Duvernoy's Gland of Colubrid Snakes," *Bulletin of the American Museum of Natural History,* CXXXVIII (1967), 1–50.
8. Marie Phisalix, *Animaux Venimeux et Venins* ("Venomous Animals and Venoms") (Paris: Masson et Cie., 1922), II, 188–195.
9. P. J. Deoras, "Studies on Bombay Snakes: Snake Farm Venom Yield Records and Their Probable Significance," in H. L. Keegan and W. V. Macfarlane, eds., *Venomous and Poisonous Animals and Noxious Plants of the Pacific Region* (Oxford: Pergamon Press, Inc., 1963), 337–349.
10. Mahmood Latifi and K. D. Shamloo, "Characteristic Electrophoretic Patterns of Serum Proteins of Several Species of Snakes of Iran," *Canadian Journal of Biochemistry,* XLIII (1965), 459–461.

11. Elazar Kochva, "A Quantitative Study of Venom Secretion by *Vipera palaestinae*," *American Journal of Tropical Medicine and Hygiene*, IX (1960), 381–390.
12. Joseph F. Gennaro, R. S. Leopold, and T. W. Merriam, "Observations on the Actual Quantity of Venom Introduced by Several Species of Crotalid Snakes in Their Bite," *Anatomical Record*, CXXXIX (1961), 303.
13. Clifford H. Pope, "Fatal Bite of Captive African Rear-fanged Snake (*Dispholidus*)," *Copeia*, No. 4 (1958), 280–282.

CHAPTER THREE: Properties and Composition of Venoms

1. The most important works relative to this controversy are: M. Charas, *New Experiments upon Vipers* (London, 1670), 1–223; Francisco Redi, *Osservazioni Intorno alle Vipere* (Florence, 1664), 1–91; Felice Fontana, *Treatise on the Venom of the Viper*, trans. J. Skinner (2 vols. London, 1787).
2. Elazar Kochva, "A Quantitative Study of Venom Secretion by *Vipera palaestinae*," *American Journal of Tropical Medicine and Hygiene*, IX (1960), 381–390.
3. Laurence M. Klauber, *Rattlesnakes* (2 vols. Berkeley, Calif.: University of California Press, 1956), II, 786.
4. Henry M. Parrish and Robert E. Thompson, "Human Envenomation from Bites of Recently Milked Rattlesnakes," *Copeia*, No. 2 (1958), 83–86.
5. Cited by Klauber, *op. cit.*, II, 778.
6. Werner Schöttler, "Toxicity of the Principal Snake Venoms of Brazil," *The Journal of Tropical Medicine*, XXXI (1951), table II, p. 497.
7. Nigel O. Wolff and Thomas S. Githens, "Record Venom Extraction from Water Moccasin," *Copeia*, No. 1 (1939), 52.
8. Klauber, *op. cit.*, II, 778.
9. Poul A. Christensen, *South African Snake Venoms and Antivenoms* (Johannesburg: The South African Institute for Medical Research, 1955), p. 4.

10. E. Grasset, "La Vipère du Gabon" ("The Gaboon Viper"), *Acta Tropica,* III (1946), 101.

11. Christensen, *loc. cit.*

12. Eric Worrell, *Reptiles of Australia* (Sydney: Angus and Robertson, Ltd., 1963), p. 137.

13. H. Alistair Reid, "Sea-Snake Bite Research," *Transactions of the Royal Society of Tropical Medicine and Hygiene,* L (1956), table II, p. 525.

14. Christensen, *loc. cit.*

15. O. N. Arrington, "Notes on the Two Poisonous Lizards with Special Reference to *Heloderma suspectum,*" *Bulletin of the Antivenin Institute of America,* IV (1930), 32–33.

16. Christensen, *op. cit.,* p. 5.

17. Wolfgang Bücherl, "Über die Ermittlung von Durchschnitt und Höchst-Giftmengen bei den häufigsten Giftschlangen Sudamerikas" ("Ascertainment of the Average and Highest Quantities of Venom from the Commonest Poisonous Snakes of South America"), in Behringwerke Mitteilungen, *Die Giftschlangen der Erde* ("The Poisonous Snakes of the World"). (Marburg/Lahn, West Germany: N. G. Elwert, 1963), tables XVI and XVII, pp. 112–113.

18. M. Freeman and C. H. Kellaway, "The Venom Yields of Common Australian Poisonous Snakes in Captivity," *Medical Journal of Australia,* II (1934), 375.

19. Walter Kocholaty and Billy D. Ashley, "Detoxification of Russell's Viper and Water Moccasin Venoms by Photooxidation," *Toxicon,* III (1966), 187–194.

20. Cited by R. Norris Wolfenden, "On the Nature and Action of the Venom of Poisonous Snakes," *Journal of Physiology,* VII (1886), p. 327.

21. *Ibid.,* p. 363.

22. Karl Slotta and Heinz Fraenkl-Conrat, "Two Active Proteins from Rattlesnake Venom," *Nature,* CXLII (1938), 213.

23. J. Moura Gonçalves, "Purification and Properties of Crotamine," in E. E. Buckley and N. Porges, eds., *Venoms* (Washington, D.C.:

American Association for the Advancement of Science, 1956), 261–274.

24. B. Ghosh, S. S. De, and D. K. Chowdhuri, "Separation of the Neurotoxin from the Crude Cobra Venom and Study of the Action of a Number of Reducing Agents upon It," *Indian Journal of Medical Research*, XXIX (1941), 367–373.

25. C. C. Chang and C. Y. Lee, "Isolation of Neurotoxins from the Venom of *Bungarus multicinctus* and Their Modes of Neuromuscular Blocking Action," *Archives International Pharmacodynamics*, CXLIV (1963), 241–257.

26. Z. Styblova and F. Kornalik, "Enzymatic Properties of *Heloderma suspectum* Venom," *Toxicon*, V (1967), 139–140.

CHAPTER FOUR: Lethal Qualities of Venoms

1. M. Annaei Lucani, *Belli Civilis* ("Civil War"), ed. A. E. Housman (Oxford: Blackwell, 1926), Vol. X, 280–281.

2. David I. Macht and Dorothy Kehoe, "The Toxicity of Snake Venoms after Administration by Stomach," *Federation Proceedings*, II (1943), 31.

3. Sherman A. Minton, Jr., "Variation in Venom Samples from Copperheads (*Agkistrodon contortrix mokeson*) and Timber Rattlesnakes (*Crotalus horridus horridus*)," *Copeia*, No. 4 (1953), 212–215.

4. Sherman A. Minton, Jr., "Observations on Toxicity and Antigenic Makeup of Venoms from Juvenile Snakes," in F. E. Russell and P. R. Saunders, eds., *Animal Toxins* (Oxford: Pergamon Press, Inc., 1967), 211–222.

5. S. Schenberg, "Geographical Pattern of Crotamine Distribution in the Same Rattlesnake Species," *Science*, CXXIX (1959), 1361–1365.

6. Donald B. Voghtman, "The Relative Efficiency of Two Types of Antivenom Sera in Neutralizing Cobra Venom," *Copeia*, No. 3 (1950), 225–228.

7. Werner H. A. Schöttler, "Problems of Antivenin Standardization," *Bulletin of the World Health Organization*, V (1952), 293–320.

8. Findlay E. Russell and Ronaldine Eventov, "Lethality of Crude and Lyophilized *Crotalus* Venom," *Toxicon,* II (1964), 81–82.
9. Helio E. Belluomini, "Extraction and Quantities of Venom Obtained from Some Brazilian Snakes," in W. Bücherl, E. Buckley, and V. Deulofeu, eds., *Venomous Animals and Their Venoms* (New York: Academic Press, 1968), 97–117.
10. Walker Van Riper, "How a Rattlesnake Strikes," *Scientific American,* CLXXXIX (October 1953), 100–102.

CHAPTER FIVE: When Snake Bites Man

1. William Plomer, "In the Snake Park," from *Collected Poems* (London: Jonathan Cape Ltd.). The poem first appeared in *The New Yorker,* September 12, 1959.
2. In this connection see: Henry M. Parrish, J. C. Goldner, and S. L. Silberg, "Poisonous Snakebites Causing No Venenation," *Postgraduate Medicine,* XXXIX (1966), 265–269; C. H. Campbell, "Venomous Snake Bite in Papua and Its Treatment," *Transactions of the Royal Society of Tropical Medicine and Hygiene,* LVIII (1967), 263–273; H. Alistair Reid, "Epidemiology of Snake Bite in North Malaya," *British Medical Journal,* I (1963), 992–997; H. Hadar and S. Gitter, "The Results of Treatment with Pasteur Antiserum in Cases of Snake Bite," *Harefuah,* LVI (1959), 1–4.
3. Archie F. Carr, "A Naturalist at Large," *Natural History,* LXXVIII (March, 1969), 18–24, 68–70.
4. Carl F. Kauffeld, "More at Home with Cobras," *Philadelphia Herpetological Society Bulletin,* XI (1963), 13–18.
5. Gary K. Clarke, "Report on a Bite by a Red Diamond Rattlesnake," *Copeia,* No. 4 (1961), 418–422.
6. Newton C. McCollough and Joseph F. Gennaro, "Evaluation of Venomous Snake Bite in the Southern United States," *Journal of the Florida Medical Association,* XLIX (1963), 959–967.
7. Clifford H. Pope, "Fatal Bite of Captive African Rear-fanged Snake, *Dispholidus,*" *Copeia,* No. 4 (1958), 280–282.

8. H. Alistair Reid, "Diagnosis, Prognosis and Treatment of Sea-Snake Bite," *The Lancet,* August 19, 1961, pp. 399–402.
9. H. Alistair Reid, "Antivene Reaction Following Accidental Sea-Snake Bite," *British Medical Journal,* II (1957), 26–29.
10. Charles M. Bogert and Rafael Martin del Campo, "The Gila Monster and Its Allies," *Bulletin of the American Museum of Natural History,* CIX (1956), 168–194.

CHAPTER SIX: Snakebite Around the World

1. Sitya Swaroop and B. Grab, "Snakebite Mortality in the World," *Bulletin of the World Health Organization,* X (1954), 35–76.
2. Henry M. Parrish, "Incidence of Treated Snakebites in the United States," *Public Health Reports,* LXXXI (1966), 269–276.
3. Henry M. Parrish, "Mortality from Snakebites, United States, 1950–54," *Public Health Reports,* LXXII (1957), 1027–1030.
4. Nicholas P. Christy, ed., "Combined Staff Clinic: Poisoning by Venomous Animals," *American Journal of Medicine,* XLII (1967), 114–118.
5. H. Tallqvist and K. Osterlund, "Huggormsbett" ("Adder-bite"), *Nordisk Medicin,* LXVIII (1962), 1073–1077.
6. T. C. Morton, "Adder-bites in Cornwall," *British Medical Journal,* II (1960), 373–376.
7. M. Leffkowitz, "On Bites and Stings in Israel," *Folia Medicina,* XXI (1962), 5–8.
8. Joseph Fayrer, "The Venomous Snakes of India and the Mortality Caused by Them," *British Medical Journal,* II (1892), 620.
9. Swaroop and Grab, *op. cit.,* pp. 57–62.
10. P. J. Deoras, *Snakes of India* (New Delhi: National Book Trust India, 1965), p. 1.
11. Swaroop and Grab, *op. cit.,* p. 63–66.
12. Michel Barme, "Venomous Sea Snakes of Viet Nam and Their Venoms," in Hugh L. Keegan and W. V. Macfarlane, eds., *Venomous and Poisonous Animals and Noxious Plants of the Pacific Region* (Oxford: Pergamon Press, Inc., 1963), p. 373.

13. Y. Sawai, Y. Kawamura, I. Ebihara, T. Okonogi, Z. Hokama, and M. Yamakawa, "Studies on the Improvement of Treatment of Habu (*Trimeresurus flavoviridis*) Bites: 7. Habu Bites on the Amami and Ryukyu Islands in 1964," *Japanese Journal of Experimental Medicine,* XXXVII (1967), 51–61.

14. Arturo Reyes and Carl Lamanna, "Snakebite Mortality in the Philippines," *Philippine Journal of Science,* LXXXIV (1955), 189–194.

15. Quoted by Jean Phillippe Vogel, *Indian Serpent Lore* (London: Arthur Probsthain, 1926), p. 1.

16. F. Kopstein, "*Bungarus javanicus,* een nieuwe Javaansche Giftslang. Mededelling over een doodelijke Bungarusbeet" (". . . a New Javanese Poisonous Snake. Account of a Fatal Krait Bite"), *Gneeskunde Tijdschrift Nederland-Indies,* LXXII (1932), 136–140.

17. M. L. Ahuja and Gurkirpal Singh, "Snake Bite in India," *Indian Journal of Medical Research,* XLII (1954), 661–680.

18. Frank Wall, *Snakes of Ceylon* (Colombo, Ceylon: Government Printer, 1921), p. 439.

19. M. W. F. Tweedie, *The Snakes of Malaya* (Singapore: Government Printing Office, 1954), p. 100.

20. G. W. Vidal, "A List of the Venomous Snakes of North Kanara Showing the Influence of *Echis carinata* on the Death-rate of the Bombay Presidency," *Journal of the Bombay Natural History Society,* V (1890), 64–71.

21. H. Alistair Reid, "Epidemiology of Snake Bite in North Malaya," *British Medical Journal,* I (1963), 992–997.

22. Malcolm A. Smith, *Monograph of the Sea-Snakes* (London: Taylor and Francis, 1926), p. xiii.

23. Swaroop and Grab, *op. cit.,* pp. 49–55.

24. Emmett R. Dunn, "Relative Abundance of Some Panamanian Snakes," *Ecology,* XXX (1949), 39–57.

25. Swaroop and Grab, *op. cit.,* pp. 39–43.

26. Norman L. Corkill, "Snake Poisoning in the Sudan," in E. E. Buckley and N. Porges, eds., *Venoms* (Washington, D.C.: American Association for the Advancement of Science, 1956), pp. 331–339.

27. David S. Chapman, "The Symptomatology, Pathology and Treatment

of the Bites of Venomous Snakes of Central and Southern Africa," in W. Bücherl, E. E. Buckley, and V. Deulofeu, eds., *Venomous Animals and Their Venoms* (New York: Academic Press, 1968), pp. 467–476.

28. Jean Doucet, "Les Serpents de la République de Côte d'Ivoire ("Snakes of the Ivory Coast"), *Acta Tropica,* XX (1963), pp. 212–213.

29. G. Salou, "Envenimation par *Echis carinatus* dans la Région de Sokode (Nord-Togo) ("Poisoning by *Echis carinatus* in the Region of Sokode [North Togo]"), *Médecine Tropique,* XI (1951), 655–660.

30. Walter Rose, *Snakes—Mainly South African* (Cape Town: Maskew Miller, Ltd., 1955), p. 105.

31. Chapman, *op. cit.,* pp. 468–469.

32. Swaroop and Grab, *op. cit.,* pp. 71–72.

33. N. Hamilton Fairley, "The Present Position of Snake Bite and the Snake Bitten in Australia," *Medical Journal of Australia,* I (1929), 296–311.

34. C. C. Reid and H. Flecker, "Snake Bite by a Taipan with Recovery," *Medical Journal of Australia,* I (1950), 82–85.

CHAPTER SEVEN: Immunity to Snake Venoms

1. Raymond Sanders, "Effects of Venom Injections in Rattlesnakes," *Herpetologica,* VII (1951), 47–52.

2. A. A. Nichol, V. Douglas, and L. Peck, "On the Immunity of Rattlesnakes to Their Venom," *Copeia,* No. 4 (1933), 211–213.

3. Henry S. Fitch, "Autecology of the Copperhead," *University of Kansas Publications Museum of Natural History,* XIII (1960), 85–288.

4. Paul Boquet, "Sur les Propriétés Antivenimeuses du Sérum de *Vipera aspis*" (On the Venom-Neutralizing Properties of the Serum of *Vipera aspis*"), *Annales de l'Institut Pasteur,* Paris, LXXI (1945), 340–345.

5. C. H. Kellaway, "The Immunity of Australian Snakes to Their Own Venoms," *Medical Journal of Australia,* II (1931), 35–53.

6. T. R. Fraser, "Address on Immunisation against Serpent's Venom and the Treatment of Snake Bites with Antivenene," *British Medical Journal,* I (1896), 957–960.
7. Eric Phillips, "Coral versus False Coral—No Survivors," *Bulletin of the Philadelphia Herpetological Society,* X (1962), 31.
8. Raymond B. Cowles, "Unusual Defense Postures Assumed by Rattlesnakes," *Copeia,* No. 1 (1938), 13–16.
9. V. B. Philpot and R. G. Smith, "Neutralization of Pit Viper Venom by King Snake Serum," *Proceedings of the Society for Experimental Biology and Medicine,* LXXIV (1950), 521–523.
10. Albert Tyler, "An Auto-Antivenin in the Gila Monster and Its Relation to a Concept of Natural Auto-Antibodies," in E. E. Buckley and N. Porges, eds., *Venoms* (Washington, D.C.: American Association for the Advancement of Science, 1956), 65–74.
11. E. Grasset, A. Zoutendyk, and A. W. Schaafsma, "Studies on the Toxic and Antigenic Properties of South African Snake Venoms with Special Reference to the Polyvalency of South African Antivenene," *Transactions of the Royal Society of Tropical Medicine and Hygiene,* XXVIII (1935), 601–612.
12. *Ibid.*
13. J. Vellard, "Résistance de Quelques Espèces Animales au Venin de Serpent" ("Resistance of Some Animal Species to Snake Venom"), *Comptes Rendus de l'Academie des Sciences,* CXLIII (1949), 5–8.
14. T. R. Fraser, *op. cit.,* p. 958.
15. Grasset *et al., loc. cit.*
16. M. Oldfield Howey, *The Encircled Serpent* (London: Rider and Co., 1928), p. 250.
17. Quoted by T. R. Fraser, *op. cit.,* p. 959.
18. Arthur Loveridge, "Notes on Snakes and Snake Bites in East Africa," *Bulletin of the Antivenin Institute of America,* I (1927), 106–109.
19. Karl P. Schmidt, "The Truth about Snake Stories," *Field Museum of Natural History, Zoology Leaflet No. 10,* 2nd edition, 1951, p. 10.
20. Quoted by Laurence M. Klauber, *Rattlesnakes* (Berkeley, Calif.: University of California Press, 1956), II, 848.

21. B. E. Schwarz, "Ordeal by Serpents, Fire and Strychnine," *Psychiatric Quarterly,* XXXIV (1960), 410.
22. Henry M. Parrish and C. B. Pollard, "Effects of Repeated Poisonous Snakebites in Man," *American Journal of the Medical Sciences,* CCXXXVII (1959), 277–286.
23. Saul Wiener, "Active Immunization of Man against Venom of the Australian Tiger Snake," *American Journal of Tropical Medicine and Hygiene,* IX (1960), 284–293.
24. Henry Sewall, "Experiments on the Preventative Inoculation of Rattlesnake Venom," *Journal of Physiology,* VIII (1887), 203–210.
25. Eduardo Vaz, "Fundamentos da Historia do Instituto Butantan seu Desenvolvimento" ("History of the Founding of the Instituto Butantan"), Special Publication of the Instituto Butantan, São Paulo, Brazil, 1949, inscription on cover.
26. Sherman A. Minton, Jr., "Paraspecific Protection by Elapid and Sea Snake Antivenins," *Toxicon,* V (1967), 47–55.
27. B. R. Criley, "Development of a Multivalent Antivenin for the Family Crotalidae," in Buckley and Porges, *op. cit.,* pp. 373–380.

CHAPTER EIGHT: Treatment of Snakebite

1. Findlay E. Russell, "Folklore Remedies Suggested for Tiger Snake Bite," *Western Medicine,* II (1961), 101–105.
2. Herschel H. Flowers and Charles Goucher, "The Effect of EDTA on the Extent of Tissue Damage Caused by the Venoms of *Bothrops atrox* and *Agkistrodon piscivorus,*" *Toxicon,* II (1965), 221–224. For clinical application of EDTA see: Y. Sawi, M. Makino, I. Tateno, T. Okonogi, and S. Mitsuhashi, "Studies on the Improvement of Treatment of Habu Snake (*Trimeresurus flavoviridis*) Bite. Clinical Analysis and Medical Treatment of Habu Snake Bites on Amami Islands," *Japanese Journal of Experimental Medicine,* XXXII (1962), 117–138.
3. Laurence M. Klauber, *Rattlesnakes* (Berkeley, Calif.: University of California Press, 1956), II, 886.

4. W. F. Beattie, "Recovery from the Bite of a Rattlesnake," *New York Medical Journal*, XVIII (1873), 619–620.

5. J. R. Thomas, "Snake Bites—Treated by Brandy," *North-Western Medical and Surgical Journal*, XII (1855), 305–306.

6. John B. DeLacerda, "O Permanganato de Potassio como Antidoto da Peconha das Cobras" ("Potassium Permanganate as an Antidote for Snakebite"), *Comptes Rendus de l'Academie des Sciences*, XCIII (1881), 466–468.

7. Joseph F. Gennaro, "Observations on the Treatment of Snakebite in North America," in H. L. Keegan and W. V. Macfarlane, eds., *Venomous and Poisonous Animals and Noxious Plants of the Pacific Region* (Oxford: Pergamon Press, 1963), pp. 427–449.

8. Herbert L. Stahnke, *The L-C Method of Treating Venomous Bites and Stings* (Tempe, Arizona: Poisonous Animals Research Laboratory, 1954), pp. 1–28.

CHAPTER NINE: Uses of Snake Venom

1. Laurence M. Klauber, *Rattlesnakes* (Berkeley, Calif.: University of California Press, 1956), II, 790.

2. J. W. Hayward, "Crotalus (Rattlesnake)," in *Materia Medica: Physiological and Applied by J. J. Drysdale* (London, 1884), I, 149–381.

3. Findlay E. Russell and Richard S. Scharffenberg, *Bibliography of Snake Venoms and Venomous Snakes* (West Covina, Calif.: Bibliographic Associates, Inc., 1964), pp. 172–193.

4. P. N. Leech, "Snake Venom Solution (Moccasin) not Acceptable for N.N.R.," *Journal of the American Medical Association*, CXIV (1940), 2218–2219.

5. Dionysio de Klobusitzky, "Snake Venom," *Journal of the American Medical Association*, CLXXIX (1962), 984.

6. H. Alistair Reid and K. E. Chan, "The Paradox in Therapeutic Defibrination," *The Lancet*, I (1968), 485–489.

7. A. A. Sharp, B. A. Warren, A. M. Paxton, M. J. Allington, "Anticoagulant Therapy with a Purified Fraction of Malayan Pit Viper Venom," *The Lancet*, I (1968), 493–499.

8. A. Monaelesser and C. Taguet, "Traitement des Algies et des Tumeurs par le 'Venin de Cobra' " ("Treatment of Pain and Tumors with Cobra Venom"), *Bulletin de l'Academie de Médecine*, Paris, CIX (1933), 371–375.

9. Arturo Castiglioni, "The Serpent in Medicine," *Ciba Symposia*, III (1942), 1177–1178.

10. Albert Calmette, "Sur la Mise en Evidence des Lipoides dans les Sérums par l'Activation du Venin de Cobra, Particulièrement au Cours de l'Infection Tuberculeuse" ("The Part Played by Serum Lipids in Activation of Cobra Venom, Particularly in Tuberculosis"), *Berliner Klinische Wochenschrift*, LI (1914), 496–500.

11. A. J. Rosanoff, "The Much-Holzmann Reaction in Insanity," *Archives of Internal Medicine*, IV (1909), 405–408.

12. H. J. Schwartz, "A Comparative Study of the Wassermann and Weil Cobra Venom Reactions for Syphilis," *New York Medical Journal*, XCV (1912), 23–27.

13. H. Lehndorff and M. J. Giannini, "The Effect of the Serum of Pregnant Women on Cobra Venom Hemolysis," *Acta Haematologia*, Basel, VIII (1952), 276–281.

14. Alton Meister, "The Use of Snake Venom L-Amino Acid Oxidase for the Preparation of Alpha-Keto Acids," in E. E. Buckley and N. Porges, eds., *Venoms* (Washington, D.C.: American Association for the Advancement of Science, 1956), p. 295.

15. Frank Padgett and Alvin S. Levine, "The Fine Structure of Rauscher Leukemia Virus as Revealed by Incubation in Snake Venom," *Virology*, XXX (1966), 623–630.

CHAPTER TEN: Snakes and Human Violence

1. W. R. Cooper, *The Serpent Myths of Ancient Egypt* (London: Robert Hardwicke, 1873), pp. 22, 66.

2. D. G. Sonneborn, "Poisonous Snake (Habu) Bites: Report of Eight Cases," *U.S. Naval Medical Bulletin*, XLVI (1946), 105–108.

3. "Asian Snakes Deadlier Than Our Own," *Journal of the American Medical Association*, CCIV (1968), 25.

4. Ramona and Desmond Morris, *Men and Snakes* (New York: McGraw-Hill, 1965), pp. 106–109.
5. H. Stilwell, "Fanged-Death Horseplay," *Field and Stream,* LIV (November 1949), 60, 110–113.
6. Steven C. Anderson, "Amphibians and Reptiles from Iran," *Proceedings of the California Academy of Sciences,* XXXI (1963), 466.
7. E. D. Williams, "The Rattlesnake Murder," in Craig Rice, ed., *Los Angeles Murders* (New York, 1947), pp. 179–188.
8. For references to arrow poisons and their composition see: "Arrow Poison," *Ciba Symposia,* III, No. 7 (1941), 994–1022; L. M. Klauber, *Rattlesnakes* (Berkeley, Calif.: University of California Press, 1956), II, 1168–1175; "Notes," *Nature,* LIII (1896), 227.
9. W. Naumann, "Historical Aspects of Curare," *Ciba Symposia,* III (1941), 996.

CHAPTER ELEVEN: The Hun-Khun and the Basilisk

1. *Dawn* (Karachi), April 6, 1962, p. 7.
2. *Ibid.,* May 27, 1962, p. 5.
3. John Stephenson, *Medical Zoology and Mineralogy* (London: John Churchill, 1838), p. 51.
4. Gerald Durrell, *The Bafut Beagles* (New York: The Viking Press, 1954), pp. 126–141.
5. Gaius Plinius Secundus, *The Historie of the World* (*Historiae Naturalis*), Philemon Holland, trans. (2 vols., London, 1634), I, 355; II, 358–359.
6. M. Oldfield Howey, *The Encircled Serpent* (London: Rider and Co., 1928), 320–327.
7. Charles M. Bogert and Rafael Martin del Campo, "The Gila Monster and Its Allies," *Bulletin of the American Museum of Natural History,* CIX (1956), 198–202.
8. Quoted by Roger Conant in "The Reptiles of Ohio," *The American Midland Naturalist,* XX (1938), 44.

9. Willy Ley, *The Lungfish, the Dodo, and the Unicorn* (New York: The Viking Press, 1948), 131–135.
10. Bogert and Martin del Campo, *op. cit.*, pp. 207–209.

CHAPTER TWELVE: Snake Cults and Snake Charmers

1. M. Oldfield Howey, *The Encircled Serpent* (London: Rider and Co., 1928), pp. 61–63.
2. J. P. Vogel, *Indian Serpent-Lore* (London: Arthur Probsthain, 1926), pp. 15–16.
3. *Ibid.*, pp. 275–280.
4. James G. Frazer, *The Golden Bough* (abridged ed., New York: Macmillan, 1955), pp. 620–621.
5. Vogel, *op. cit.*, pp. 268–270.
6. *Ibid.*, p. 35.
7. *Ibid.*, pp. 223–228, 250.
8. *Ibid.*, p. 34.
9. *Ibid.*, p. 102.
10. *Ibid.*, pp. 106, 116.
11. *Ibid.*, p. 208.
12. Plutarch, *Lives,* Dryden's translation revised by A. H. Clough (Boston: Little Brown, 1906), IV, 160–161.
13. Vogel, *op. cit.*, p. 192.
14. *Ibid.*, p. 267.
15. *Ibid.*, pp. 199–201.
16. Howey, *op. cit.*, p. 48.
17. Vogel, *op. cit.*, p. 37.
18. Nelly De Rooij, *The Reptiles of the Indo-Australia Archipelago* (Leiden: E. J. Brill, 1917), II, 288.
19. Post Wheeler, *The Sacred Scriptures of the Japanese* (New York: Henry Schuman, Inc., 1952), p. 555.
20. Kilton Stewart, *Pygmies and Dream Giants* (New York: Norton, 1954), p. 233.
21. John Gasperetti, "Survey of the Reptiles of the Sheikhdom of Abu

Dhabi, Arabian Peninsula. Part I. A Geographical Sketch of the Sheikhdom of Abu Dhabi," *Proceedings of the California Academy of Sciences,* XXXV (1967), 154–155.

22. Ramona and Desmond Morris, *Men and Snakes* (New York: Mc-Graw-Hill, 1965), pp. 140–141.

23. U. T. Thakur, *Sindhi Culture* (Bombay: University of Bombay Press, 1959), 110–113.

24. *Ibid.*

CHAPTER THIRTEEN: Myths from Africa and the Middle East

1. M. Leffkowitz, "Description of a Snake Bite More than 3500 Years Ago," *Dapim Refuim,* XIII (1954), v–vi.

2. M. O. Howey, *The Encircled Serpent* (London: Rider and Co., 1928), p. 207.

3. Gaius Plinius Secundus, *Historiae Naturalis* (*The Historie of the World*), Philemon Holland, trans. (London, 1634), I, 154.

4. Howey, *op. cit.,* p. 208.

5. *Ibid.,* p. 209.

6. *Ibid.*

7. André Villiers, *Les Serpents de l'Ouest Africain* ("West African Serpents"), (2nd ed. Dakar, Senegal: Institut Français d'Afrique Noire, 1963), p. 64.

8. *Ibid.,* pp. 63–64.

9. Walter Rose, *Snakes, Mainly South African* (Cape Town: Maskew Miller, 1955), p. 180.

10. Alan H. Gardiner, "Magic (Egyptian)," in James Hastings, ed., *Encyclopedia of Religion and Ethics* (New York: Charles Scribner's Sons, 1908–1927), VIII, 266.

11. R. M. Isemonger, *Snakes of Africa* (Johannesburg: Thomas Nelson and Sons, 1962), p. 6.

12. W. R. Cooper, *The Serpent Myths of Ancient Egypt* (London: Robert Hardwicke, 1873), p. 66.

13. J. E. Hanauer, *Folk-Lore of the Holy Land* (London: Duckworth and Co., 1907), p. 283.

14. Villiers, *op. cit.*, p. 60.
15. S. B. St John, *Hayti, the Black Republic* (London, 1884), p. 185.
16. Howey, *op. cit.*, p. 239.
17. T. J. Hutchinson, *Impressions of Western Africa* (London, 1858), p. 196.
18. Howey, *op. cit.*, p. 250.
19. W. D. Hambly, "Serpent Worship in Africa," *Field Museum of Natural History Publications,* XXI (1931), 43.
20. A. J. N. Tremearne, *The Ban of the Bori* (London: Heath, Cranton and Ourseley, 1914), p. 172.
21. Villiers, *op. cit.*, p. 61.

CHAPTER FOURTEEN: European Snake Worship and Myths

1. Jane Ellen Harrison, *Prolegomena to the Study of Greek Religion* (Cambridge: The University Press, 1922), pp. 17–23.
2. J. A. MacCulloch, "Serpent Worship (Introductory and Primitive)," in James Hastings, ed., *Encyclopedia of Religion and Ethics* (New York: Charles Scribner's Sons, 1908–1927), XI, 406.
3. Jane Ellen Harrison, *Themis: A Study of the Social Origins of Greek Religion* (2nd ed. Cambridge: The University Press, 1927), pp. 261–263.
4. William S. Fox, "Greek and Roman," in *The Mythology of All Races* (Boston: Marshall Jones Co., 1916), I, 34.
5. *Ibid.*, p. 279.
6. James G. Frazer, *Adonis, Attis, Osiris* (London: Macmillan Co., 1922), p. 90.
7. Fox, *op. cit.*, p. 279.
8. J. E. Harrison, *Themis, op. cit.*, pp 294–297.
9. Enid Welsford, "Serpent Worship (Teutonic and Balto-Slavic)," in Hastings, ed., *op. cit.*, XI, 419.
10. *Ibid.*, 420–421.
11. Ramona and Desmond Morris, *Men and Snakes* (New York: McGraw-Hill, 1965), p. 47.

12. R. B. Cowles and R. L. Phelan, "Olfaction in Rattlesnakes," *Copeia,* No. 2 (1958), 77–83.

13. Gaius Plinius Secundus, *Historiae Naturalis (The Historie of the World),* Philemon Holland, trans. (London, 1634), II, 358.

14. MacCulloch, *op. cit.,* p. 404.

15. Gaius Plinius Secundus, *op. cit.,* pp. 154–155.

16. MacCulloch, *op. cit.,* p. 404.

17. Jacob Grim, *Teutonic Mythology,* J. S. Stallybrass, trans. (New York: Dover Publications Inc., 1966), IV, 684–685.

18. MacCulloch, *op. cit.,* p. 404.

19. M. Oldfield Howey, *The Encircled Serpent* (London: Rider and Co., 1928), pp. 6–13.

20. Katharine Kuh, "The Circuitous Odyssey of Irish Art," *Saturday Review,* March 23, 1968, pp. 25–26.

21. James G. Frazer, *The Golden Bough* (abridged ed.; New York: Macmillan, 1955), pp. 759–760.

22. R. Chambers, *The Book of Days* (Edinburgh: W. & R. Chambers, 1881), pp. 382–383.

23. *Ibid.*

24. Welsford, *op. cit.,* p. 420.

25. P. Grappin, "Germanic Lands: The Mortal Gods," in Pierre Grimal, ed., *Larousse—World Mythology* (New York: Putnam, 1965), p. 378.

26. H. A. Guerber, *Myths of Northern Lands* (New York: American Book Co., 1895), pp. 19–21, 264–270.

CHAPTER FIFTEEN: The Belled Vipers of America

1. Laurence M. Klauber, *Rattlesnakes* (2 vols. Berkeley, Calif.: University of California Press, 1956), II, 1091–1092.

2. *Ibid.,* pp. 1159, 1164–1167.

3. J. A. MacCulloch, "Serpent Worship (Introductory and Primitive)," in James Hastings, ed., *Encyclopedia of Religion and Ethics* (New York: Charles Scribner's Sons, 1908–1927), XI, 401–406.

4. Klauber, *op. cit.,* II, 1091.

5. J. W. Powell, "Mythology of the North American Indians," *Bureau of American Ethnology, First Annual Report,* 1879–1880, p. 88.
6. Hastings, *op. cit.,* I, 324.
7. Matilda Coxe Stevenson, "The Sia," *Bureau of American Ethnology, Eleventh Annual Report,* 1894, p. 88.
8. George A. Dorsey and H. R. Voth, "The Mishongnovi Ceremonies of the Snake and Antelope Fraternities," *Field Columbian Museum Publication Anthropology Series,* III (1902), 180.
9. Klauber, *op. cit.,* II, 1113–1122.
10. Charles M. Bogert, "Notes on the Snake Dance of the Hopi Indians," *Copeia,* No. 4 (1933), 219–221.
11. James A. Oliver, *Snakes in Fact and Fiction* (New York: Macmillan, 1959), 101–108.
12. Matilda Coxe Stevenson, "The Zuni Indians," *Bureau of American Ethnology, Twenty-third Annual Report,* 1904, pp. 73–102.
13. Frank Russell, "The Pima Indians," *Bureau of American Ethnology. Twenty-sixth Annual Report,* 1908, pp. 215–216.
14. Hastings, *op. cit.,* VI, 829.
15. Klauber, *op. cit.,* II, 1093.
16. Daniel G. Brinton, *American Hero Myths* (Philadelphia: H. C. Watts and Co., 1882), pp. 159–163.
17. *Ibid.,* pp. 126–130.
18. *Ibid.,* pp. 136–141.
19. Bernal Diaz del Castillo, *The True History of the Conquest of New Spain,* Alfred P. Maudslay, trans. (London: The Hakluyt Society, 1910), II, 67.

CHAPTER SIXTEEN: Snakes in the Space Age

1. Laurence M. Klauber, *Rattlesnakes* (Berkeley, Calif.: University of California Press, 1956), II, 977–978.
2. Rheua Vaughn Medden, "Tales of the Rattlesnake: From the Works of Early Travelers in America," *Bulletin of the Antivenin Institute of America,* V (1931), 25.
3. Weston LaBarre, *They Shall Take Up Serpents* (Minneapolis: University of Minnesota Press, 1962), pp. 11–14.

4. Washington (D.C.) *Evening Star,* August 20, 1968.
5. William Sargant, "Some Cultural Group Abreactive Techniques and Their Relation to Modern Treatments," *Proceedings of the Royal Society of Medicine,* XLII (1949), 367–374.
6. John A. Womeldorf, "Rattlesnake Religion," *The Christian Century,* December 10, 1947, pp. 1517–1518.
7. Berthold Schwarz, "Ordeal by Serpents, Fire and Strychnine," *Psychiatric Quarterly,* XXXIV (1960), 422–424.
8. Klauber, *op. cit.,* p. 947.
9. LaBarre, *op. cit.,* pp. 19–20.
10. Schwarz, *op. cit.,* pp. 410–411, fig. 2.
11. Alva W. Taylor, "Snake Handling Cults Flourish," *The Christian Century,* October 23, 1947, p. 1308.
12. LaBarre, *op. cit.,* pp. 49–50.

CHAPTER SEVENTEEN: How Snakes Acquired Charisma

1. Lucien Levy-Bruhl, *Les Fonctions Mentales dans les Sociétés Inférieures*; English edition, *How Natives Think,* Lilian A. Clare, trans. (New York: Washington Square Press, 1966), pp. 91–92.
2. James G. Frazer, *The Golden Bough* (abridged ed.; New York: Macmillan, 1955), I, 574–575.
3. *Ibid.,* I, 689–703.
4. Gaius Plinius Secundus, *Historiae Naturalis* (*The Historie of the World*), Philemon Holland, trans. (London, 1634), I, 163.
5. Marcos Freiberg, *Vida de Batracios y Reptiles Sudamericanos* (Life of South American Amphibians and Reptiles) (Buenos Aires: Cesarini Hnos., 1954), pp. 152–153.
6. Frazer, *op. cit.,* 696.
7. G. M. Foster, "A Summary of Yuki Culture," *University of California Anthropological Records,* V (1944), 214.
8. Walter E. Roth, "Animism and Folklore of the Guiana Indians," *Bureau of American Ethnology, 30th Annual Report* (1908–09), 313.
9. R. Berndt and C. Berndt, *The World of the First Australians* (Sydney: Ure Smith, 1964), pp. 153–154.

10. Roland Robinson, *The Feathered Serpent* (Sydney: Edwards and Shaw, 1956), p. 30.

11. Franz Boas, "Tsimshian Mythology," *Bureau of American Ethnology, 31st Annual Report* (1909–10), pp. 604, 614, 809.

12. Roth, *op. cit.,* 135.

13. Indianapolis *Star,* October 20, 1968, p. 42.

14. J. H. Rivett-Carnac, "The Snake Symbol in India," *Journal of the Asiatic Society of Bengal,* L (1881), 419–420.

15. Jane Ellen Harrison, *Prolegomena to the Study of Greek Religion* (Cambridge, The University Press, 1903), p. 122.

16. Samuel Noah Kramer, *Sumerian Mythology* (New York, Harper, 1961), pp. 33–34.

17. G. C. Vaillant, *The Aztecs of Mexico* (Harmondsworth, England: Penguin Books, Ltd., 1950), p. 177, pl. 54.

18. T. Volker, *The Animal in Far Eastern Art* (Leiden: E. J. Brill, 1950), p. 148.

19. Levy-Bruhl, *op. cit.,* pp. 245–250.

20. Weston LaBarre, *They Shall Take Up Serpents* (Minneapolis: University of Minnesota Press, 1962), pp. 79–80.

21. James G. Frazer, *Folk-lore in the Old Testament* (London: Macmillan Co., 1918), p. 45.

22. James G. Frazer, *The Worship of Nature* (New York: Macmillan, 1926), I, 201.

23. *Ibid.,* p. 199.

24. James G. Frazer, *The Golden Bough* (3rd ed.; London: Macmillan Co., 1913), IV, 303.

25. Roth, *op. cit.,* pp. 143–144.

26. Laurence M. Klauber, *Rattlesnakes* (Berkeley, Calif.: University of California Press, 1956), II, 1088–1089, 1095.

27. Robert E. Kuntz, *Snakes of Taiwan* (Taipei, Taiwan: U.S. Naval Medical Research Unit No. 2, 1963), frontispiece.

28. Ramona and Desmond Morris, *Men and Snakes* (New York: McGraw-Hill, 1965), pp. 23–24.

29. Robinson, *op. cit.,* p. 56.

Glossary

~~~~~~

ALLOPATHIC MEDICINE

Originally, the method of curing disease by inducing a different or opposite reaction in the body, now occasionally used to designate a system of medical practice which makes use of all therapeutic measures that have proved of value.

ANAMNESTIC RESPONSE

A prompt and marked rise in ANTIBODY production following a second or later contact with the substance originally used to elicit the antibody. Also known as "recall phenomenon" or "immune memory."

ANAPHYLACTIC SHOCK

A severe reaction of allergy or hypersensitivity usually following injection of a foreign substance. There may be respiratory, circulatory, and neurological symptoms; the condition is often fatal if untreated.

ANTIBODY

A protein of the globulin type produced by the body in response to introduction of a foreign substance (usually a protein or polysaccharide). The antibody reacts specifically with the substance that has elicited its production.

ANTICOAGULANT FRACTION

The portion or component of a venom or other substance which inhibits the clotting of blood.

ANTISERUM

The serum (fluid portion of the blood that remains after clotting) of an animal injected or otherwise immunized against a foreign substance (usually a protein or an infectious organism). This serum combines specifically with the substance against which it is produced.

ANTIVENIN (ANTIVENENE, ANTIVENOM)

An antiserum produced against a venom and capable of neutralizing its effects.

AVATAR

A manifestation or incarnation of a supernatural being in an earthly form.

BELLY SCUTES

Transversely enlarged scales seen on the under surface of most snakes.

BEZOAR STONE

A concretion or a hair ball found in the stomach; formerly prized as medicine. Bezoar goats were once raised for these stones.

BIOASSAY

Determination of the presence or potency of a substance by comparing its effect on a living organism or on a living, isolated organ or tissue with that of a standard preparation.

BIOCHEMISTRY

The chemistry of living organisms and of life processes.

BIOSYNTHETIC REACTIONS

Chemical reactions within living tissue that result in the synthesis of new substances.

CENTRIFUGE

An apparatus for spinning fluids rapidly in order to separate substances of different densities.

CHERUBIM (sing. CHERUB)

Mythical winged figures with human heads and animal bodies, usually the guardians of some holy place.

CHTHONIC

Literally "in or under the earth"; a term applied to infernal deities of pre-classical Greece, some of whom manifested themselves as snakes.

COLORIMETER

An instrument for determining or comparing colors, especially colors produced by chemical reactions, in an objective manner—for example, by comparison with light of a given wave length.

CORTICOSTEROIDS

A group of compounds chemically related to cholesterol and normally produced in the adrenal cortex. They are potent substances with a wide range of biological effects, including the reduction of inflammation and allergy and the suppression of the body's immune defenses.

CORTICOTROPIN

A hormone, also known as ACTH, secreted by the pituitary and acting on the adrenal gland to increase the secretion of hydrocortisone and certain other substances produced in the adrenal cortex.

CRYOTHERAPY

Treatment of a disease or injury by application of cold.

CURARE

A muscle-paralyzing poison derived from certain South American plants. Originally an arrow poison, it is now also used in medicine.

DAIMON

A mythical spirit; often a demon.

DUVERNOY'S GLAND

The venom-producing gland of the rear-fanged colubrid snakes, usually located between the eye and the angle of the mouth. Named for D. M. Duvernoy, the French anatomist who first described it.

ECOLOGY

The study of the interrelationship of plants and animals with each other and with their physical environment.

ENTEROLITH

A stone or concretion found in the intestine.

ENZYME

A protein catalyst that initiates or promotes a biochemical reaction without being itself permanently changed in the reaction.

EPIDEMIOLOGY

The science that deals with the incidence, distribution, and control of disease in a population.

EPITHELIUM

A sheet of cellular tissue covering a free surface or lining a tube or cavity of an animal body. The cells may be involved in processes of secretion, excretion, or absorption.

ETHYLENEDIAMINETETRACETIC ACID (EDTA)

A chemical that inactivates certain venom enzymes which cause the local NECROSIS seen with some snakebites.

EXTRAPOLATE

To project or extend known data into an unknown area.

GANGRENE

Local death of tissue due to interference with the blood supply.

GEL DIFFUSION TEST

A chemical or physiochemical procedure in which the reacting substances diffuse toward each other through a gel instead of being mixed as liquids. In immunodiffusion, the reacting substances are antiserum and solutions of proteins or other high molecular weight substances.

GLOBULIN FRACTION

That portion of the blood serum proteins which is insoluble in distilled water and half-saturated ammonium sulfate solution. It contains the IMMUNE GLOBULINS.

HEMOLYSIN

A substance that breaks down the red blood corpuscles with the liberation of hemoglobin.

HEMOLYSIS

The breakdown of red blood corpuscles with liberation of hemoglobin.

HEMORRHAGIC

Pertaining to or characterized by hemorrhage or bleeding.

HISTAMINE

A derivative of the amino acid histidine. It causes dilation and increased permeability of small blood vessels, as well as other biological effects. Its production is increased in many allergic conditions.

HOMEOPATHIC MEDICINE

A system of therapeutics based on the doctrine that diseases are cured by drugs producing effects similar to the symptoms of the disease and that the effect of drugs is increased by giving them in minute doses. (Compare ALLOPATHIC MEDICINE.)

HOMOLOGOUS

Used in comparative anatomy to refer to structures having a common origin but not necessarily the same function—for example, the forearm of a man and the wing of a bat.

IDIOPATHIC

Self-originated or of unknown origin.

IMMUNE GLOBULIN

That part of the blood serum containing or made up of ANTIBODIES. There are several types of immune globulins; most of the antibodies induced by conventional methods of immunization are of the gamma globulin type with a molecular weight of about 160,000 and low electrophoretic mobility.

IMMUNITY

Ability to resist a particular disease.

IMMUNOLOGY

The science that deals with the phenomena and causes of immunity.

LIPIDS

Structural components of living tissue that are only slightly soluble in water but more freely soluble in ether, alcohol, and other fat solvents; they include fats, waxes, phosphatides, and compounds related to or derived from these.

LYSIS

The destruction of cells or tissue by action of a specific toxin, enzyme, or antibody.

MAXILLARY BONE

One of the bones of the upper jaw. In all venomous snakes it bears the poison fangs and is lateral to and usually extends anterior to the other tooth-bearing bones of the upper jaw.

MOLECULAR WEIGHT

The weight of a molecule of a substance calculated as the sum of the atomic weights of the constituent atoms. Hydrogen, with an atomic weight of 1.008, is a unit of this system.

MONKEY-WALLAH

An itinerant sidewalk performer whose act features one or more trained monkeys. In Pakistan and India, the term "wallah" is widely used in much the same sense as "fellow" or "guy" in America. Snake charmers are often called "snake-wallahs."

MONOVALENT

Containing antibodies specific for the single substance or organism; a term applied to ANTIVENINS produced against venom of a single species of snake.

NECROSIS

Localized death of a circumscribed area of tissue.

NEUROTOXIC

Poisonous or destructive to the nervous system.

PALEONTOLOGY

The science that deals with the organisms of past geological periods as based on the study of fossils.

PARALLEL EVOLUTION

The development of a series of similar species by two distantly related groups. The evolution of marsupials in Australia parallels the evolution of rodents in other parts of the world.

PAROTID GLANDS

A pair of large serous salivary glands of most mammals. In man these are located in front of and slightly below each ear.

PERIORBITAL TISSUES

The tissues around the eyes.

PETROGLYPH

A low-relief carving or inscription on a rock.

PIPAL TREE

A type of fig tree (*Ficus religiosa*) noted for its longevity and great size and prized for its sap (lac). Pipal trees in India are often honored as shrines.

POLYVALENT

Containing antibodies specific for several substances or organisms. Applied to ANTIVENINS produced against venoms of several species of snakes.

PRECIPITATE

An insoluble substance separated from solution by a chemical or physical change.

PSYCHOGENIC

Originating in the mind, or resulting from mental or emotional conflict.

PURPURA

Condition in which reddish or purplish patches appear beneath the skin and mucous membranes as a result of local hemorrhage from small blood vessels.

RADIOISOTOPE TAGGING

Attachment of a radioactive isotope of an element to a nonradioactive substance in order to make the latter more readily detectable. Often used in biology to follow the course of a substance introduced into the body of an organism.

RAGA

A traditional melodic pattern in Hindu music.

SACHEM

An American Indian chief or important tribal elder.

SCHISTOSOMIASIS

Infection with schistosomes, or blood flukes.

SEROTONIN

An aromatic amine (5-hydroxytryptamine) present in small amounts

in normal tissues and in large amounts in venoms of various inverte-
brates (hornets, centipedes, scorpions) as well as in snake venoms.
It has multiple biological activities including contraction of small
blood vessels and the production of pain.

STUPA

A round shrine built of wood or stone to house holy relics of Buddha or a Buddhist saint.

TAXONOMY

The science of classification of organisms.

TETANY

Prolonged contraction or spasm of muscle.

TOXICOLOGY

The science that deals with poisons and their effects on living organisms and with the detection of poisons.

TOXINOLOGY

A subdivision of toxicology which deals with poisons produced by
plants and animals particularly as they occur in their natural form.

VASODILATING

Causing dilation of the blood vessels.

VENOM FRACTIONS

Components of venom obtained after chemical or physical separation
procedures such as electrophoresis, dialysis, and so on. Many of
these components are identified by their biological activity.

ZOOGEOGRAPHY

The study of the geographical distribution of animals.

Selected Bibliography

BEHRINGWERKE MITTEILUNGEN. *Die Giftschlangen der Erde.* ("The Poisonous Snakes of the World"). Marburg/Lahn, West Germany: N. C. Elwert, 1963.

BELLAIRS, ANGUS, and UNDERWOOD, GARTH. "The Origin of Snakes," *Biological Reviews of the Cambridge Philosophical Society,* XXVI (1951), 193–237.

BOGERT, CHARLES M., and MARTIN DEL CAMPO, RAFAEL. "The Gila Monster and Its Allies," *Bulletin of the American Museum of Natural History,* CIX (1956), 1–238.

BÜCHERL, W., BUCKLEY, E. E., and DEULOFEU, V., eds. *Venomous Animals and Their Venoms.* 3 vols. New York: Academic Press, 1968–.

BUCKLEY, E. E., and PORGES, N., eds. *Venoms.* Washington, D.C.: American Association for the Advancement of Science, 1956.

CHRISTENSEN, POUL A. *South African Snake Venoms and Antivenoms.* Johannesburg: The South African Institute for Medical Research, 1953.

CHRISTY, NICHOLAS P. "On Fear of Serpents and Ophiolatry," *Transactions of the American Clinical and Climatological Association,* LXXIX (1967), 21–33.

COOPER, W. R. *The Serpent Myths of Ancient Egypt.* London: Robert Hardwicke, 1873.

FITCH, HENRY S. "The Autecology of the Copperhead," *University of Kansas Publications Museum of Natural History,* XIII (1960), 85–288.

FRASER, THOMAS R. "Address on Immunisation Against Serpents' Venom and the Treatment of Snake Bites with Antivenene," *British Medical Journal*, I (1896), 957–961.

FRAZER, JAMES G. *The Golden Bough*. Abridged ed. New York: Macmillan, 1955.

GRIMM, JACOB. *Teutonic Mythology*. 4 vols. London: George Bell and Sons, 1883–1888. Reprinted 1966 by Dover Publications Inc., New York.

HARRISON, JANE ELLEN. *Prolegomena to the Study of Greek Religion*. London: Cambridge University Press, 1903.

————. *Themis, a Study of the Social Origins of Greek Religion*. 2nd ed. London: Cambridge University Press, 1927.

HOWEY, M. OLDFIELD. *The Encircled Serpent*. London: Rider and Co., 1928.

ISEMONGER, R. M. *Snakes of Africa, Southern, Central and East*. Johannesburg: Thomas Nelson and Sons, 1962.

KAISER, ERICH, and MICHL, M. *Die Biochemie der Tierischen Gifte* ("The Biochemistry of Animal Venoms"). Vienna: F. Deuticke, 1958.

KEEGAN, HUGH L., and MACFARLANE, W. V. (eds.). *Venomous and Poisonous Animals and Noxious Plants of the Pacific Region*. Oxford: Pergamon Press, Inc., 1963.

KLAUBER, LAURENCE M. *Rattlesnakes*. 2 vols. Berkeley, Calif.: University of California Press, 1956.

LABARRE, WESTON. *They Shall Take Up Serpents*. Minneapolis: University of Minnesota Press, 1962.

MERTENS, ROBERT. *The World of Amphibians and Reptiles*. Trans. H. W. Parker. London: George G. Harrap and Co., 1960.

MORRIS, RAMONA, and MORRIS, DESMOND. *Men and Snakes*. New York: McGraw-Hill, 1965.

OLIVER, JAMES A. *Snakes in Fact and Fiction*. New York: Macmillan, 1959.

PHISALIX, MARIE. *Animaux Venimeux et Venins* ("Venomous Animals and Venoms"). 2 vols. Paris: Masson et Cie., 1922.

POPE, CLIFFORD H. *The Reptile World*. New York: Knopf, 1955.

ROSE, WALTER. *Snakes—Mainly South African*. Cape Town: Maskew Miller, Ltd., 1955.

RUSSELL, F. E., and SAUNDERS, P. R. (eds.). *Animal Toxins*. Oxford: Pergamon Press, Inc., 1967.

SCHMIDT, KARL P., and INGER, ROBERT F. *Living Reptiles of the World*. Garden City, N.Y.: Hanover House, 1957.

SWAROOP, SITYA, and GRAB, B. "Snakebite Mortality in the World," *Bulletin of the World Health Organization*, X (1954), 35–76.

THOMPSON, STITH. *Motif Index of Folk Literature*. Bloomington, Ind.: Indiana University Press, 1932–1936.

UNDERWOOD, GARTH. *A Contribution to the Classification of Snakes*. London: British Museum (Natural History), 1967.

U.S. NAVY BUREAU OF MEDICINE AND SURGERY. *Poisonous Snakes of the World*. Rev. ed. Washington, D.C.: U.S. Government Printing Office, 1968.

VILLIERS, ANDRÉ. *Les Serpents de l'Ouest Africain* ("The Serpents of West Africa"). Dakar, Senegal: Institut Français d'Afrique Noire, 1963.

VOGEL, JEAN P. *Indian Serpent Lore*. London: Arthur Probsthain, 1926.

WORRELL, ERIC. *Reptiles of Australia*. Sydney: Angus and Robertson, 1964.

ACKNOWLEDGMENTS

INDEX

Acknowledgments

We would like to thank the many people who helped us in the preparation of this book. Some are long-time friends; others were total strangers; all responded generously to our requests for aid. Dr. Carl Gans of the Department of Biology, State University of New York at Buffalo, read most of the herpetological sections of the manuscript and made numerous helpful suggestions. Dr. Joseph F. Gennaro of the Department of Anatomy, University of Louisville Medical School, sent us a preprint of his important paper on the ultrastructure of pit-viper venom.

Herpetologists and toxinologists who responded to our inquiries for specific information or generally allowed us to pick their brains include Dr. H. B. Bechtel of Valdosta, Georgia; W. Leslie Burger of Franklin College, Franklin, Indiana; Dr. Willard B. Elliott of the Department of Biochemistry, State University of New York at Buffalo; Major Herschel Flowers, Veterinary Corps, U. S. Army; Dr. Mahmood Latifi, Razi Serum and Vaccine Institute, Tehran, Iran; Dr. James A. Peters and Simon Camden-Main of the U. S. National Museum; Dr. H. Alistair Reid of the Liverpool School of Tropical Medicine; and Dr. Philip W. Smith of the Illinois Natural History Survey. Dr. Weston LaBarre of the Department of Anthropology, Duke University, and Dr. Samuel Noah Kramer of the University of Pennsylvania Museums advised us regarding specific problems in their areas of interest. Mrs. Thomas D. Wilson of Indianapolis gathered material on North American Indian snake myths and read sections of the manuscript. Dr. Findlay E. Russell of the University of Southern California School of Medicine and Dr. Gastão Rosenfeld of the Instituto Butantan, São Paulo, Brazil, supplied data on snakebite cases from their files.

Dr. Roy Sieber, director of Indiana University's Fine Arts Museum, read parts of the manuscript and helped us to locate illustration materials in the museum collections. Dr. Saul Reisenberg and Robert M. Laughlin of the Smithsonian Office of Anthropology permitted us to use pictures from the annual reports of the Bureau of American Ethnology.

Allan Roberts of Richmond, Indiana, took some photographs at our request, including two of pictures published by the Smithsonian Institution, and made others available to us from his collection. Still other photographs were provided by William Oates of Indianapolis; H. F. Pickett of Durham, North Carolina; Dr. Herbert Rosenberg of the Langmuir Laboratory, Cornell University; and John Tashjian of Oakland, California. The Illustration Department of Indiana University Medical Center generously made black-and-white prints from many of our color slides.

For assistance in obtaining reference material and for bringing to our attention literature we might otherwise have overlooked, we are indebted to Dr. Theodore Bowie of the Fine Arts Department of Indiana University, Dr. Richard Davis of Butler University Library, Indianapolis, and Dr. Herndon Dowling and Itzchak Gilboa of the Department of Herpetology, American Museum of Natural History. David Randall and Jo Bennett permitted us to examine certain rare books in the collection of the Lilly Library of Indiana University. Mary Jane Laatz and her staff at the Indiana University Medical Center Library were most helpful in many ways. Juanita Derry and Marie Glass of Indiana University Medical Center typed sections of the manuscript.

Index

About the Authors

~~~~~~

SHERMAN A. MINTON, JR., was born in Indiana and received his M.D. from Indiana University in 1942. He has been Associate Professor of Microbiology at the School of Medicine of Indiana University since 1948. A noted herpetologist who has contributed to numerous scientific and technical journals, Dr. Minton has served as President of the International Society of Toxinology. He is a Fellow and Council Member of the Herpetologists League and Research Associate in Herpetology of the American Museum of Natural History.

MADGE RUTHERFORD MINTON, also born in Indiana, studied at Medill School of Journalism and Indiana University and received her A.B. from Butler University in 1941. She has assisted her husband with various procedures, particularly the extracting of snake venom, and has worked closely with him in the field.